Longman
Preparation Course
for the TOEFL®

Deborah Phillips

Longman
New York & London

Longman Preparation Course for the TOEFL®

Longman, 10 Bank Street, White Plains, N.Y. 10606

Associated companies:
Longman Group Ltd., London
Longman Cheshire Pty., Melbourne
Longman Paul Pty., Auckland
Copp Clark Pitman, Toronto
Pitman Publishing Inc., New York

Special thanks to Marjorie Fuchs for her helpful ideas, her calm and cheerful demeanor, and her
dedication to quality.

Executive editor: Joanne Dresner
Development editor: Marjorie Fuchs
Production editor: Elsa van Bergen
Text design: Jill Francis Wood
Cover design: Joseph De Pinho
Production supervisor: Judith Stern

Published in the United Kingdom by Longman Group Ltd., Longman House, Burnt Mill,
Harlow, Essex CM20 2JE, England, and by associated companies, branches, and
representatives throughout the world.

Library of Congress Cataloging-in-Publication Data

Phillips, Deborah, 1952–
    Longman preparation course for the TOEFL.

    1. English language—Textbooks for foreign speakers.
2. English language—Examinations, questions, etc.
I. Title.   II. Title: Preparation course for the
TOEFL.
PE1128.P46   1989   428.2'4   88-9149

ISBN 0-8013-0141-6

7 8 9 10-KE-95949392

CONTENTS

INTRODUCTION

ABOUT THIS BOOK

PURPOSE OF THE BOOK

This book is intended to prepare students for the TOEFL (Test of English as a Foreign Language). It is based on the most up-to-date information available on the format and style of actual TOEFL tests.

Longman Preparation Course for the TOEFL® can be used in a variety of ways, depending on the needs of the reader:

1. It can be used as the primary classroom text in a course emphasizing TOEFL preparation.
2. It can be used as a supplementary text in a more general ESL course.
3. It can be used as a tool for individualized study by students preparing for the TOEFL outside of the ESL classroom.

WHAT'S IN THE BOOK

This book contains a variety of materials which together provide a comprehensive TOEFL preparation program:

1. **Pre-tests** for each section measure students' level of performance on each section of the TOEFL and allow students to determine specific areas of weakness.
2. **Skills and Strategies** for each of the sections of the TOEFL, including the new Test of Written English, provide students with clearly defined steps to take to improve performance on the TOEFL.
3. **Exercises,** some in TOEFL format and others in a format more suited to the specific skill, allow students to practice each skill individually.
4. **Review Exercises** incorporate a number of skills and reinforce previously taught skills.
5. **TOEFL Exercises** demonstrate how skills will be tested on the TOEFL.
6. **TOEFL Review Exercises** incorporate a number of skills in TOEFL format.
7. **Post-Tests** for each section measure the progress students have made after working through the skills and strategies in the text.
8. **The Scoring information** allows students to determine their approximate TOEFL scores on the Pre-Test and Post-Test.
9. **A Chart** allows students to record their progress from the Pre-Test to the Post-Test.
10. **TOEFL Answer Sheets** allow practice in using the test forms correctly; both horizontal and vertical ovals are used in the test and in this book.

OTHER AVAILABLE MATERIALS

Additional materials are available to supplement the materials included in the text.

1. *Longman Preparation Course for the TOEFL®: Tapescript and Answer Key.* The **answer key** includes answers to all questions in the Pre-Tests, Exercises, and Post-Tests. A **Tapescript** gives a transcription of all listening comprehension exercises included on the cassette tapes accompanying this text.
2. *Longman Practice Tests for the TOEFL®* contains five TOEFL-format tests, Listening Comprehension Tapescripts, answer keys, scoring information, and charts to record progress.
3. **Cassettes** (*Longman Preparation Course for the TOEFL® Cassettes* and *Longman Practice Tests for the TOEFL® Cassettes*) contain, respectively, recordings of the Listening Comprehension Pre-Test, Listening Exercises, and Listening Comprehension Post-Test; and the Listening Comprehension sections of the Practice Tests.

ABOUT THE TOEFL

DESCRIPTION OF THE TOEFL

The Test of English as a Foreign Language (TOEFL) is a test to measure the level of English proficiency of non-native speakers of English. It is required primarily by English-language colleges and universities. Additionally, institutions such as government agencies or scholarship programs may require this test.

The test currently has the following sections:

1. **Listening Comprehension** (multiple choice): To demonstrate their ability to understand spoken English, examinees must listen to a tape and respond to various types of questions.
2. **Structure and Written Expression** (multiple choice): To demonstrate their ability to recognize grammatically correct English, examinees must choose the correct way to complete sentences and must find errors in sentences.
3. **Vocabulary and Reading Comprehension** (multiple choice): To demonstrate their ability to understand written English, examinees must answer vocabulary questions and must also answer questions about reading passages.
4. **Test of Written English** (written): Examinees must write an essay on a given topic in 30 minutes to demonstrate their ability to produce correct and meaningful English. The Test of Written English is not given with every administration of the TOEFL. You should check the *Bulletin of Information for TOEFL and TSE* for upcoming dates for this test.

The following chart outlines the probable format of a TOEFL test. It should be noted that on certain occasions a longer version of the TOEFL is given.

	TOEFL	TIME
LISTENING COMPREHENSION	50 questions	30 minutes*
STRUCTURE AND WRITTEN EXPRESSION	40 questions	25 minutes
VOCABULARY AND READING	60 questions	45 minutes
TEST OF WRITTEN ENGLISH	1 essay question	30 minutes

*Approximate time.

WHAT YOUR TOEFL SCORE MEANS

The TOEFL is scored on a scale of 200 to 700 points. There is no passing score on the TOEFL, but various institutions have their own TOEFL score requirements. You must find out from each institution what TOEFL score is required.

When you take the TOEFL Pre-Tests and Post-Tests in this book, it is possible for you to estimate your TOEFL score. A description of how to estimate your TOEFL score has been provided at the back of this book on pages 268–270.

The score of the Test of Written English is not included in your overall TOEFL score. It is a separate score on a scale of 1 to 6.

WHERE TO GET ADDITIONAL INFORMATION

Additional information is available in the *Bulletin of Information for TOEFL and TSE*. This bulletin can be obtained free of charge by sending a request to the following address:

TOEFL/TSE Services
P.O. Box 6151
Princeton, NJ 08541-6151
USA

TO THE STUDENT

HOW TO PREPARE FOR THE TOEFL

The TOEFL is a **test** of **English.** To do well on this test you should therefore work in two areas to improve your score:

1. You must work on improving your knowledge of the English language.
2. You must work on the skills and strategies specific to the TOEFL test.

An understanding of the TOEFL strategies and skills presented in this text can improve your TOEFL score. However, skills and strategies alone will not make you successful; a good basic knowledge of the English language is also necessary. Therefore do not forget the general study of the English language as you work to prepare for the TOEFL.

HOW TO USE THIS BOOK

1. Take the Pre-Test at the beginning of a section (Listening, Structure and Written Expression, Vocabulary and Reading); when you take the Pre-Test, try to reproduce the conditions and time pressure of a real TOEFL.

   - Take each section of the test without interruption.
   - Work on only one section at a time.
   - Use the answer sheets from the back of this book. One set is to be used for all Pre-Tests and the other for all Post-Tests.
   - Use a pencil to *completely* fill in the answer oval that corresponds to the answer you choose.
     Example: Ⓐ ● Ⓒ Ⓓ
     TOEFL answer sheets may include ovals either horizontally or vertically arranged.
   - Erase *completely* any changes you make on the answer sheet.
   - Time yourself for each test section. You need to experience the time pressure that exists on actual TOEFL tests.
   - Play the listening cassette one time only during the test.
   - Mark only your answer sheet. You cannot write in a TOEFL test booklet.

   Record your answers on the Pre-Test Answer Sheet beginning on page 271. After you finish the Pre-Test, you can determine your TOEFL score for that section using the table on page 268. Then record the results in the chart on page 270. Analyze the results of the Pre-Test to determine what types of questions you find the most difficult.

2. Work through the explanations and exercises for each section. Pay particular attention to the skills you had problems with in the Pre-Test.

3. Each time you complete a TOEFL-format exercise, try to simulate the conditions and time pressure of a real TOEFL.

   - For structure questions, allow yourself 1 minute for 2 questions. (For example, you should take 5 minutes for an exercise with 10 questions.)
   - For vocabulary questions, allow yourself 1 minute for 4 questions. (For example, you should take 2½ minutes for an exercise with 10 questions.)
   - For reading questions, allow yourself 1 minute for 1 question. (For example, if a reading passage has 5 questions, you should allow yourself 5 minutes to read the passage and answer the 5 questions.)

4. When you have completed all the skills exercises for a section, take the Post-Test for that section, recording your answers on the Post-Test Answer Sheet on page 275. Determine your TOEFL score using the table on page 268, and record your results in the chart on page 270.

TO THE TEACHER

HOW TO GET THE MOST OUT OF THE EXERCISES

The exercises are a vital part of the TOEFL preparation process presented in this text. Maximum benefit can be obtained from the exercises if the students are properly prepared for the exercises and if the exercises are carefully reviewed after completion.

1. Be sure that the students have a clear idea of the appropriate skills and strategies involved in each exercise. Before beginning each exercise review the skills and strategies that are used in that exercise. Then when you review the exercises, reinforce what skills and strategies can be used to determine the correct answers.
2. As you review the exercises, be sure to discuss each answer, the incorrect answers as well as the correct answers. Discuss how students can determine that each correct answer is correct and each incorrect answer is incorrect.
3. Two different methods are possible to review the listening exercises. One good way to review these exercises is to play back the tape, stopping after each question to discuss the skills and strategies involved in determining which answer is correct and which is incorrect. Another method is to have the students refer to the tapescript in the *Longman Preparation Course for TOEFL®: Tapescript and Answer Key* to discuss each question.
4. The structure exercises in the correct/incorrect format present a challenge for the teacher. In exercises in which the students are asked to indicate which sentences are correct and which are incorrect, it is extremely helpful for the students to correct the incorrect sentences. It should be noted, however, that many of the incorrect sentences can be corrected in several ways. The role of the teacher is to assist the students in finding the various ways that the sentences can be corrected.
5. The exercises are designed to be completed in class rather than assigned as homework. The exercises are short and take very little time to complete, particularly since it is important to keep the students under time pressure while they are working on the exercises. Considerably more time should be spent in reviewing the exercises than in actually doing them.

HOW TO GET THE MOST OUT OF THE PRE-TEST AND POST-TEST

It is essential for the Pre-Tests and Post-Tests to be taken under conditions as similar as possible to actual TOEFL conditions (see page 4).

Since the Pre-Tests and Post-Tests serve two different functions, review of these two types of tests should have different emphases. While reviewing the Pre-Tests, the teacher should encourage students to determine in which areas they are weak and need the most practice. While reviewing the Post-Tests, the teacher has one final time to emphasize the skills and strategies involved in determining the correct answer to each question.

SECTION ONE

LISTENING COMPREHENSION

TOEFL PRE-TEST

SECTION 1
LISTENING COMPREHENSION

In this section of the test, you will have an opportunity to demonstrate your ability to understand spoken English. There are three parts in this section, with special directions for each part.

Part A

<u>Directions:</u>   For each question in Part A, you will hear a short sentence. Each sentence will be spoken just one time. The sentences you hear will not be written out for you. Therefore, you must listen carefully to understand what the speaker says.

After you hear a sentence, read the four choices in your test book, marked (A), (B), (C), and (D), and decide which <u>one</u> is closest in meaning to the sentence you heard. Then, on your answer sheet, find the number of the question and fill in the space that corresponds to the letter of the answer you have chosen. Fill in the space so the letter inside the oval cannot be seen.

Example I

Sample Answer

● Ⓑ Ⓒ Ⓓ

You will hear:

You will read: (A) John outran the others.
(B) John was the fastest hunter in the chase.
(C) John wasn't the slowest in the race.
(D) John was the last runner to finish the race.

The speaker said, "John was the fastest runner in the race." Sentence (A), "John outran the others," is closest in meaning to the sentence you heard. Therefore, you should choose answer (A).

Example II

Sample Answer

Ⓐ Ⓑ ● Ⓓ

You will hear:

You will read: (A) Could you help me use the rest?
(B) Do you mind using the other desk?
(C) Would you mind helping me carry this piece of furniture?
(D) If you move my desk, I'll help you with your work.

GO ON TO THE NEXT PAGE

The speaker said, "Could you help me move my desk?" Sentence (C), "Would you mind helping me carry this piece of furniture?" is closest in meaning to the sentence you heard. Therefore, you should choose answer (C).

1. (A) The student couldn't finish closing the library book.
   (B) The student hadn't finished the library assignment, but he was close.
   (C) The student was working on the assignment when the library closed.
   (D) The homework was incomplete because the library wasn't open.

2. (A) Housing in New York that is within my budget is hard to locate.
   (B) It's hard to find his house in New York.
   (C) I can't afford to move my house to New York.
   (D) Housing in New York is unavailable.

3. (A) The plane is going to take off soon.
   (B) The fight will start in a while.
   (C) They are frightened about the departure.
   (D) A few minutes ago the flight departed.

4. (A) The movie wasn't very good.
   (B) The film was terrific.
   (C) He thinks that moving would be wonderful.
   (D) The movie was a fantasy.

5. (A) He'll take his driving test for a second time.
   (B) He passed another driver two times.
   (C) He failed the test the first time.
   (D) He tried for a second time to drive past the test facility.

6. (A) The concert series was temporarily delayed.
   (B) He phoned to find out when the concert started.
   (C) It was absolutely necessary to start the concert.
   (D) The concert was postponed from last season.

7. (A) He reported that the time for the budget meeting had been set.
   (B) He's always late in reporting his accounting figures.
   (C) The manager never budgets his time well.
   (D) It's never too late to turn in a report.

8. (A) The professor divided the lecture into parts.
   (B) The lecture was long and boring.
   (C) The biologist tried to sell the results of the experiment.
   (D) The teacher ran all around the subdivision.

9. (A) The coffee is much better this morning.
   (B) The coffee tastes extremely good today.
   (C) The coffee isn't very good.
   (D) This morning I definitely want some coffee.

10. (A) Marlene's roommate went to a great restaurant.
    (B) It was good of Marlene to take her roommate out to dinner.
    (C) Marlene told her roommate that she wanted to take her to dinner.
    (D) Marlene described a fantastic restaurant.

GO ON TO THE NEXT PAGE

11. (A) The agents were standing in line with their passports.
    (B) The line to get new passports is very long.
    (C) You must wait your turn to get your passport checked.
    (D) The agent needs to understand what is in your passport.

12. (A) The sale was on for three hours, so I bought a lot.
    (B) I purchased several pens because of the good price.
    (C) I brought three of my friends to the sale.
    (D) I got three new pans on sale.

13. (A) The two of them rode quickly across the field.
    (B) They went to watch a couple of horse races.
    (C) The horses were very mellow after the race.
    (D) A couple of horses were lolling in the meadow.

14. (A) The students were angry that the teacher was around.
    (B) The teacher angered the students with the exam results.
    (C) The boisterous students made the teacher mad.
    (D) The angered students complained to the teacher.

15. (A) The free meals include rice.
    (B) Drinks aren't included with meals.
    (C) The cost of food is in addition to the fee.
    (D) Meals are included in the price.

16. (A) Several sheep were driven to the port this morning.
    (B) Several ships departed in the morning.
    (C) This morning they dried part of the sheets.
    (D) Some boats entered the harbor early today.

17. (A) The poorly prepared food was returned to the cook.
    (B) He went back to the kitchen to meet the chef.
    (C) The diner was not happy with the overcooked meal.
    (D) The diner thanked the chef for the meal.

18. (A) The driver accidentally drove back to the intersection.
    (B) An accident was the cause of the congested traffic.
    (C) An accident occurred at the intersection when a car backed up.
    (D) There was a traffic accident in the back section of the lot.

19. (A) New employees are rarely initiated into the company.
    (B) New workers don't generally undertake actions on their own.
    (C) New employees are initially rated.
    (D) It's rare for employees to make new suggestions.

20. (A) The repairs that the mechanic had indicated were made.
    (B) The car needed a lot of repairs.
    (C) Buying a new car would be quite expensive.
    (D) The auto mechanic extended the repair warranty.

GO ON TO THE NEXT PAGE ➤

Part B

Directions: In Part B you will hear short conversations between two speakers. At the end of each conversation, a third person will ask a question about what was said. You will hear each conversation and question about it just one time. Therefore, you must listen carefully to understand what each speaker says. After you hear a conversation and the question about it, read the four possible answers in your test book and decide which one is the best answer to the question you heard. Then, on your answer sheet, find the number of the question and fill in the space that corresponds to the letter of the answer you have chosen.

Look at the following example.

You will hear:

You will read: (A) The exam was really awful.
(B) It was the worst exam she had ever seen.
(C) It couldn't have been more difficult.
(D) It wasn't that hard.

Sample Answer

Ⓐ Ⓑ Ⓒ ●

From the conversation you learn that the man thought the exam was very difficult and that the woman disagreed with the man. The best answer to the question "What does the woman mean?" is (D), "It wasn't that hard." Therefore, you should choose answer (D).

21. (A) She thinks the tuition should be raised.
(B) The semester's tuition is quite affordable.
(C) She doesn't have enough money for her school fees.
(D) She has more than enough for tuition.

22. (A) He hasn't yet begun his project.
(B) He's supposed to do his science project next week.
(C) He needs to start working on changing the due date.
(D) He's been working steadily on his science project.

23. (A) The boss was working on the reports.
(B) He would have to finish the reports before the end of next month.
(C) He was directed to stay late and finish some work.
(D) He could finish the reports at home.

24. (A) At the post office.
(B) In a florist shop.
(C) In a restaurant.
(D) In a hospital delivery room.

GO ON TO THE NEXT PAGE ➤

25. (A) He must see his dentist.
    (B) He doesn't want to go to his appointment.
    (C) He will cancel his dental appointment.
    (D) He's sorry he must meet with the woman.

26. (A) It was quite a success.
    (B) It was huge.
    (C) She agrees with the man.
    (D) She thought it was terrible.

27. (A) She isn't sure she likes the class.
    (B) The class gets out after 9:00.
    (C) She isn't certain when the buses run.
    (D) She will definitely take the bus.

28. (A) She needs to make an itemized list.
    (B) They haven't gone shopping for a long time.
    (C) They should be finished quickly.
    (D) She's in a hurry.

29. (A) He's not going on vacation.
    (B) He's not sure when he can get away.
    (C) He still has all his vacation plans to make.
    (D) The vacation is completely planned.

30. (A) He'd like to get some insurance.
    (B) He'd like to help the agent.
    (C) He's strongly against it.
    (D) He can't help it that he's busy.

31. (A) He should look for another typist.
    (B) He should locate a typist tomorrow morning.
    (C) He should try harder to find a typist.
    (D) He should complete the paper without help.

32. (A) She needs someone to take care of her children.
    (B) She can't find her baby.
    (C) She prefers to sit down with her baby.
    (D) She only has time for her child.

33. (A) She'd like some pie.
    (B) It's easy to prepare pie.
    (C) The task the man's working on isn't difficult.
    (D) It's easier to prepare pie than do what the man is doing.

34. (A) He's read all fifty books.
    (B) He's read more than fifty books.
    (C) There are too many books on the list.
    (D) He'd prefer a longer reading list.

35. (A) In a theater.
    (B) In an auto dealership.
    (C) In a forest.
    (D) In a factory.

GO ON TO THE NEXT PAGE ➤

Part C

Directions: In this part of the test, you will hear short talks and conversations. After each of them, you will be asked some questions. You will hear the talks and conversations and the questions about them just one time. They will not be written out for you. Therefore, you must listen carefully to understand what each speaker says.

After you hear a question, read the four possible answers in your test book and decide which one is the best answer to the question you heard. Then, on your answer sheet, find the number of the question and fill in the space that corresponds to the letter of the answer you have chosen.

Listen to this sample talk.

You will hear:

Now look at the following example.

You will hear: Sample Answer

You will read: (A) Art from America's inner cities.   Ⓐ Ⓑ Ⓒ ●
                 (B) Art from the central region of
                     the U.S.
                 (C) Art from various urban areas in
                     the U.S.
                 (D) Art from rural sections of
                     America.

The best answer to the question "What style of painting is known as American regionalist?" is (D), "Art from rural sections of America." Therefore, you should choose answer (D).

Now look at the next example.

You will hear: Sample Answer

You will read: (A) *American Regionalist.*   Ⓐ Ⓑ ● Ⓓ
                 (B) *The Family Farm in Iowa.*
                 (C) *American Gothic.*
                 (D) *A Serious Couple.*

The best answer to the question "What is the name of Wood's most successful painting?" is (C), "*American Gothic.*" Therefore, you should choose answer (C).

GO ON TO THE NEXT PAGE ➤

36. (A) She's a senior.
    (B) She's a junior.
    (C) She's a transfer student.
    (D) She's a graduate student.

37. (A) How to transfer to a junior college.
    (B) How to find his way around campus.
    (C) The course requirements for a literature major.
    (D) Who won the campus election.

38. (A) Three.
    (B) Five.
    (C) Eight.
    (D) Ten.

39. (A) Introduction to Literary Analysis.
    (B) Survey of World Literature.
    (C) American Literature.
    (D) Literature Electives.

40. (A) American Literature.
    (B) World Literature.
    (C) Literary Analysis.
    (D) Surveying.

41. (A) To protect its members.
    (B) To save the natural environment.
    (C) To honor the memory of John Muir.
    (D) To improve San Francisco's natural beauty.

42. (A) For less than a year.
    (B) Only for a decade.
    (C) For approximately a century.
    (D) For at least two centuries.

43. (A) San Francisco.
    (B) All fifty states.
    (C) The Sierra Nevada.
    (D) The eastern U.S.

44. (A) All over the world.
    (B) In the entire United States.
    (C) Only in California.
    (D) Only in the Sierra Nevadas.

45. (A) A newsletter.
    (B) A magazine.
    (C) Statistical studies.
    (D) Books.

46. (A) Science.
    (B) Art.
    (C) Literature.
    (D) Music.

47. (A) They are completely different.
    (B) They are somewhat similar but have an essential difference.
    (C) They are the same.
    (D) They are unrelated.

48. (A) A strong belief in idealism.
    (B) The expression of natural laws.
    (C) A philosophic bent.
    (D) Fidelity to actual experience.

49. (A) Objective.
    (B) Idealistic.
    (C) Philosophical.
    (D) Environmental.

50. (A) Heredity.
    (B) Environment.
    (C) Idealism.
    (D) Natural laws.

THIS IS THE END OF THE LISTENING COMPREHENSION SECTION OF THE TEST

THE NEXT PART OF THE TEST IS SECTION 2. TURN TO THE
DIRECTIONS FOR SECTION 2 IN YOUR TEST BOOK.
READ THEM, AND BEGIN WORK.
DO NOT READ OR WORK ON ANY OTHER SECTION OF THE TEST.

LISTENING COMPREHENSION

The first section of the TOEFL is the Listening Comprehension Section. This section consists of 50 questions (some tests may be longer). You will listen to recorded material and respond to questions about the material. You must listen carefully, because you will hear the tape one time only, and the material on the tape is not written in your test booklet.

There are three types of questions in the Listening Comprehension Section of the TOEFL:

1. **Part A** (questions 1–20) consists of 20 sentences. You must choose, from the four choices in your test booklet, the sentence that is closest in meaning to the sentence you hear on the tape.
2. **Part B** (questions 21–35) consists of 15 short conversations, each followed by a question. You must choose the best answer to each question from the four choices in your test booklet.
3. **Part C** (questions 36–50) consists of longer conversations or talks, each followed by a number of questions. You must choose the best answer to each question from the four choices in your test booklet.

GENERAL STRATEGIES

1. **During the directions, look ahead at the answers.** The directions on every TOEFL are the same, so it is not necessary to listen carefully to them each time. You should be completely familiar with the directions before the day of the test. You can then use the time when the directions are being given to look ahead at the answers to any questions on the same page as the directions. (You may not look ahead at another page during the directions.)

2. **Listen carefully to the sentences, conversations, and short talks.** You should concentrate fully on what the speakers are saying in questions 1–50.

3. **Choose the best answer to each question.** You should guess even if you are not sure; never leave any answers blank. (There is no penalty for guessing on the TOEFL.)

4. **Use any remaining time to look ahead at the answers to the questions that follow.** When you finish with one question, you may have time to look ahead at the answers to the next question.

LISTENING SKILLS PART A

For each of the 20 questions in Part A of the Listening Comprehension Section of the TOEFL, you will hear a short sentence on tape. After you hear the sentence, you must choose from the test booklet the answer closest in meaning to the sentence you hear.

Example

You will hear:
[Don read the book from cover to cover.]*

You will read:
(A) Don read the cover of the book.
(B) Don read all of the book.
(C) Don put a cover on the book.
(D) Don was under the bed covers when he read the book.

Answer (B) is closest in meaning to the sentence you hear on the tape. The expression *from cover to cover* means *all of the book.*

STRATEGIES FOR LISTENING COMPREHENSION—PART A

1. **During the directions to Listening Comprehension—Part A, look ahead at the answers to questions 1–20.** Look ahead at the answers to the questions that are on the same page as the directions. You may **not** turn the page during the directions.

2. **Listen carefully as the sentences in questions 1–20 are spoken.** As you listen to the sentences, remember the following:

   - Be careful of answers that sound similar to what you hear on the tape. They are usually not the correct ones.
   - Be careful of negatives. An idea expressed negatively on the tape may be expressed positively in the answers or vice versa.
   - Pay attention to the time (past, present, future) of the verb.
   - Pay attention to *who* is doing *what*.

3. **Choose the best answer to each question.** Remember to answer each question even if you are not sure of the correct response.

4. **Use any remaining time to look ahead at the answers to the questions that follow.**

---

*In this book, sentences in brackets [. . .] indicate what you will actually hear on the tape. *Italics* are used when words from the tape are discussed in the text. (On actual TOEFL tests, quotation marks " . . . " are used when words from the tape are discussed in the sample exercises.)

The following skills will help you to implement these strategies in Part A of the Listening Comprehension Section.

PROBLEMS WITH SIMILAR SOUNDS

SKILL I: RECOGNIZE SIMILAR SOUNDS

When working on Listening—Part A, you should recognize words with similar sounds in the answer choices for each question. If the answer choices contain several words with similar sounds, you know that these are important words. You must listen carefully when the statement is spoken to determine which word is actually spoken. For example, the answer choices might contain both *pin* and *pan*. If so, you must listen carefully to the statement to determine which one the speaker says.

This skill serves two purposes. First, you will begin to recognize how words with similar sounds can cause confusion in Listening—Part A. Second, you will have practice in looking ahead at answers. When you look ahead at answers in Listening—Part A, it is extremely important for you to recognize words with similar sounds in the answers, because those are the words that are being tested.

EXERCISE I: In this exercise you will see four answer choices. (You will not hear the statement on the tape.) Compare the answer choices, and underline the words or groups of words with similar sounds. The first question has been answered for you.

1. (A) There was plenty of work to do.
   (B) They worked to plant a tree.
   (C) Their work was plain to see.
   (D) Their work was carefully planned.

2. (A) Sue sent a note to the leader.
   (B) Sue said it was not a letter.
   (C) Sue will need it later.
   (D) Sue knotted a rope to the ladder.

3. (A) The crowd gave a big cheer.
   (B) The audience jeered the singer.
   (C) The speaker chaired the meeting.
   (D) The people were jarred by the news.

4. (A) Larry walked on the hard sand.
   (B) Larry thought he heard a sound.
   (C) Larry was happy that he had a son.
   (D) Larry hardly saw the accident.

5. (A) It will hurt less in the morning.
   (B) Do you understand the lesson?
   (C) He will come unless his son is sick.
   (D) I believe there is less than one.

6. (A) He wished me good luck on the project.
   (B) He told me to lock the projector.
   (C) He said that I should look for a new process.
   (D) He believed there was a lack of progress.

7. (A) Mary felt a great deal of pain.
   (B) Mary wrote a letter with a new pen.
   (C) Mary pinned the skirt.
   (D) Mary cooked the soup in a pan.

8. (A) Can you put the water in a glass?
   (B) Can you help me water the grass?
   (C) Can the waiter take cash?
   (D) Can you wait for me after class?

9. (A) Will you take the bus to the park?
   (B) When will the bus depart?
   (C) Where is the bus depot?
   (D) Have you taken the bus in the past?

10. (A) George parked the car in the garage.
    (B) George packed the box with care.
    (C) George picked the fruit in the garden.
    (D) George backed into the carton.

SKILL 2: CHOOSE THE ANSWER THAT SOUNDS DIFFERENT

It is important for you to understand that the correct answer in Listening—Part A is often the answer that sounds the most different from the sentence that you hear on the tape. The incorrect answers will often contain words and phrases that have sounds similar to the sentence on the tape.

Example

You will hear:
    [This isn't the right key for that door.]

You will read:
    (A) Do not put the key in the drawer.
    (B) Can you write the message on the door?
    (C) This is the wrong key.
    (D) The right key isn't in the drawer.

In this example, incorrect answers (A) and (D) contain the word *drawer* because it sounds like *door,* and incorrect answer (B) contains the word *write* because it sounds like *right.* The correct answer in this case is (C); notice that the correct answer uses the word *wrong* because it has the same meaning as *not . . . right* but it has a different sound.

EXERCISE 2: In this exercise, first look ahead at the answer choices quickly, looking for words with similar sounds. Underline the words. Then listen to the statements on the tape and choose the answer that is closest in meaning to the statement you heard. (Remember that the correct answer is often the one that sounds different.) The first question has been underlined for you.

▶ NOW BEGIN THE TAPE AT EXERCISE 2.

1. (A) Sally had no <u>sense</u> of responsibility.
   (B) Sally was <u>sent</u> with her friend.
   (C) Sally had no money.
   (D) Sally was on the <u>set</u> with her.

2. (A) The sweater's the wrong size.
   (B) The girl's feet aren't sweating.
   (C) The girl doesn't like the sweater.
   (D) The sweet girl doesn't feel like going.

3. (A) Bob thought the lesson didn't matter.
   (B) Bob couldn't learn the lesson.
   (C) Bob wasn't the master of the class.
   (D) Bob didn't like most of the lesson.

4. (A) Animals try to avoid fire.
   (B) Animals are killed by forest fires.
   (C) In the first frost, animals die.
   (D) Frost can kill animals.

5. (A) They locked the map in a car.
   (B) They looked many times in the car.
   (C) It cost a lot of money when the car leaked oil.
   (D) They didn't have enough money to buy another car.

6. (A) I assure you that I know the truth.
   (B) I am sure that isn't the truth.
   (C) I believe that you know the truth.
   (D) I soon will know the truth.

7. (A) The weather saved the meal.
   (B) The waiter arrived at the table with dinner.
   (C) Water was served with the meal.
   (D) He was waiting to be served the meal.

8. (A) Tom tended to dislike biology lab.
   (B) Attendance wasn't necessary at biology lab.
   (C) Tom went to biology lab.
   (D) There was a tendency to require biology lab.

9. (A) The attorney seemed to think about the problem.
   (B) The lawyer appeared to take a drink.
   (C) The lawyer happened to think of a solution.
   (D) The lawyer poured a drink.

10. (A) The meal will be served at noon.
    (B) The males should drive there by noon.
    (C) The ice will melt before noon.
    (D) The letters ought to be delivered at 12:00.

PROBLEMS WITH NEGATIVES

SKILL 3: BE CAREFUL OF NEGATIVE MEANINGS

Negatives are very common in Listening—Part A, and the most common kind of correct response to a negative statement is a positive statement with an opposite meaning word.

Example

You will hear:
[They didn't drive slowly to Maine.]

You will read:
(A) They drove rather quickly to Maine.
(B) They couldn't have driven more slowly to Maine.
(C) They wanted to travel slowly to Maine.
(D) They didn't drive to Maine.

The correct answer is answer (A). If they did not drive slowly to Maine, this means that they drove rather quickly. Notice that the correct answer uses *quickly*, the opposite of *slowly*. The answers that use *slowly* are not correct.

Various types of negatives occur in English. Review the following negative structures, because they are very common in Listening—Part A.

1. The most common type of negative is the word *not,* or its contraction *n't.*

    Tom isn't sad about the results.
    (This means that Tom is happy with the results.)

2. Other negative words such as *nobody, nothing, never,* and *none* can also cause comprehension problems in Listening—Part A.

    Nobody was in the room.
    (This means that the room was empty.)

    None of the bottles was empty.
    (This means that each of the bottles had something in it.)

3. You should also be careful about negative prefixes such as *un-* or *in-.* These prefixes have the effect of making the meaning negative.

    She was unfamiliar with the city.
    (This means that she was not familiar with the city.)

    The doctor decided that the girl was insane.
    (This means that the doctor felt that she was not sane.)

EXERCISE 3: Choose the letter of the sentence that is closest in meaning to the sentence you hear on the tape.

Now Begin the Tape at Exercise 3.

1. (A) The laboratory assistant completed one experiment.
   (B) The laboratory assistant couldn't finish one experiment.
   (C) The laboratory assistant didn't want to do more experiments.
   (D) None of the experiments could be completed.

2. (A) He helped me say what I couldn't say.
   (B) I was unable to say anything about him.
   (C) He hasn't helped me very much.
   (D) What he said was very helpful.

3. (A) Nothing was very difficult.
   (B) That exam wasn't easy.
   (C) The exam couldn't have been easier.
   (D) The exam had nothing difficult on it.

4. (A) He couldn't take his luggage to the store.
   (B) He stored his luggage at the train station.
   (C) There were no lockers for his bags.
   (D) He carried his luggage from the train station to the store.

5. (A) These paintings aren't very interesting.
   (B) I wasn't fascinated by these paintings.
   (C) Do you think these paintings are interesting?
   (D) I find these paintings quite interesting.

6. (A) I want that job very much.
   (B) Nobody wants that job very much.
   (C) Everybody wants that job as much as I do.
   (D) They all want that job more than I do.

7. (A) I'm feeling terrific.
   (B) I felt a lot worse today.
   (C) I'm not feeling too well today.
   (D) I'm a bit better today.

8. (A) I don't like this meal too much.
   (B) This food tastes wonderful to me!
   (C) Don't you like this food?
   (D) I can't stand this meal!

9. (A) The service at this hotel isn't too good.
   (B) The service at the hotel could be improved.
   (C) This hotel's service is equal to the service at other hotels.
   (D) This hotel gives excellent service.

10. (A) He told his kids to leave.
    (B) He seriously wanted you to go.
    (C) He was joking when he told you to leave.
    (D) When did he tell you to leave?

SKILL 4:   BE CAREFUL OF DOUBLE NEGATIVES

It is sometimes possible for two negative ideas to appear in one sentence, and the result can be quite confusing.

Example

> You will hear:
> [It isn't impossible for the concert to take place.]

> You will read:
> (A) There is no possibility that the concert will take place.
> (B) The concert will definitely not take place.
> (C) The concert might take place.
> (D) The concert can't take place.

The correct answer to this question is answer (C). If it *isn't impossible* for the concert to take place, then it *is possible*.

Review the following structures with two negatives. These structures can be heard in Listening—Part A.

1. The most common situation in which you would find two negatives in one sentence is when you have one negative word (such as *not, none, nothing, nobody*) and one negative prefix (such as *in-, un-*).

    > He didn't like the unclean office.
    > (This means that he would have preferred a clean office.)

2. It is also possible to have two negative verbs in one sentence.

    > It wasn't snowing, so they didn't go to the mountains.
    > (This means that they would have gone to the mountains if it had been snowing.)

3. The following negative structure with *neither* or *either* is also very common on the TOEFL.

    > Sue didn't like the movie, and neither did Mark.
    > (This means that Sue did not like the movie, and Mark also did not like the movie.)

    > The teacher wasn't late, and the students weren't either.
    > (This means that the teacher was not late, and the students also were not late.)

EXERCISE 4:   Choose the letter of the sentence that is closest in meaning to the sentence that you hear on the tape.

  NOW BEGIN THE TAPE AT EXERCISE 4.

1. (A) Mike was extremely friendly
       when I met him.
   (B) Mike could have met me
       sooner.
   (C) Mike didn't seem to like me at
       all.
   (D) When I met Mike, he didn't
       have a friend.

2. (A) Steve wanted to finish his
       paper, and so did Paul.
   (B) Both Steve's and Paul's papers
       were incomplete.
   (C) Steve and Paul were busy doing
       their term papers.
   (D) When Steve wasn't able to
       finish his paper, Paul couldn't
       help.

3. (A) She has problems that others
       aren't aware of.
   (B) She knows she's been a
       problem.
   (C) Others aren't aware of her
       problems.
   (D) She doesn't have a care in the
       world.

4. (A) The first essay was better than
       the second.
   (B) The first and second drafts
       couldn't be better.
   (C) The second draft of the essay
       was much better than the
       first.
   (D) Both versions of the essay were
       poorly written.

5. (A) The union elections have
       bothered him greatly.
   (B) He wasn't the least bit
       disturbed by the elections.
   (C) The elections had little effect on
       him.
   (D) He recently effected new
       elections in the union.

6. (A) The patient absolutely didn't
       need the surgery.
   (B) The necessity for the surgery
       was unquestionable.
   (C) The surgeon felt that the
       operation was necessary.
   (D) It was essential that the
       surgery be performed
       immediately.

7. (A) With so many members
       present, the committee
       couldn't reach a decision.
   (B) The committee should've waited
       until more members were
       present.
   (C) The issue shouldn't have been
       decided by all the committee
       members.
   (D) The issue wasn't decided
       because so many members
       were absent.

8. (A) He always tells me that he
       doesn't like my work.
   (B) I hope that he never tells me
       that my work is bad.
   (C) I want his work always to be
       acceptable.
   (D) He never says that my work is
       unacceptable.

9. (A) Neither Tim nor Sylvia is
       taking care of Art.
   (B) Sylvia likes modern art even
       less than Tim does.
   (C) Sylvia doesn't care for anything
       Tim does.
   (D) Sylvia and Tim agree in their
       opinion of modern art.

10. (A) Mary's an exacting person.
    (B) Mary can't be counted on to
        forgive you.
    (C) Mary generally forgives others.
    (D) Mary isn't exact about what she
        gives to others.

SKILL 5: BE CAREFUL OF "ALMOST NEGATIVE" EXPRESSIONS

Certain expressions in English have "almost negative" meanings. These expressions are common on the TOEFL and need to be reviewed.

1. The words *hardly, barely, scarcely,* and *only* mean *almost none.*

   > Steve <u>hardly</u> talked.
   > (This means that Steve talked just a little; he almost did not talk at all.)

   > Wendy had <u>barely</u> enough money.
   > (This means that Wendy did have enough money, but she did not have any extra.)

   > Martha <u>scarcely</u> finished reading in time.
   > (This means that Martha did finish reading, but she did not have any extra time.)

   > Robert was the <u>only</u> student to go to class.
   > (This means that Robert did go to class, but all the other students did not.)

2. The words *rarely* and *seldom* mean *almost never.*

   > The children <u>rarely</u> play outside.
   > (This means that the children almost never play outside.)

   > The students <u>seldom</u> work in the computer lab.
   > (This means that the students almost never work in the computer lab.)

EXERCISE 5: Choose the letter of the sentence that is closest in meaning to the sentence that you hear on the tape.

  NOW BEGIN THE TAPE AT EXERCISE 5.

1. (A) Theresa could've gotten a higher grade.
   (B) Anyone could get a good grade.
   (C) No one else is capable of doing as well as Theresa.
   (D) A high grade is impossible for anyone.

2. (A) They always work hard in the afternoon.
   (B) They don't do much after lunch.
   (C) After noon they never work.
   (D) It's never hard for them to work in the afternoon.

3. (A) He was unable to pay his tuition.
   (B) He was scared that he didn't have enough for tuition.
   (C) He couldn't pay tuition because money was scarce.
   (D) He had just enough to pay his school fees.

4. (A) This math project was extremely complex.
    (B) This math project was less complicated than the last.
    (C) They seldom complete their math projects.
    (D) Complicated math projects are often assigned.

5. (A) This was a very long staff meeting.
    (B) This was the only staff meeting in a long time.
    (C) The meeting lasted only until 1:00.
    (D) The one staff meeting should've lasted longer.

6. (A) Meat tastes delicious to me when it is cooked rare.
    (B) Do you think this food is delicious?
    (C) This meat is the best I've tasted in a long time.
    (D) I'd like to eat some meat from this delicatessen.

7. (A) I often have long waits in Dr. Roberts' office.
    (B) I must always wait patiently for Robert.
    (C) Dr. Roberts is generally punctual.
    (D) I don't mind waiting for Dr. Roberts.

8. (A) Although he did pass, Mark's exam grade wasn't too good.
    (B) Mark failed his history exam.
    (C) The highest grade on the history exam went to Mark.
    (D) Professor Franks didn't pass Mark on the history exam.

9. (A) It's hard for the supermarket to sell its fruit.
    (B) All of the fresh fruit at the market is hard.
    (C) I hardly ever go to the supermarket to buy fresh fruit.
    (D) There's a scarcity of fresh fruit at the supermarket.

10. (A) I advise you to get another dormitory key.
    (B) To get another key, see your advisor.
    (C) The dormitory advisor can only give you one key.
    (D) This is the only dormitory to which you can get a key.

REVIEW EXERCISE (Skills 3–5): Choose the letter of the sentence that is closest in meaning to the sentence you hear on the tape.

Now Begin the Tape at Review Exercise (Skills 3–5).

1. (A) We've always been late for the bus.
   (B) The bus has always been late.
   (C) The bus only left on time once.
   (D) Only on this trip has the bus been on time.

2. (A) They couldn't find her phone number, so they didn't call her.
   (B) They couldn't give her the list over the phone.
   (C) When they went to call her, they couldn't find the list.
   (D) They couldn't recollect the number that was on the list.

3. (A) Sam usually spends this much time on his school work.
   (B) Sam has rarely worked so hard.
   (C) Sam took too much time on this paper.
   (D) Sam should've worked harder on this paper.

4. (A) This party hasn't been any fun at all.
   (B) Did you enjoy yourself?
   (C) Are you having fun at this party?
   (D) I've enjoyed myself tremendously.

5. (A) Betty often takes vacations in winter.
   (B) Betty prefers to take vacations in winter.
   (C) Does Betty like to go on vacation in winter?
   (D) A winter vacation is unusual for Betty.

6. (A) It's hard for me to work when it gets warm.
   (B) Whenever it gets warm, we turn on the air conditioner.
   (C) The air conditioner only works when we don't need it.
   (D) We like to use the air conditioner when it is warm.

7. (A) The art professor didn't believe Tom.
   (B) Tom's art work was amazing.
   (C) The catches that Tom made were incredible.
   (D) Tom didn't believe that the art professor detested his work.

8. (A) Sue's unhappy to end the semester.
   (B) Sue's glad to be finishing school.
   (C) Sue couldn't be happier to begin the semester.
   (D) The end of the semester is making Sue feel sad.

9. (A) There wasn't enough soup to go around.
   (B) We had so much soup that we couldn't finish it.
   (C) Everyone got one serving of soup, but there wasn't enough for seconds.
   (D) Everyone at the table ordered soup for dinner.

10. (A) They passed the library at six o'clock.
    (B) The library opens at six o'clock in the summer.
    (C) You can't check out more than six books in the summer.
    (D) The library closes at six o'clock.

REVIEW EXERCISE (Skills 1–5): Choose the letter of the sentence that is closest in meaning to the sentence you hear on the tape.

▭ NOW BEGIN THE TAPE AT REVIEW EXERCISE (SKILLS 1–5).

1. (A) She's unable to take her
        vacation this year.
   (B) Her vacation next week has
        been postponed.
   (C) She'll go on vacation next
        week.
   (D) She's leaving now for a
        week-long vacation.

2. (A) His bank account has too much
        money in it.
   (B) He believes there isn't enough
        money in his account.
   (C) He thinks he should go over to
        his bank.
   (D) He wants to think over whether
        he should have a bank
        account.

3. (A) It's fortunate that he was
        accepted.
   (B) It's good that he wasn't
        admitted.
   (C) Fortunately the university
        didn't admit him.
   (D) It's too bad he was rejected.

4. (A) The pilot made an emergency
        landing.
   (B) The pilot was forced to leave
        the plane in a hurry.
   (C) The pilot fielded questions
        about the forced landing.
   (D) The plane was damaged when it
        landed forcefully.

5. (A) The salesman only sold the
        required amount.
   (B) The salesman almost reached
        his goal.
   (C) The salesman rarely used
        quotes in his research.
   (D) This month the salesman
        reached his highest sales level
        ever.

6. (A) The oranges are almost ready
        to be picked.
   (B) The fruit on the trees is too
        ripe.
   (C) The orange trees have little
        fruit.
   (D) The children are in the trees
        eating fruit.

7. (A) You should never be late for
        school.
   (B) You can always return to
        school.
   (C) You should never go back to
        school.
   (D) If you're late to school, you
        should go through the back
        door.

8. (A) Twenty pairs of shoes are on
        sale.
   (B) The shoe salesman spent
        twenty dollars on pears.
   (C) The shoes cost twenty dollars.
   (D) The shoes could be repaired for
        twenty dollars.

9. (A) It wasn't his responsibility to
        pay the bill.
   (B) Bill was irresponsible about
        paying the rent.
   (C) He acted carelessly by not
        taking care of the bill.
   (D) He took responsibility for the
        unpaid bill.

10. (A) There's little rain in July.
    (B) In July it never rains.
    (C) It rains hard in July.
    (D) When it rains in July, it rains
         hard.

PROBLEMS WITH VERBS

SKILL 6: BE CAREFUL OF SENTENCES WITH ONE VERB

You need to be very careful with the time of the verb in Listening—Part A. It is not unusual for the verb in the spoken sentence to take place in one time and for the incorrect answers to be in different times.

Example

You will hear:
[The boy read the book last week.]

You will read:
(A) The boy is reading the book this week.
(B) The book exhibit lasted for a week.
(C) The boy has been reading the book for a week.
(D) The boy completed the book a week ago.

In this example, the correct answer is (D) because it gives the same meaning as the sentence you heard, but in different words; in both sentences the action of reading the book was finished last week. Answer (A) is incorrect because it takes place now (in the present), and Answer (C) is incorrect because it means that the boy started reading the book a week ago and is still reading it now. Answer (B) is incorrect because it has a completely different meaning from the sentence you heard.

You should review the following verb problems, because they occur again and again in Part A of the Listening Section.

1. If the present tense is used in a sentence, it usually means **habitual, repeated action** in the present. It does not mean *right now*.

    They play soccer on Saturday.
    (This means that every Saturday they play soccer. It does not mean that they are playing soccer right now.)

2. If the *be* + *ing* form of the verb is used, it can mean either **right now** or **future**.

    She is going to her doctor's appointment.
    (This can mean either that she is going to her doctor's appointment right now or that she will go there in the future.)

3. If the word *ago* is used, the action definitely **occurred and finished in the past.**

    The boy ate his dinner a long time ago.
    (The boy began eating his dinner and finished eating his dinner in the past.)

4. If the *have* + *ed* form of the verb is used, this usually means that the action **began in the past and is still continuing in the present.**

I <u>have lived</u> in New York for five years.
(This means that I began living in New York five years ago, and I am still living there now.)

EXERCISE 6: Choose the letter of the sentence that is closest in meaning to the sentence that you hear on the tape.

Now Begin the Tape at Exercise 6.

1. (A) The wait has taken close to an hour.
   (B) Most of us were stranded in our car.
   (C) We almost always have to stand in line.
   (D) We stood in line hour after hour.

2. (A) Walter has been regularly using a computer in Boston.
   (B) Walter is traveling to Boston regularly from now on.
   (C) Walter regularly goes to communities around Boston.
   (D) Walter was and still is making trips to Boston.

3. (A) Ellen will try to get her driver's license in two days.
   (B) Ellen passed her driving test the day before yesterday.
   (C) Ellen's driver's license expired two days ago.
   (D) The day before yesterday, Ellen's license was found.

4. (A) You can't meet with the vice president now.
   (B) No one has seen the vice president.
   (C) It's impossible to see what the vice president has done.
   (D) The vice president won't accept visitors when he returns.

5. (A) Yesterday, Stan went to school, worked, and then studied.
   (B) After class, Stan went to work and studied.
   (C) Stan has a regular schedule every day.
   (D) Stan has a tendency to go to class in the morning, in the afternoon, and at night.

6. (A) It took a long time for Susan to finish her degree.
   (B) Susan was awarded a degree long ago.
   (C) In a few minutes, Susan will receive her degree.
   (D) Susan has been quiet about the time it took to finish her degree.

7. (A) He's moved from an apartment to a house.
   (B) He's decided to move into an apartment.
   (C) He'll be moving at the beginning of the month.
   (D) He's been in his new house since the beginning of the month.

8. (A) Was your mother sad about the car accident?
   (B) Did your mother tell you about the dent in the car?
   (C) Will your mother tell you to rent a car?
   (D) Will your mother be upset about the car?

9. (A) His piano playing has improved.
    (B) He's been taking piano lessons since the beginning of the year.
    (C) He made a lot of progress before taking piano lessons.
    (D) He's expected to progress rapidly because of the piano lessons.

10. (A) He spent part of last Saturday in his dentist's office.
    (B) He's looking for a job in a dentist's office.
    (C) He works for a dentist a few hours a week.
    (D) Every Saturday his dentist only works part of the day.

Skill 7: Be Careful of Sentences with Two Verbs

When sentences have two verbs, you must be very careful of the meaning shown by the combination of the two verbs.

Example

You will hear:
[When he has time, he will make a trip.]

You will read:
(A) He has time, so he is taking a trip.
(B) He will have some free time, and then he will take a trip.
(C) Whenever he has time, he takes trips.
(D) If he had had time, he would've taken a trip.

The meaning of the spoken sentence is in the future: when he has time (in the future), he will take a trip (in the future). Answer (A) is incorrect because it means *right now* (in the present). Answer C is incorrect because it refers to repeated actions in the present. Answer (D) is incorrect because it means he did not have the time (in the past) and he did not take a trip. The correct answer is answer (B).

You should be careful of certain time expressions and constructions with two verbs, because they occur again and again in Listening—Part A.

1. The words *before, after,* and *as soon as* indicate that one action occurred before the other.

    Before you go to bed, you should brush your teeth.
    (This means that first you brush your teeth, and then you go to bed.)

    The baby learned to talk after she learned to walk.
    (This means that first the baby learned to walk, and then she learned to talk.)

    As soon as she opens a checking account, she will write the check.
    (This means that first she will open the checking account, and then she will write the check.)

2. The words *as* and *while* indicate that the two actions occurred at the same time.

> <u>As</u> the bell was ringing, the students left the class.
> (This means that the students left at the same time that the bell was ringing.)

> <u>While</u> he was driving down the highway, he listened to the radio.
> (This means that he did two things at the same time: he drove and he listened to the radio.)

3. The word *whenever* means that an action has been repeated several times.

> <u>Whenever</u> he watched a scary movie, he couldn't sleep.
> (This means that he watched several scary movies, and each time he did that he could not sleep.)

4. When one verb is in the *had + ed* form and the other verb is in the past, the *had + ed* verb occurred in the past before the other verb.

> They <u>had finished</u> the report when the chairman <u>asked</u> for it.
> (This means that they finished the report in the past, and after they finished the report the chairman asked for it.)

5. When a *had + ed* verb is in the inverted form, it means *if*.

> <u>Had</u> she <u>known</u> the truth, she would not have come.
> (This sentence has the same meaning as: *If she had known the truth, she would not have come.* Both sentences mean that she did not know the truth, and she did come.)

EXERCISE 7: Choose the letter of the sentence that is closest in meaning to the sentence you hear on the tape.

 NOW BEGIN THE TAPE AT EXERCISE 7.

1. (A) She didn't work as hard as possible because she didn't know what the reward was.
   (B) She couldn't have put more effort into the project to win the prize.
   (C) She won first prize because of her hard work on the art project.
   (D) She worked so hard that she knew first prize was hers.

2. (A) Pat only overate on his last vacation.
   (B) Wherever Pat goes on vacation, he likes to sample the food.
   (C) Pat's overeating on this vacation.
   (D) As a rule, Pat eats too much on vacation.

3. (A) She couldn't finish the soup or the salad.
   (B) The waitress brought the soup after the salad.
   (C) Soup was served before salad.
   (D) The waitress finished the soup and the salad.

4. (A) The computers are still used by the lab assistants.
   (B) They will open the lab if you want to use the computers.
   (C) You should use the computers before the lab closes.
   (D) While you are in the lab, use of the computers is limited.

5. (A) It's better for him to do his homework than to watch television.
   (B) When his homework is done, he can watch television.
   (C) He watches television while he does his homework.
   (D) His homework always gets done after television.

6. (A) She got up from her seat to sharpen her pencil.
   (B) She sharpened her pencil and then took a seat.
   (C) While she was writing, she needed to sharpen her pencil.
   (D) After she sat down, she decided that her pencil needed sharpening.

7. (A) When he saw the car coming, he tried to get out of the way.
   (B) He was able to get out of the way because he saw the car coming.
   (C) He jumped out of the way of the oncoming car.
   (D) Because he didn't see the car coming, he couldn't get out of the way.

8. (A) It was so hot that her son didn't want to get up.
   (B) In the late afternoon, it was extremely hot.
   (C) It wasn't too hot even after the sun came up.
   (D) The heat got stronger and stronger in the early morning.

9. (A) She saw that her grade was amazingly good.
   (B) She didn't want the grades to be posted because she wanted to be surprised.
   (C) She knew how well she had done before the grades were posted.
   (D) When the postman brought the grades, she was surprised.

10. (A) It took the passport office several months to process his application.
    (B) His passport arrived several months before he filled out the forms.
    (C) It was necessary to wait several months to fill out the forms for the passport.
    (D) He arrived several months before his passport was ready.

SKILL 8: BE CAREFUL OF MODALS

You must be careful of the meanings of modals such as *may, might, could,* and *should* in Part A of the Listening Section of the TOEFL.

Example

You will hear:
[He might look for a job next summer.]

You will read:
(A) He may leave his job next summer.
(B) He must have a job next summer.
(C) It's possible that he will hunt for summer work.
(D) He can't spend the summer looking for a job.

The correct answer is answer (C). The modal *might* indicates the **possibility** that he will look for a job.

Review the following expressions with modals. They are very common in Listening—Part A.

1. The modal *can* shows that you have the **ability** to do something, the **permission** to do something, or the **possibility** of doing it.

     He <u>can</u> play the piano better than everyone else.
     (This means that he has the ability to play the piano very well.)

     His mother says that he <u>can</u> stay until 11:00.
     (This means that his mother has given him permission to stay until 11:00.)

     Where <u>can</u> I buy gasoline around here?
     (This means that the speaker wants to know where it is possible to buy gasoline.)

2. The modals *may* and *might* show that there is a **possibility** that something will happen.

     The weatherman said that it <u>may</u> rain tonight.
     (This means that according to the weatherman, there is a possibility that it will rain.)

     They <u>might</u> go to the circus with us.
     (This means that it is possible that they will go with us to the circus.)

3. The modal *must* can show **obligation** or **assumption.**

     He <u>must</u> arrive on time.
     (This means that he has an obligation to arrive on time.)

     It <u>must</u> be Monday.
     (This means that it is assumed to be Monday.)

4. The modals *should* and *ought to* can mean that it is **advisable** to do something.

> She should study for that exam.
> (This means that she has not studied for the exam, but it is advisable to study for it.)
>
> He ought to buy a car.
> (This means that it is advisable for him to purchase a car.)

The modals *should* and *ought to* can also express the idea of **probability**.

> The meeting should be starting soon.
> (This means that the meeting will probably start soon.)
>
> The suitcase ought to be in your room.
> (This means that the suitcase is probably in your room.)

5. The modal *must have* shows that something has **probably already happened.**

> He must have returned the books to the library.
> (This means that he has probably already returned the books to the library.)

6. The modals *could have* and *should have* show that something that was **possible** or **advisable** in the past **did not happen.**

> He could have taken the art course.
> (This means that it was possible for him to take the art course, but he did not take it.)
>
> Mary should have mailed the letter on time.
> (This means that it was advisable for Mary to mail the letter on time, but she did not do it.)

EXERCISE 8: Choose the letter of the sentence that is closest in meaning to the sentence you hear on the tape.

 NOW BEGIN THE TAPE AT EXERCISE 8.

1. (A) Mark needs to pay his bill today.
    (B) Mark didn't pay his bill on time.
    (C) Mark's bill was paid when it should have been.
    (D) Mark's bill wasn't sent to him on time.

2. (A) It's possible that your grade will be higher if your report looks better.
    (B) Your grade depends on the type of report that you do.
    (C) Your typing grade will be better if you turn in the report.
    (D) The type of report you choose might have an impact on your grade.

3. (A) I'm positive that the machine is
         working.
    (B) I should be getting my work
         done on the machine.
    (C) The machine ought to be fixed
         by now.
    (D) The photocopies should be
         ready now.

4. (A) Gordon isn't here because he
         has left for home.
    (B) Gordon must have his briefcase
         at home.
    (C) I believe that Gordon has
         already left.
    (D) Gordon must have left his
         briefcase at home.

5. (A) If you take the coat to the
         cleaner, he'll certainly remove
         the spot.
    (B) If the coat is dry, the cleaner
         can get the spot out.
    (C) Maybe the cleaner can dry the
         sports coat.
    (D) It's possible that the spot can
         be removed.

6. (A) Your registration might be
         voided if your fees are late.
    (B) You shouldn't pay your tuition,
         or your registration will
         be cancelled.
    (C) You can cancel your tuition
         check if your registration is
         on time.
    (D) If you don't want to pay your
         tuition, you can register late.

7. (A) I finished the chapter before
         lunch.
    (B) I ought to complete my reading
         before eating.
    (C) It's better to read the chapter
         in the cafeteria.
    (D) After I've had some lunch, I
         can read the chapter.

8. (A) Can we miss classes on Friday?
    (B) When will you know how long
         your Friday classes will last?
    (C) Can we leave class early on
         Friday?
    (D) Will we be able to leave after
         classes are over at the end
         of the week?

9. (A) It was the agent's job to take
         trips.
    (B) I believe that the travel agent
         made an error.
    (C) The travel agent mistakenly
         made me mad.
    (D) It was a mistake to use a travel
         agent.

10. (A) We had a lot of time for the
         assignment.
    (B) The professor gave us more
         time than we needed.
    (C) The professor really didn't give
         us enough time to complete
         the work.
    (D) He couldn't have used more
         time for the assignment.

REVIEW EXERCISE (SKILLS 6–8): Choose the letter of the sentence that is closest in meaning
to the sentence you hear on the tape.

Now Begin the Tape at Review Exercise (Skills 6–8).

1. (A) They knew that they had to
         prepare for the exam.
    (B) They didn't prepare for the exam.
    (C) As soon as they knew about the
         exam, they began to prepare
         for it.
    (D) They knew that the preparation
         for the exam would take a
         lot of time.

2. (A) It was good that Betty went to
         the biology lab this afternoon.
    (B) There should've been a biology
         lab this afternoon.
    (C) Betty didn't go to the biology
         lab today.
    (D) The biology professor attended
         the afternoon seminar with
         Betty.

3. (A) Keith has succeeded on his
         doctoral exams.
    (B) Keith hopes to pass his doctoral
         exams soon.
    (C) Keith passed his exam results
         to his doctor.
    (D) The quality of Keith's exams
         wasn't passing.

4. (A) The policeman wrote a ticket
         and then tried to stop the
         motorist.
    (B) The policeman wrote that the
         motorist should have stopped.
    (C) The policeman wrote a report
         about the motor.
    (D) The policeman gave a ticket to
         the motorist at the side of
         the road.

5. (A) Bob's running to find the
         treasure.
    (B) The treasury department didn't
         like how Bob ran his business.
    (C) Bob wants to hold an office in
         the business club.
    (D) Bob has taken up running at his
         health club.

6. (A) The Miller family has bought a
         new Ford this year.
    (B) Perhaps the Miller family will have
         enough money for a new car.
    (C) If the Miller family buys a new
         car, it will be a Ford.
    (D) It might be possible to care for
         a horse this year.

7. (A) The movie star entered the
         dimly lit room.
    (B) It was dumb that the movie
         star was late.
    (C) The movie began after the
         lights were turned down.
    (D) The lights in the movie were
         quite damp.

8. (A) I believe that this is a different
         lock.
    (B) His luck must have changed.
    (C) They need change to open the
         lock.
    (D) We need to have the lock
         changed.

9. (A) The bell indicates when class
         finishes.
    (B) After class began, they heard
         the sound of the bell.
    (C) They will begin to hand out
         class rings today.
    (D) Class starts after you hear the
         bell.

10. (A) The customer submitted the
         fees and the application.
    (B) He admitted that the application
         fee was customary.
    (C) It's standard for the money to
         accompany the application.
    (D) The customer's free to apply
         for admittance.

REVIEW EXERCISE (SKILLS 1–8):   Choose the letter of the sentence that is closest in meaning to the sentence you hear on the tape.

NOW BEGIN THE TAPE AT REVIEW EXERCISE (SKILLS 1–8).

1. (A) It's impossible to leave at noon.
    (B) Can we leave the room?
    (C) Can't the four of us leave at noon?
    (D) Is it possible to go by 12:00?

2. (A) The fire started to attack the building.
    (B) The fireman stared at the attacker.
    (C) The fire probably began at the top of the building.
    (D) The fireman started to attack the fire.

3. (A) It's difficult to sleep when there's a lot of moonlight.
    (B) The moon was so bright that I couldn't sleep.
    (C) When I have trouble sleeping, I like to watch the moon.
    (D) I don't feel too bright in the morning whenever I have trouble sleeping at night.

4. (A) Hospital visiting hours begin at 10:00.
    (B) This hospital doesn't allow visitors.
    (C) People may visit only the hospital's lower floors.
    (D) Visitors must leave before 10:00.

5. (A) Although Mark couldn't get tickets, Paul did.
    (B) Both were unable to obtain tickets.
    (C) Neither Mark nor Paul wanted to go to the concert.
    (D) Mark tried to get tickets, but Paul didn't.

6. (A) Would you please do the grocery shopping?
    (B) Would you prefer cooked vegetables or salad?
    (C) Could you help prepare the salad?
    (D) He minds shopping for vegetables.

7. (A) They filled up the gas tank at the last service station.
    (B) Although they filled up the tank, they still ran out of gas.
    (C) They ran out of gas because they didn't stop at the gas station.
    (D) Even though they didn't stop at the service station, they didn't run out of gas.

8. (A) He only parks his car there once in a while.
    (B) He's parked his car there a lot.
    (C) He only parks his car there for short periods of time.
    (D) He left his car there on just one occasion.

9. (A) The company was founded about a year ago.
    (B) It was just established that he could go into business.
    (C) The business only lasted a year.
    (D) They're going into business this year.

10. (A) I'm so happy we don't have to work on Friday.
    (B) It would be nice if we could finish our work on Friday.
    (C) Could you be nice enough to come in to work in my place on Friday?
    (D) It's too bad we must work on Friday.

PROBLEMS WITH WHO IS DOING THE ACTION _____

SKILL 9:   BE CAREFUL OF ACTIVE AND PASSIVE MEANINGS

It is sometimes confusing to understand who is doing the action in a passive sentence. This problem is often tested in Listening—Part A.

Example

You will hear:
[Sue was given a book on Roman history by Mary.]

You will read:
(A) Sue gave a book to Mary.
(B) Mary was given a book on Roman history.
(C) A book on Roman history was given to Mary.
(D) Mary gave a book on Roman history to Sue.

The correct answer is (D). Answers (A), (B), and (C) all say that Sue gave the book to Mary. Answer (D) says that Mary gave the book to Sue.

Remember the following tips about passive and active sentences in Listening—Part A.

1. If the spoken sentence is in the passive, often the correct response is in the active.

> The letter was sent by John last week.
> (A possible correct answer for this passive statement is the active version: *John sent the letter last week.*)

2. If the spoken sentence is in the active, sometimes the correct response is in the passive.

> The students finished the exercises before lunch.
> (A possible correct answer for this active statement is the passive version: *The exercises were finished before lunch.*)

EXERCISE 9:   Choose the letter of the sentence that is closest in meaning to the sentence you hear on the tape.

 NOW BEGIN THE TAPE AT EXERCISE 9.

1. (A) I drank some water on the lawn this morning.
    (B) I waited for you on the lawn this morning.
    (C) The lawn has already been watered today.
    (D) I wanted a new lawn this morning.

2. (A) The road the horses took was long and hard.
    (B) It was hard to find the hidden houses.
    (C) The riders worked the horses too much.
    (D) It was hard for people to ride the horses for long.

3. (A) The bicycle rider didn't want to help the motorists.
   (B) The bicycle rider passed by several motorists.
   (C) The motorists could be helped by the bicycle rider.
   (D) Many drivers didn't stop to assist the bicycle rider.

4. (A) We need new print for the additional copies.
   (B) We can make extra copies if necessary.
   (C) Printers are needed for the additional copies.
   (D) Additional copies are needed immediately.

5. (A) The musical was very crowded.
   (B) The cannon exploded near the musician.
   (C) The performer was applauded by those sitting in the audience.
   (D) The musical attracted large crowds.

6. (A) The lights in the trees were destroyed in the storm.
   (B) The storm damaged the trees.
   (C) The falling trees destroyed a store.
   (D) In the light the destruction of the storm could be seen.

7. (A) Harry admitted that he wanted to go to law school in the fall.
   (B) The law school accepted Harry as a student.
   (C) The law professor admitted that Harry would be a student in the fall semester.
   (D) Harry would be admitted to law school after the fall semester.

8. (A) Mark's plants were cared for in his absence.
   (B) Mark's plan was to be out of town.
   (C) Mark was careful about his planned trip out of town with me.
   (D) I was careful while Mark was gone.

9. (A) She was broke from skiing.
   (B) She went skiing in spite of her broken leg.
   (C) Her leg was hurt on a skiing trip.
   (D) Her skis were broken in the mountains.

10. (A) Angela asked how to find her way to class.
    (B) Angela was present when the class asked about foundlings.
    (C) Angela found a present to give to the class.
    (D) Angela spoke to the class about her research results.

Skill 10: Recognize Who Is Doing the Action with Certain Verbs

Even when **active vs. passive** is not the problem, it is sometimes difficult to recognize who is doing the action because of the verb that is used.

Example

You will hear:
[Mara replaced Robert in the band.]

You will read:
(A) Robert became a new member of the band.
(B) Robert took Mara's place in the band.
(C) Mara didn't have a place in the band.
(D) Mara took Robert's place in the band.

The spoken sentence *Mara replaced Robert in the band* means that Robert is no longer in the band, and Mara is in the band. Answers (A) and (B) are incorrect because they say that Robert is in the band. Answer (C) is incorrect because it says that Mara was not in the band. Answer (D) is correct.

Although there can be confusion over who is doing the action with any verb, there are two structures that often cause this type of confusion. Review the following two structures, because they are very common in Listening—Part A.

1. Sentences with *had + a noun, made + a noun,* or *let + a noun* often cause confusion over who is doing the action.

    The teacher had the students fill out the forms.
    (This means that the students filled out the forms. The teacher did not fill out the forms.)

    The mother made the child eat the apple.
    (This means that the child ate the apple. The mother did not eat the apple.)

    The officer let the soldiers have a weekend pass.
    (This means that the soldiers had a weekend pass. The officer did not have a weekend pass.)

2. Certain verbs (such as *name, appoint, call, elect*) can have two nouns after them, and this causes confusion about who is doing what.

    The teacher named Marie homecoming queen.
    (This says that Marie became homecoming queen. The teacher did not become homecoming queen.)

    The governor appointed Mr. Benson judge.
    (This means that Mr. Benson became judge. The governor did not become judge.)

EXERCISE 10: Choose the letter of the sentence that is closest in meaning to the sentence you hear on the tape.

  NOW BEGIN THE TAPE AT EXERCISE 10.

1. (A) The students pointed at Mac.
    (B) Mac was present when the other students made the appointment.
    (C) The class representative suggested Mac to the other students.
    (D) Mac was chosen by his classmates to represent them.

2. (A) The manager went to the supply room.
    (B) The clerk sent supplies to the floor.
    (C) The clerk went to the supply room at the manager's request.
    (D) The clerk backed into the manager in the supply room.

3. (A) The passenger waited at the corner.
    (B) The passenger looked for a taxi at the corner.
    (C) The cab driver waited for the passenger.
    (D) The passenger cornered the waiting taxi driver.

4. (A) Mr. Swansen discussed politics at the party.
    (B) Mr. Swansen was selected by the committee to become the head of the party.
    (C) Mr. Swansen voted for a committee to head the political party.
    (D) The political committee was selected by the party chairman.

5. (A) Mary became the new class president.
    (B) Sue took her place as class president.
    (C) In place of Mary, Susan became senior class president.
    (D) The senior class president replaced Sue and Mary.

6. (A) The police officer was stationed near the tourist.
    (B) The tourist was forced to accompany the policeman.
    (C) The tourist became mad at the police station.
    (D) The tourist stated that the police officer never came.

7. (A) John received an inheritance when his uncle died.
    (B) It's a benefit that John's name is the same as his uncle's.
    (C) John knows that his uncle will come to the benefit.
    (D) John's uncle gave him a beneficial name.

8. (A) The librarian was quite reserved with the students for two days.
    (B) Within two days the librarian had the books for the students.
    (C) The librarian reserved the books for the students.
    (D) The students put the books on hold for two days.

9. (A) It was hard for me to hear Jane last night.
    (B) Jane gave a harp recital last night.
    (C) Jane was playing hard while I was hurt.
    (D) I played the harp last night for Jane.

10. (A) The baby-sitter went to bed quite early.
    (B) The children didn't like going to bed early.
    (C) The baby-sitter made the bed after the children got up.
    (D) The children were forced to go to bed early.

REVIEW EXERCISE (SKILLS 9–10): Choose the letter of the sentence that is closest in meaning to the sentence that you hear on the tape.

NOW BEGIN THE TAPE AT REVIEW EXERCISE (SKILLS 9–10).

1. (A) The students were told to go listen to the speaker.
   (B) The professor attended that evening's lecture.
   (C) The students listened to the lecturer give them directions.
   (D) The professor was directed to the lecture hall.

2. (A) I didn't want the coffee that Carol ordered.
   (B) I wasn't sure if Carol wanted coffee.
   (C) I was unaware that coffee had already been ordered.
   (D) I already had coffee before Carol ordered it.

3. (A) The chairman decided that Tony would serve on the board for another year.
   (B) Tony's chairman was elected by the board.
   (C) The board decided Tony could be chairman after one year.
   (D) Tony became chairman for one more year.

4. (A) The judge defended the murderer.
   (B) The judge tried to protect the defendant from the murderer.
   (C) The judge said that the defendant was a criminal.
   (D) The defense couldn't make a judgment about the murderer.

5. (A) The cars were in the left parking lot at the airport.
   (B) The passengers parked their cars at the airport.
   (C) The airport couldn't hold a lot of cars.
   (D) There were a lot of cars to the left of the parking lot.

6. (A) Sam went into the house next door.
   (B) While Martha was out walking, she saw Sam's house.
   (C) Martha served Sam at a neighbor's house.
   (D) Sam walked over to his neighbor Martha's house.

7. (A) The man taught his son about football.
   (B) The boy received the ball from his dad.
   (C) The ball was tossed into the air by the boy.
   (D) The man played with the ball in the sun.

8. (A) The doctor decided to take some time off from work.
   (B) The doctor told him he was too weak to work.
   (C) He was mad when the doctor took some time off.
   (D) He took a vacation on his doctor's orders.

9. (A) The attendant checked the oil
         in Mark's car.
    (B) Mark checked to see if he had
         enough oil in his car.
    (C) Mark checked with the service
         station attendant.
    (D) Mark wrote a check for the oil.

10. (A) He approached a woman to find
         out the time.
    (B) He approached the woman just
         in time.
    (C) He wanted to ask the woman
         what time she would be
         ready.
    (D) The woman asked the man
         what time it was.

REVIEW EXERCISE (SKILLS 1–10):   Choose the letter of the sentence that is closest in meaning to the sentence you hear on the tape.

NOW BEGIN THE TAPE AT REVIEW EXERCISE (SKILLS 1–10).

1. (A) The professor bought two
         books.
    (B) The students had to purchase
         two books.
    (C) The students sold two books to
         the professor.
    (D) The students were required to
         read two books by the
         professor.

2. (A) The managers will take the
         train later this week.
    (B) A program to develop new
         managers will commence
         soon.
    (C) The new management program
         is very weak.
    (D) The start of the training
         program has been delayed
         by management.

3. (A) The client presented his case to
         the lawyer.
    (B) The client was upset about the
         lawyer's rejection.
    (C) That the lawyer returned the
         suitcase made the client
         unhappy.
    (D) The client made the lawyer
         unhappy about the case.

4. (A) After the earthquake, the
         insurance company came out
         to inspect the damage.
    (B) The insurance company insisted
         that the building be repaired
         to meet earthquake safety
         standards.
    (C) The inhabitants paid their
         insurance premiums after
         the earthquake.
    (D) The insurance company paid for
         the earthquake damage.

5. (A) The prices of microcomputers
         are increasing.
    (B) Better technology should lead
         to decreased prices.
    (C) The decreased prices should
         make the technology better.
    (D) Because the prices of
         microcomputers are
         extremely high, they should
         come down.

6. (A) The instructor selected several
         passages.
    (B) The conductor was fair to the
         passengers.
    (C) The stamp collector conducted
         his business.
    (D) The riders paid for their train
         trip.

7. (A) The referee blew his whistle to end the game.
   (B) The game started when the whistle had blown.
   (C) When the game began, the referee blew his whistle.
   (D) After the referee began the game, the whistle was blown.

8. (A) Unauthorized people aren't allowed at the testing location.
   (B) The security guard is prohibited from entering the test site.
   (C) Everyone is prohibited from entering the test site.
   (D) The authorities have prohibited security personnel from entering the test site.

9. (A) Paul is getting married this summer.
   (B) Paul's sister is returning from Vermont to get married.
   (C) Paul will be there when his sister gets married this summer.
   (D) Paul's sister is coming to his wedding in Vermont.

10. (A) She dresses in three different styles.
    (B) There are three different dresses for you to try on.
    (C) Would you like to come in and see the different dresses?
    (D) Those dresses are carried in various sizes.

For each of the 15 questions in Part B of the Listening Comprehension Section of the TOEFL, you will hear a short conversation between two speakers followed by a question. After you listen to the conversation and the question, you must choose the best answer to the question from your test booklet.

Example

You will hear:
    Man: [I've always wanted to visit Hawaii with you.
    Woman: Why not next month?
              WHAT DOES THE WOMAN MEAN?]

You will read:
    (A) Next month isn't a good time for the trip.
    (B) She doesn't want to go to Hawaii.
    (C) She suggests taking the trip next month.
    (D) She's curious about why he doesn't want to go.

Answer (C) is the best answer to the question. *Why not next month?* is a suggestion that they take the trip next month.

STRATEGIES FOR LISTENING COMPREHENSION—PART B

1. **During the directions for Listening Comprehension—Part B, look ahead at the answers to questions 21–35.** Look ahead at the answers to the questions that are on the same page as the directions. You may **not** turn the page during the directions.

2. **Listen carefully as the conversations in questions 21–35 are spoken.** As you listen to the conversations, remember the following:

   - Be careful of answers that sound similar to what you hear on the tape. They are usually not the correct ones.
   - Be careful of the meanings of negatives on the tape and in the answers. (Note: The above two skills are also used in Listening—Part A.)
   - Listen carefully to the second line of the conversation, because it often contains the answer to the question.
   - Draw conclusions about *who, what,* and *where.*

3. **Choose the best answer to each question.** Remember to answer each question even if you are not sure of the correct response.

4. **Use any remaining time to look ahead at the answers to questions that follow.**

The following skills will help you to implement these strategies in Part B of the Listening Comprehension Section.

PROBLEMS SIMILAR TO LISTENING—PART A————————

SKILL 11: CHOOSE THE ANSWER THAT SOUNDS DIFFERENT

In Listening—Part B as well as Listening—Part A the correct answer is often the answer that sounds most different from what you heard on the tape. The incorrect answers will often contain words and phrases that have sounds similar to the conversation on the tape.

Example

You will hear:
   Woman: [Does your broken arm hurt very much?
   Man: Only if I try to move.
              WHAT DOES THE MAN MEAN?]

You will read:
   (A) He broke his arm trying to move it.
   (B) He only hurt the broken arm.
   (C) He only tries to move the broken arm.
   (D) There's no pain if he rests quietly.

Answer (D) is the best answer to the question because the man hurts himself only when he moves, and he therefore does not hurt himself if he does not move. You should notice that answer (D) is the only answer that does not contain the words *broken, arm, hurt,* or *try.*

EXERCISE 11:   In this exercise listen carefully to the short conversation and question on the tape, and then choose the best answer to the question. Remember that the best answer is often the one that sounds most different from what you hear on the tape.

  NOW BEGIN THE TAPE AT EXERCISE 11.

1. (A) It's been partly fixed.
    (B) It's unrepaired.
    (C) It was left exactly as it had
          been.
    (D) Bob left only part of it.

2. (A) She's marked it on her
          calendar.
    (B) She's not sure if she's free.
    (C) She'll write a check for the
          calendar.
    (D) Her calendar says she has to
          have a meeting at 3:00.

3. (A) He never wants it to stop.
   (B) He'd like it to rain again.
   (C) He thinks it's finally stopped.
   (D) He's tired of it.

4. (A) It's important to pack the suitcases.
   (B) One should call the porter before he packs.
   (C) The man should put the package in the suitcase.
   (D) They need help with their bags.

5. (A) It's too dark where she usually studies.
   (B) She doesn't like working with a lamp on the desk.
   (C) She isn't working in the living room.
   (D) There's no lamp on her desk.

6. (A) The cafeteria opens at 10 o'clock in the morning.
   (B) Breakfast is served for three hours.
   (C) She thinks the cafeteria is open for seven to ten hours.
   (D) In the morning the cafeteria opens sometime between 7 o'clock and 10 o'clock.

7. (A) The firemen saved the homes for last.
   (B) A fireman saved the hillside last night.
   (C) The homes on the hillside were burned.
   (D) The houses weren't destroyed.

8. (A) There's no more wood inside.
   (B) The wood in the fireplace should be put outside.
   (C) There's a fire outside.
   (D) He needs to bring some wood outside.

9. (A) There's enough soup.
   (B) The spices are adequate.
   (C) She thinks the soup's too salty.
   (D) He should add more salt and pepper.

10. (A) She'd like to work on her social skills at the football game.
    (B) She wishes she could work on her term paper for sociology.
    (C) She can't attend the game because of her schoolwork.
    (D) Sociology is less important to her than football this weekend.

SKILL 12:   BE CAREFUL OF NEGATIVES

In Listening—Part B as well as Listening—Part A you must pay careful attention to negatives.

Example

You will hear:
   Woman: [Are you planning to go to college next year?
   Man: I'm not too happy with that idea.
   Q: WHAT DOES THE MAN MEAN?]

You will read:
   (A) He's happy about going to college.
   (B) He isn't very happy with her plans.
   (C) His idea is to go to college.
   (D) He'd rather do something else.

In the conversation the man says that he is not happy with the idea of going to college. This implies that he would rather do something other than going to college. The best answer is therefore answer (D). Notice that the incorrect answers (A), (B), and (C) contain the words *happy, college, plans,* and *idea,* which are heard in the conversation.

EXERCISE 12: In this exercise listen carefully to the short conversation and question on the tape, and then choose the best answer to the question. Be particularly careful of negatives in this exercise.

NOW BEGIN THE TAPE AT EXERCISE 12.

1. (A) She does want to see the movie.
   (B) It's extremely important to her to go.
   (C) She doesn't want to go there anymore.
   (D) She really couldn't move there.

2. (A) Mona hasn't worked hard.
   (B) Mona's experience has been hard.
   (C) The manager's job is hard work.
   (D) Mona hasn't worked for very long.

3. (A) Finishing the paper today.
   (B) Not working on the paper now.
   (C) Never typing the paper.
   (D) Taking time out from the paper now.

4. (A) She doesn't mind an hour more.
   (B) She'd rather stay more than an hour.
   (C) It's better to stay than go.
   (D) She prefers to leave.

5. (A) He'll definitely be elected.
   (B) The election is now complete.
   (C) She has high hopes for his chances.
   (D) He has little chance.

6. (A) His attendance was perfect.
   (B) He has almost all the notes.
   (C) He went to all the lectures but one.
   (D) He missed more than one psychology class.

7. (A) She barely rode the bicycle.
   (B) She paid for the bicycle.
   (C) The bicycle didn't need to be paid for.
   (D) She didn't have enough money.

8. (A) He prefers to watch sports.
   (B) He'll watch the movie if he has time.
   (C) He never watches movies on television.
   (D) He had the idea at the same time that she did.

9. (A) Information about the problem is unavailable.
   (B) No one has been informed.
   (C) Everybody knows what is going on.
   (D) Nobody is aware that the problem is serious.

10. (A) The project will take all their effort.
    (B) They have no other work to do.
    (C) It's impossible to finish.
    (D) They aren't even close to finishing the project.

REVIEW EXERCISE (SKILLS 11–12): In this exercise listen carefully to the short conversation and question on the tape. Then choose the best answer to the question.

🔲 NOW BEGIN THE TAPE AT REVIEW EXERCISE (SKILLS 11–12).

1. (A) The convention was disorganized.
   (B) She didn't plan to attend the convention.
   (C) She planned the convention last week.
   (D) She wasn't pleased with the last week of the convention.

2. (A) He rarely spends time on his courses.
   (B) He's an excellent student.
   (C) He never studies.
   (D) His books are always open.

3. (A) He should take the pie out.
   (B) He should try something else.
   (C) He shouldn't try cherry pie.
   (D) He should feel sorry.

4. (A) She'd rather go running.
   (B) She doesn't want to go into the pool.
   (C) She'll go swimming after she changes clothes.
   (D) She needs a sweatsuit to go running.

5. (A) He finished the exam in plenty of time.
   (B) He was scared he wouldn't finish.
   (C) He used every possible minute to finish.
   (D) He was unable to complete the exam.

6. (A) The newspaper headlines described a bad storm.
   (B) The weather will probably get worse later.
   (C) There was news about a headstrong man.
   (D) He had a tan hat on his head.

7. (A) She believes the plan will solve the problems.
   (B) She thinks her vote isn't the best solution.
   (C) She's unsure of the plan's effectiveness.
   (D) She's against a solution to the parking problem.

8. (A) He can easily type for fifty minutes.
   (B) This is the easiest of fifty jobs he has applied for.
   (C) He's able to type very quickly.
   (D) This job is easy for anyone to do.

9. (A) She hopes her work will be well received.
   (B) She knows no one is happy with what she has done.
   (C) She's arranged to take a trip because she's unhappy.
   (D) Everyone's happy with the condition of the field.

10. (A) He always watches television from 1:00 to 2:00.
    (B) He'll watch in an hour or two.
    (C) He just got a television this week.
    (D) He doesn't see many programs.

PROBLEMS SPECIFIC TO LISTENING—PART B _____

SKILL 13: LISTEN FOR THE SECOND LINE OF THE CONVERSATION

In the majority of questions in Part B of the Listening Comprehension Section, the question is answered in the second line of the conversation. Many students make the mistake of listening carefully to the first line of the conversation, thinking about it, and missing the second line. But you should be listening carefully to the second line of the conversation, because that line generally contains the answer.

Example

You will hear:
    Man: [Will you be back by 4:00?
    Woman: I'll be back as quickly as I can.
    Q: WHAT DOES THE WOMAN MEAN?]

You will read:
    (A) She'll try to return fast.
    (B) She'll definitely be back by 4:00.
    (C) She can give it back by 4:00.
    (D) She'll call back quickly.

Answer (A) is the correct answer, and this answer is based on the second line of the conversation: *I'll be back as quickly as I can. I'll be back* means that she will return, and *as quickly as I can* means that she will try to be fast. Notice that the correct answer has the same meaning as the second line of the conversation, but it sounds very different. The incorrect answers have many sounds similar to the conversation.

EXERCISE 13: In this exercise listen carefully to the second line of the conversation and the question on the tape. Then choose the best answer to the question based on the second line of the conversation.

NOW BEGIN THE TAPE AT EXERCISE 13.

1. (A) He can help her tonight.
    (B) He's always busy with his homework.
    (C) He's sorry he can't ever help her.
    (D) He'll help her tomorrow night.

2. (A) She worked late at a conference.
    (B) Her meeting was cancelled.
    (C) She called a conference at work.
    (D) She was late to a conference.

3. (A) Water the plants once a day.
    (B) Give the plants no more water.
    (C) Water the plants often while he's gone.
    (D) Give the plants a limited amount of water.

4. (A) She doesn't like the place he chose.
    (B) She doesn't want to get into the car.
    (C) It's impossible to put the car there.
    (D) She'd prefer anywhere else.

5. (A) He was the second to arrive.
   (B) He had no time to spare.
   (C) He should've checked before he came.
   (D) He arrived too early.

6. (A) He should try to borrow some from a neighbor.
   (B) He should take a check to Tom.
   (C) He should work on his math assignment with Tom.
   (D) He should check behind the door.

7. (A) There's plenty to eat.
   (B) The refrigerator's broken.
   (C) The food isn't in the refrigerator.
   (D) She's not sure if there's enough.

8. (A) Her eyes hurt.
   (B) She thought the lecture was great.
   (C) The class was boring.
   (D) She didn't want to watch Professor Martin.

9. (A) Not all the bills have been paid.
   (B) They don't have enough credit to pay the bills.
   (C) She used a credit card to pay some of the bills.
   (D) They don't have any credit cards.

10. (A) The team hasn't won often.
    (B) He usually doesn't pay attention to the football team.
    (C) It's out of the ordinary for the team to lose.
    (D) He usually hears about the football games.

SKILL 14: MAKE INFERENCES ABOUT WHO, WHAT, AND WHERE

It is common in Listening—Part B to ask you to draw some kind of conclusion. In this type of question the answer is not clearly stated; instead you must draw a conclusion based on clues given in the conversation. One kind of conclusion that is common in Listening—Part B is to determine what type of job one of the speakers has, based on the clues given in the conversation.

Example

You will hear:
Woman: [Can you tell me what assignments I missed when I was absent from your class?
Man: You missed one homework assignment and a quiz.
Q: **WHO** IS THE MAN (WHAT IS HIS JOB?)

You will read:
(A) A newspaper assignment editor.
(B) A police officer.
(C) A teacher.
(D) A student.

The clues *your class, homework,* and *quiz* in the conversation tell you that the man is probably a teacher. Answer (C) is therefore the correct answer.

Another type of conclusion that is common in Listening—Part B is to determine what will probably happen next, based on the clues given in the conversation.

Example

You will hear:
Woman: [Are you going to read those books here in the library?
Man: I think I'd rather check them out now and take them home.
Q: **WHAT** WILL THE MAN PROBABLY DO NEXT?]

You will read:
(A) Sit down in the library.
(B) Look for some more books.
(C) Return the books to the shelves.
(D) Go to the circulation desk.

The man says that he would like to check the books out now. Since the circulation desk is where you go to check books out from a library, the man will probably go to the circulation desk next. The correct answer is therefore answer (D).

A final type of conclusion that is common in Listening—Part B is to determine where the conversation probably takes place, based on the clues given in the conversation.

Example

You will hear:
Man: [Are you going into the water or are you just going to lie there on the sand?
Woman: I think I need to put on some suntan lotion.
Q: **WHERE** DOES THIS CONVERSATION PROBABLY TAKE PLACE?]

You will read: (A) At a beauty salon.
(B) At the beach.
(C) In a sandbox.
(D) At an outdoor restaurant.

The clues *water, sand,* and *suntan lotion* in the conversation tell you that this conversation probably takes place at the beach. Therefore answer (B) is the correct answer.

EXERCISE 14: In this exercise listen carefully to the short conversation and question on the tape, and then choose the best answer to the question. You will have to draw conclusions about *who, what,* and *where.*

Now Begin the Tape at Exercise 14.

1. (A) In a photography studio.
   (B) In a biology laboratory.
   (C) In an office.
   (D) In the library.

2. (A) He's a pilot.
   (B) He's a flight attendant.
   (C) He's a member of the grounds
       crew.
   (D) He works clearing land.

3. (A) Wash the dishes immediately.
   (B) Use as many dishes as possible.
   (C) Wash the dishes for as long as
       possible.
   (D) Wait until later to clean up.

4. (A) In a bank.
   (B) In a coffee shop.
   (C) At a service station.
   (D) In a beauty salon.

5. (A) Salesman.
   (B) Shoe repairman.
   (C) Party caterer.
   (D) Sales clerk in a fixtures
       department.

6. (A) A playground.
   (B) A parking lot.
   (C) A zoo.
   (D) A photo studio.

7. (A) Respond to the mail.
   (B) Put the letters in a file.
   (C) It depends on where the file is.
   (D) File the answers she received
       to the letters.

8. (A) In an airplane.
   (B) In a police car.
   (C) In a theater.
   (D) At a fireworks exhibition.

9. (A) At a department store.
   (B) At a service station.
   (C) At a collection agency.
   (D) In a delivery room.

10. (A) In a restaurant.
    (B) At a bakery.
    (C) On a farm.
    (D) In a market.

REVIEW EXERCISE (SKILLS 13–14):   In this exercise listen carefully to the short conversation and question on the tape. Then choose the best answer to the question.

 NOW BEGIN THE TAPE AT REVIEW EXERCISE (SKILLS 13–14).

1. (A) Earn his paycheck.
   (B) Write a check for a deposit on
       an apartment.
   (C) Go to a bank.
   (D) Make a list of errands to run.

2. (A) She doesn't like to listen to
       turkeys.
   (B) She thinks the dinner sounds
       special.
   (C) She especially likes the roast
       turkey.
   (D) She'd prefer a different dinner.

3. (A) In a doctor's office.
   (B) At a bar.
   (C) In a travel agency.
   (D) In a business office.

4. (A) She's very lucky to get the last
       book.
   (B) It's too bad she can't get the
       book today.
   (C) She always has good luck with
       books.
   (D) She just wanted to look at the
       book.

5. (A) Barb answered the bell.
   (B) The house was probably empty.
   (C) The bell wasn't in the house.
   (D) The house doesn't have a bell.

6. (A) A worker at the county fair.
   (B) A bus driver.
   (C) A traffic officer.
   (D) A museum guide.

7. (A) Sometimes the postman arrives after noon.
   (B) She usually reads her mail while eating lunch.
   (C) She doesn't always check the mail at lunchtime.
   (D) The mail delivery is extremely predictable.

8. (A) In a hospital.
   (B) At a police station.
   (C) At the beach.
   (D) In a locker room.

9. (A) She has no time to work now.
   (B) She doesn't want to work on the report either.
   (C) It's best to get it over with now.
   (D) There's no time to present the report now.

10. (A) Go to work in the lab.
    (B) Sample the work from the lab.
    (C) Have the samples delivered.
    (D) Send a note to the lab.

REVIEW EXERCISE (SKILLS 11–14): In this exercise listen carefully to the short conversation and question on the tape, and then choose the best answer to the question.

NOW BEGIN THE TAPE AT REVIEW EXERCISE (SKILLS 11–14).

1. (A) She's not very happy.
   (B) She didn't do very well on the exam.
   (C) She could be somewhat happier.
   (D) She's delighted with the results.

2. (A) In a department store.
   (B) In a stationary store.
   (C) At the post office.
   (D) At the airport.

3. (A) The man prefers his own restaurant.
   (B) She doesn't really like that restaurant.
   (C) Each of them has his own restaurant.
   (D) Everyone has different tastes.

4. (A) It's unlikely that he'll go to the interview.
   (B) The interview was apparently quite unsuccessful.
   (C) He thinks he'll be recommended for a high-level job.
   (D) He had an excellent interview.

5. (A) Take care of Bob.
   (B) Invite Bob to dinner.
   (C) Let Bob know that they accept his invitation.
   (D) Respond to the woman's question.

6. (A) She's told Matt he'll go far.
   (B) Matt has far from enough talent.
   (C) She told Matt to roll farther.
   (D) She believes Matt has the ability for the part.

7. (A) She refuses to help him.
   (B) She's afraid she can't be of
        much assistance.
   (C) He doesn't know enough for
        her to help him.
   (D) He should try to do it on his
        own.

8. (A) A pharmacist.
   (B) A dentist.
   (C) A teacher.
   (D) A business manager.

9. (A) The man's never late.
   (B) It's good that he was fifteen
        minutes late.
   (C) It's never better to be late for
        class.
   (D) It's good that he went to class.

10. (A) He hasn't seen Steve.
    (B) Steve was there only for a
         moment.
    (C) Steve was around a short time
         ago.
    (D) He needs to think a moment
         about where Steve is.

LISTENING SKILLS—PART C

Listening—Part C consists of longer passages, each followed by a number of questions. You will hear the passages and the questions on a tape; they are not written in your test booklet. You must choose the best answer to each question from the four choices that are written in your test booklet.

The long passages in Listening—Part C of the TOEFL may be in the form of either a conversation between two people or a talk by one. The conversations are often about some aspect of school life:

- how difficult a class is
- how to write a research paper
- how to sell a textbook at the end of the semester
- how to register for a course

The conversations can also be about topics currently in the news in the United States:

- desalination of the water supply
- recycling of used products
- preventing damage from lightning

The talks are most often lectures from university courses on subjects relating to the United States:

- United States history
- United States art and literature
- United States geography

QUESTIONS AND ANSWERS

There are three common kinds of questions about the passages in Listening—Part C.

1. **Main Idea, Subject, or Topic Questions**
   For almost every passage in Listening—Part C of the TOEFL, there is one main idea, subject, or topic question. This refers to the entire passage rather than just one detail. The following are examples of this type of question:

   - What is the topic of this talk?
   - What is the main idea of this passage?
   - What is the subject of this conversation?

   This type of question is generally answered in the first line of the passage, because the first line of the passage is most often a topic or main idea sentence. Therefore, **it is extremely important to listen very carefully to the first line of the passage when it is spoken.** It probably contains the answer to the subject, topic, or main idea type of question.

2. **Inference Questions**

It is very common to have one inference question about each passage in Listening—Part C of the TOEFL. An inference question is a question that is not answered directly in the passage; you must draw a conclusion from information given in the passage. (You have already used this type of skill in Listening—Part B.) The words *probably* and *most likely* indicate that a question is not answered directly in the passage. The following are examples of inference questions:

- Where does this conversation **probably** take place?
- Who is **most likely** giving this talk?
- In what course would this talk **most likely** be given?

Notice that these inference questions are all about the situation of the talk or conversation in Listening—Part C. You are often asked to draw conclusions about where a conversation is taking place or about who is talking, or, in the case of a lecture, about which course the lecture might be a part of. Therefore, when you listen to each passage **you should try to picture the situation: Who is talking and where or in which course is it happening?**

3. **Detail Questions**

The majority of questions in Listening—Part C are detail questions. This means that the questions are answered directly in the passage. The following are examples of detail questions:

- In what year did the action occur?
- What caused him to act that way?
- How did he find out that he was wrong?

There are two important ideas to remember when answering detail questions. First, **the detail questions are generally answered in order in the passage.** The first detail question is answered near the beginning of the passage, and the last detail question is answered near the end of the passage. Next, the answers in Listening—Part C do not always sound different from what you hear on the tape. Remember that the correct answers in Listening—Part A and Part B very often **sound different** from what is said on the tape. In Listening—Part C this is not true. **The answers in Listening—Part C very often sound the same as what is said on the tape.** Sometimes, however, the correct answer sounds different from what is said on the tape.

A SAMPLE LISTENING COMPREHENSION—PART C PASSAGE

You will hear:

[The settling of the vast farmlands in central North America was delayed at least partly because of an error by one man. In the early nineteenth century, Lieutenant Zebulon Pike of the U.S. Army was sent out to explore and chart the huge expanses of land in the center of the continent. When he returned from his explorations, he wrote a report in which he erroneously stated that the vast plains in the central part of the continent were desertlike, comparable to the Sahara in Africa. In reality, however, these vast plains contained some of the most fertile farmland in the world. Because of Pike's mistake, the maps of the day depicted the central part of what is today the United States as a vast desert rather than the excellent and available farmland that it was. This mistaken belief about the nature of those lands caused settlers to avoid the central plains for years.]

You will hear:
   [1. What is the topic of this talk?]

You will read:
   (A) Zebulon Pike's career.
   (B) A mistake that influenced the
       settlement of America.
   (C) A report for the army.
   (D) The farmlands of America.

You will hear:
   [2. What area was Lieutenant Pike
       sent to explore?]

You will read:
   (A) The entire North American
       continent.
   (B) A farm in the center of the United
       States.
   (C) The mountainous areas to the
       east of the plains.
   (D) The central part of the North
       American continent.

You will hear:
   [3. How did Pike describe this area?]

You will read:
   (A) As a desert.
   (B) As usable for army purposes.
   (C) As located in the Sahara.
   (D) As available for farmland.

You will hear:
   [4. What was this area really like?]

You will read:
   (A) It was a vast desert.
   (B) It was covered with farms.
   (C) It was excellent farmland.
   (D) It was similar to the Sahara.

You will hear:
   [5. This talk would probably be given
       in which of the following courses?]

You will read:
   (A) Agricultural Science.
   (B) American History.
   (C) Geology of the United States.
   (D) Military Science.

Question 1 asks about the topic of the passage. The topic of the passage is found in the first sentence of the passage *The settling of the vast farmlands in central North America was delayed at least partly because of an error by one man.* Therefore, the best answer to this question is (B).

Question 2 is a detail question that asks, *What area was Lieutenant Pike sent to explore?* The passage indicates that Pike was *sent out to explore and chart the huge expanses of land in the center of the continent.* Therefore, the best answer to this question is (D).

Question 3 is another detail question that asks, *How did Pike describe this area?* It is stated in the passage that Pike *wrote a report in which he erroneously stated that the vast plains in the central part of the continent were desertlike. . . .* Therefore, the best answer to this question is (A).

Question 4 is an additional detail question that asks, *What was this area really like?* Because the passage indicates that *in reality . . . these vast plains contained some of the most fertile farmland in the world,* the best answer to this question is (C).

Question 5 is an inference question. It asks in which course this lecture would probably be given. The word *probably* indicates to you that the question is not answered directly in the passage. You must draw a conclusion from the information in the passage to answer this question. Because this passage takes place *in the early nineteenth century* and discusses the *settling of the vast farmlands in central North America,* this talk would probably be given in an American History course. The best answer to this question is (B).

STRATEGIES FOR LISTENING COMPREHENSION—PART C

1. **During the directions to Listening Comprehension—Part C, look ahead at the answers to questions 36–50.** Look ahead at the answers to the questions that are on the same page as the directions. You may **not** turn the page during the directions. While you are looking ahead at the answers, you should try to do the following:

   - Anticipate the **topics** of the passages you will hear.
   - Anticipate the **questions** for each of the groups of answers.

2. **Listen carefully to the first line of the passage.** It often contains the main idea, subject or topic of the passage.

3. **As you listen to the passage, draw conclusions about who is talking and where the talk or conversation takes place.** You will often be asked to make such inferences in the questions about the passage.

4. **As you listen to the passage, follow along with the answers in your test booklet, and try to determine the correct answers.** Detail questions are generally answered in order in the passage, and the answers often sound the same as what is said on the tape.

5. **You should guess even if you are not sure;** never leave any answers blank.

6. **Use any remaining time to look ahead at the answers to the questions that follow.**

The following skills will help you to implement these strategies in Part C of the Listening Comprehension Section.

WHAT TO DO BEFORE LISTENING TO THE PASSAGES————————

SKILL 15: ANTICIPATE THE TOPICS

It is very helpful to your overall comprehension if you know what topics to expect in Listening—Part C. You should therefore try to anticipate the topics you will be hearing. For example, are the passages about American history, or literature, or art?

The best time to try to anticipate the topics of the listening passages is while the directions to Listening—Part C are being read on the tape. The directions to Listening—Part C are very long, and you can use this time to look ahead at the answers in the test booklet and try to determine what the passage topics are.

EXERCISE 15: Before you hear the passages, you should study the answers in the test booklet and try to determine the topics of the passages you will hear. Look at the answers to the five questions together and try to anticipate the topic of the passage for those five questions. (Of course, you cannot always determine exactly what the topic is, but you often can get a general idea.) Questions 1–5 have been answered for you.

1. (A) Find work on campus.
   (B) Work in the employment office.
   (C) Help students find jobs.
   (D) Ask the woman questions.

2. (A) In the library.
   (B) In a classroom.
   (C) In a campus office.
   (D) In an apartment.

3. (A) No more than ten.
   (B) At least twenty.
   (C) Not more than twenty.
   (D) Up to ten.

4. (A) Every morning.
   (B) Afternoons and weekends.
   (C) When he's in class.
   (D) Weekdays.

5. (A) Fill out a form.
   (B) Give her some additional
       information.
   (C) Tell her some news.
   (D) Phone her.

What is the topic of the passage for questions 1 through 5?

Finding a job on campus.

You can guess this because of the following clues:

• work on campus
• employment office
• students/jobs

Now look ahead at answers 6–10 and try to determine the topic of the passage.

6. (A) During a biology laboratory
       session.
   (B) In a biology study group.
   (C) On the first day of class.
   (D) Just before the final exam.

7. (A) Once a week.
   (B) Two times a week.
   (C) Three times a week.
   (D) For fifteen hours.

8. (A) To do the first laboratory
       assignment.
   (B) To take the first exam.
   (C) To study the laboratory manual.
   (D) To read one chapter of the text.

9. (A) Room assignments.
   (B) Exam topics.
   (C) Reading assignments.
   (D) The first lecture.

10. (A) Exams and lab work.
    (B) Reading and writing
        assignments.
    (C) Class participation and grades
        on examinations.
    (D) Lecture and laboratory
        attendance.

What do you think is the topic of the passage for questions 6 through 10?

Now look ahead at answers 11–15 and try to determine the topic of the passage.

11. (A) All kinds of pollution.
    (B) How acid rain has harmed the
        earth.
    (C) Pollution from cars and
        factories.
    (D) The causes and possible effects
        of acid rain.

12. (A) Nuclear power.
    (B) Electricity.
    (C) Burning coal and oil.
    (D) Solar power.

13. (A) From sulfur dioxide and water
        vapor.
    (B) From sulfur dioxide and
        nitrogen oxide.
    (C) From nitric acid and sulfur
        dioxide.
    (D) From water vapor and nitric
        acid.

14. (A) Only in North America.
    (B) At the north and south poles.
    (C) In parts of several northern
        continents.
    (D) In equatorial areas.

15. (A) She should protect herself from
        the rain.
    (B) She should clean up the water
        supply.
    (C) She should read a novel.
    (D) She should get more
        information about acid rain.

What do you think is the topic of the passage for questions 11 through 15?

SKILL 16: ANTICIPATE THE QUESTIONS

It is very helpful to your ability to answer individual questions if you can anticipate what the questions are and listen specifically for the answers to those questions.

Example

You will read:
(A) In the airport.
(B) In the library.
(C) In the dormitory.
(D) In the travel agent's office.

You will try to anticipate the question:
[Where does the conversation probably take place?]

While the speaker on the tape is giving the directions to Listening—Part C, you should be studying the answers and trying to anticipate the questions. Of course, you cannot predict exactly what the questions will be. However, you can often determine if the questions will be about *who, when, where, how many,* etc.

EXERCISE 16: Before you hear the passages, you should try to anticipate the questions that will be asked. Study the following answers and try to determine what the questions will be. Perhaps you will not be able to predict the question at all, or you will only be able to predict part of the question. If you cannot predict the question in a short period of time, then move on to the next group of answers. Question 1 has been answered for you.

1. Question: *What will he/she try to do?*
   (A) Find work on campus.
   (B) Work in the employment office.
   (C) Help students find jobs.
   (D) Ask the woman questions.

2. Question: _____
   (A) In the library.
   (B) In a classroom.
   (C) In a campus office.
   (D) In an apartment.

3. Question: _____
   (A) No more than ten.
   (B) At least twenty.
   (C) Not more than twenty.
   (D) Up to ten.

4. Question: _____

    (A) Every morning.
    (B) Afternoons and weekends.
    (C) When he's in class.
    (D) Weekdays.

5. Question: _____

    (A) Fill out a form.
    (B) Give her some additional information.
    (C) Tell her some news.
    (D) Phone her.

6. Question: _____

    (A) During a biology laboratory session.
    (B) In a biology study group.
    (C) On the first day of class.
    (D) Just before the final exam.

7. Question: _____

    (A) Once a week.
    (B) Two times a week.
    (C) Three times a week.
    (D) For fifteen hours.

8. Question: _____

    (A) To do the first laboratory assignment.
    (B) To take the first exam.
    (C) To study the laboratory manual.
    (D) To read one chapter of the text.

9. Question: _____

    (A) Room assignments.
    (B) Exam topics.
    (C) Reading assignments.
    (D) The first lecture.

10. Question: _____

    (A) Exams and lab work.
    (B) Reading and writing assignments.
    (C) Class participation and grades on examinations.
    (D) Lecture and laboratory attendance.

11. Question: _____

    (A) All kinds of pollution.
    (B) How acid rain has harmed the earth.
    (C) Pollution from cars and factories.
    (D) The causes and possible effects of acid rain.

12. Question: _____
    (A) Nuclear power.
    (B) Electricity.
    (C) Burning coal and oil.
    (D) Solar power.

13. Question: _____
    (A) From sulfur dioxide and water vapor.
    (B) From sulfur dioxide and nitrogen oxide.
    (C) From nitric acid and sulfur dioxide.
    (D) From water vapor and nitric acid.

14. Question: _____
    (A) Only in North America.
    (B) At the north and south poles.
    (C) In parts of several northern continents.
    (D) In equatorial areas.

15. Question: _____
    (A) She should protect herself from the rain.
    (B) She should clean up the water supply.
    (C) She should read a novel.
    (D) She should get more information about acid rain.

WHAT TO DO WHILE LISTENING TO THE PASSAGES _____

SKILL 17:   DETERMINE THE TOPIC

As you listen to each passage, you should be thinking about the topic (subject) or main idea for each passage. Since the first sentence is generally a topic sentence, you should be asking yourself what the topic is while you are listening carefully to the first sentence.

    Example

    You will hear:
        [The major earthquake that occurred east of Los Angeles in 1971 is still affecting the economy of the area today.]

    You will think:
        [The topic of the passage is the effect of the 1971 earthquake on Los Angeles today.]

EXERCISE 17:   Listen to the first line of each of the passages and decide on the topic of each passage.

   NOW BEGIN THE TAPE AT EXERCISE 17.

1. What is the topic of Passage 1?

    _____

2. What is the topic of Passage 2?

    _____

3. What is the topic of Passage 3?

    _____

SKILL 18: DRAW CONCLUSIONS ABOUT *WHO*, *WHAT*, AND *WHERE*

As you listen to each passage, you should be trying to set the situation in your mind. You should be thinking: *Who is talking, where are they,* and *what kind of course or topic is being discussed?*

Example

You will hear:
Man:	[Why do you have so many books?
Woman:	I need them for my paper on George Washington. Do you know how I can check them out?
Man:	Yes, you should go downstairs to the circulation desk and fill out a card for each book.]

You will think:
Who is probably talking?	(two students)
Where are they?	(in the library)
What course are they discussing?	(American History)

EXERCISE 18: Listen to the beginning lines of each of the passages, and try to imagine the situation. Ask yourself the following questions:

- Who is probably talking?
- Where are they?
- What course or topic are they discussing?

NOW BEGIN THE TAPE AT EXERCISE 18.

Passage 1:

1. Who is probably talking?   _____
2. Where are they?   _____
3. What topic is being discussed?   _____

Passage 2:

1. Who is probably talking?   _____
2. Where is he?   _____
3. What course is being discussed?   _____

Passage 3:

1. Who is probably talking?   _____
2. Where are they?   _____
3. What topic is being discussed?   _____

SKILL 19: READ ALONG WITH THE ANSWERS

There are two possible methods to use while you listen to the passage.

1. You can just listen to the passage (and ignore the answers).
2. You can follow along with the answers while you listen.

Some students prefer to just listen to the passage while it is being spoken, and if that method works out well for you, then that is what you should do. Other students find that they can answer more questions correctly if they read along with the answers while the passage is being spoken. Because the detail questions are answered in order in the passage, it is possible to read along while you listen to the passage on the tape.

Example

You will hear:

[The great Chicago Fire began on October 8, 1871, and according to legend began when a cow knocked over a lantern *in Mrs. O'Leary's barn*. No matter how it began, it was a disastrous fire. *The preceding summer had been exceedingly dry in the Chicago area, and the extreme dryness accompanied by Chicago's infamous winds created an inferno that destroyed 18,000 buildings and killed more than 300 people* before it was extinguished the following day.

1. According to legend, where did the Chicago fire begin?

2. Which of the following is **not** true about the Chicago fire?]

You will read (same time):

1. (A) In a barn.
   (B) In Mrs. O'Leary's home.
   (C) In a cow pasture.
   (D) In a lantern factory.

2. (A) The dry weather prior to the fire made it worse.
   (B) It happened during the summer.
   (C) Chicago's winds made it worse.
   (D) It killed many people.

When you read the answers to the first question, you can anticipate that the first question is: *Where did something happen?* As you listen, you determine that the fire began in Mrs. O'Leary's barn. Therefore, you can anticipate that the best answer to the first question is (A).

If you read the answers to the second question while you listen to the passage, you can determine that answers (A), (C), and (D) are true. Answer (B) is not true: the fire did not begin in the summer, it began in October, which is in the autumn. Therefore, answer (B) is the best answer to the question *Which of the following is **not** true about the Chicago fire?*

EXERCISE 19: In this exercise you will hear the complete passages. See if you can follow along with the answers while you listen to the passages on the tape. Then try to choose the best answer to each question.

NOW BEGIN THE TAPE AT EXERCISE 19.

1. (A) Find work on campus.
   (B) Work in the employment office.
   (C) Help students find jobs.
   (D) Ask the woman questions.

2. (A) In the library.
   (B) In a classroom.
   (C) In a campus office.
   (D) In an apartment.

3. (A) No more than ten.
   (B) At least twenty.
   (C) Not more than twenty.
   (D) Up to ten.

4. (A) Every morning.
   (B) Afternoons and weekends.
   (C) When he's in class.
   (D) Weekdays.

5. (A) Fill out a form.
   (B) Give her some additional information.
   (C) Tell her some news.
   (D) Phone her.

6. (A) During a biology laboratory session.
   (B) In a biology study group.
   (C) On the first day of class.
   (D) Just before the final exam.

7. (A) Once a week.
   (B) Two times a week.
   (C) Three times a week.
   (D) For fifteen hours.

8. (A) To do the first laboratory assignment.
   (B) To take the first exam.
   (C) To study the laboratory manual.
   (D) To read one chapter of the text.

9. (A) Room assignments.
   (B) Exam topics.
   (C) Reading assignments.
   (D) The first lecture.

10. (A) Exams and lab work.
    (B) Reading and writing assignments.
    (C) Class participation and grades on examinations.
    (D) Lecture and laboratory attendance.

11. (A) All kinds of pollution.
    (B) How acid rain has harmed the earth.
    (C) Pollution from cars and factories.
    (D) The causes and possible effects of acid rain.

12. (A) Nuclear power.
    (B) Electricity.
    (C) Burning coal and oil.
    (D) Solar power.

13. (A) From sulfur dioxide and water vapor.
    (B) From sulfur dioxide and nitrogen oxide.
    (C) From nitric acid and sulfur dioxide.
    (D) From water vapor and nitric acid.

14. (A) Only in North America.
    (B) At the north and south poles.
    (C) In parts of several northern continents.
    (D) In equatorial areas.

15. (A) She should protect herself from the rain.
    (B) She should clean up the water supply.
    (C) She should read a novel.
    (D) She should get more information about acid rain.

REVIEW EXERCISE (SKILLS 15–19):   In this exercise you will use all of the skills you learned in sections 15 through 19.

Before the tape begins, you should read over the answers to questions 1 through 15 and do the following:

1. Anticipate the topics you will hear.
2. Anticipate the questions.

While you are listening to the passages, you should do the following:

1. Listen for the topic in the first sentence.
2. Draw conclusions about who is speaking, where the passage takes place, and what course or topic is being discussed.
3. Read along with the answers and try to determine the correct answers to the questions.

NOW BEGIN THE TAPE AT REVIEW EXERCISE (SKILLS 15–19).

1. (A) To a concert.
   (B) To a rehearsal.
   (C) To a lecture.
   (D) To the library.

2. (A) Five minutes.
   (B) Twenty minutes.
   (C) Less than a day.
   (D) For the last week.

3. (A) One.
   (B) Two.
   (C) Three.
   (D) Four.

4. (A) The bus does not go directly to the Music Building.
   (B) The bus goes very slowly to the Music Building.
   (C) The bus sometimes does not come.
   (D) The bus will not arrive for a while.

5. (A) To walk.
   (B) To wait for the bus.
   (C) To miss the lecture.
   (D) To think of another plan.

6. (A) How and when we celebrate
      Thanksgiving.
   (B) The traditional Thanksgiving
      dinner.
   (C) When Thanksgiving began.
   (D) Abraham Lincoln.

7. (A) With colonists in
      Massachusetts.
   (B) Alone and thinking about how
      Thanksgiving developed.
   (C) With a big Thanksgiving dinner.
   (D) In an untraditional manner.

8. (A) The terrible winter.
   (B) The corn harvest.
   (C) The development of
      Thanksgiving day.
   (D) For getting the whole family
      together.

9. (A) At many different times.
   (B) In July.
   (C) Anytime in November.
   (D) On a Thursday in November.

10. (A) Before the Civil War.
    (B) At the end of the Civil War.
    (C) At the beginning of the
       twentieth century.
    (D) Within the last decade.

11. (A) The Civil War ended.
    (B) The U.S. government issued a
       large amount of paper
       currency.
    (C) The price of gold plummeted.
    (D) The value of gold became
       inflated.

12. (A) An excessive amount of paper
       currency had been issued.
    (B) The price of gold was extremely
       low.
    (C) The value of paper currency
       was inflated.
    (D) The gold market had been
       cornered.

13. (A) The president.
    (B) The president's brother.
    (C) The president's brother-in-law.
    (D) The president's wife.

14. (A) Issue greenbacks.
    (B) Sell gold.
    (C) Corner the gold market.
    (D) Hold its gold reserves.

15. (A) Black gold.
    (B) The crash of the gold market.
    (C) The issuance of paper currency.
    (D) The economic role of the U.S.
       president.

TOEFL POST-TEST
FOLLOWS

TOEFL POST-TEST

SECTION 1
LISTENING COMPREHENSION

In this section of the test, you will have an opportunity to demonstrate your ability to understand spoken English. There are three parts in this section, with special directions for each part.

Part A

Directions: For each question in Part A, you will hear a short sentence. Each sentence will be spoken just one time. The sentences you hear will not be written out for you. Therefore, you must listen carefully to understand what the speaker says.

After you hear a sentence, read the four choices in your test book, marked (A), (B), (C), and (D), and decide which one is closest in meaning to the sentence you heard. Then, on your answer sheet, find the number of the question and fill in the space that corresponds to the letter of the answer you have chosen. Fill in the space so the letter inside the oval cannot be seen.

Example I   Sample Answer

You will hear: ●
                                                                                     Ⓑ
You will read: (A) John outran the others.   Ⓒ
                 (B) John was the fastest hunter in   Ⓓ
                     the chase.
                 (C) John wasn't the slowest in the
                     race.
                 (D) John was the last runner to
                     finish the race.

The speaker said, "John was the fastest runner in the race." Sentence (A), "John outran the others," is closest in meaning to the sentence you heard. Therefore, you should choose answer (A).

Example II   Sample Answer

You will hear: Ⓐ
                                                                                     Ⓑ
You will read: (A) Could you help me use the rest?   ●
                 (B) Do you mind using the other   Ⓓ
                     desk?
                 (C) Would you mind helping me
                     carry this piece of furniture?
                 (D) If you move my desk, I'll help
                     you with your work.

GO ON TO THE NEXT PAGE ➡

The speaker said, "Could you help me move my desk?" Sentence (C), "Would you mind helping me carry this piece of furniture?" is closest in meaning to the sentence you heard. Therefore, you should choose answer (C).

1. (A) The cake was extremely good.
   (B) He never tasted the cake.
   (C) He wished he hadn't tasted the cake.
   (D) The cake was never this delicious.

2. (A) I remember what my brother said.
   (B) I recall my brother wearing that shirt.
   (C) My brother told me he recalled hearing that.
   (D) I believe my brother heard me say that.

3. (A) I never liked reading the newspaper.
   (B) The front page of the newspaper is too much for me to read.
   (C) I usually read only the front page.
   (D) I like to read the whole paper.

4. (A) She knew that grapes were cheaper than cherries.
   (B) She didn't know that grapes were cheaper than cherries.
   (C) She bought grapes because they were cheaper than cherries.
   (D) She didn't buy either cherries or grapes because of the price.

5. (A) I gave Tom money to pay the rent.
   (B) I was given money for rent.
   (C) Tom borrowed money for rent.
   (D) Tom didn't have enough money for rent.

6. (A) At the corner, he ran into another car.
   (B) He ran to her because he cared.
   (C) At the party he met one of his relatives.
   (D) At the reunion, Carl was running from place to place.

7. (A) Walter's had a lack of success with his business.
   (B) Walter's failed in business.
   (C) Walter's new company is doing rather well.
   (D) Walter hoped to succeed in business.

8. (A) Martha applied for a visa last month.
   (B) Martha's visa will last only a month.
   (C) Martha arrived last month without her visa.
   (D) One month ago Martha got her visa.

9. (A) The professor required the class to prepare an outline.
   (B) There was a long line to register in the required class.
   (C) It is a requirement for each professor to teach at least one course.
   (D) The professor described what the students needed to do.

10. (A) The postman was eager to leave his job.
    (B) The postman was unhappy at the thought of retiring.
    (C) The postman couldn't be unhappier about retiring.
    (D) The postman was retiring too soon.

11. (A) I need to use the car for my shopping trip.
    (B) We should leave the car and go shopping.
    (C) Would you like to go on a shopping trip in the car?
    (D) Do you know where you left the car keys?

GO ON TO THE NEXT PAGE

12. (A) The astronomy department has a new observatory.
    (B) The university is moving the astronomy department to a new building.
    (C) The astronomy department has plans for a new observatory.
    (D) The university is observing the building of the astronomy department.

13. (A) The farm's yield was down.
    (B) The man went out onto his farm early in the morning.
    (C) The farmer went down to the field in the late afternoon.
    (D) The farmer wanted another field quickly.

14. (A) The landlord failed to collect rent on the first of last month.
    (B) The tenants absolutely must pay rent at the beginning of the month.
    (C) The landlord will not fail to collect your rent on the first of next month.
    (D) You should call the landlord about rent on the first of the month.

15. (A) Jill and Beth both spend too much money on vacation in New Mexico.
    (B) Jill doesn't like New Mexico, but Beth does.
    (C) Beth and Jill prefer New Mexico for their vacations.
    (D) New Mexico doesn't seem like a good vacation spot to either Jill or Beth.

16. (A) Mr. Drew pointedly asked the president about the committee.
    (B) The president pointed to Mr. Drew's head.
    (C) Mr. Drew became head of the new commission.
    (D) Mr. Drew was committed to the president's appointments.

17. (A) You should arrive at the rehearsal at five o'clock.
    (B) You have to remain outside the rehearsal until five o'clock.
    (C) You'll probably be practicing until five o'clock.
    (D) At five o'clock, your expectations about the rehearsal will be known.

18. (A) The Commerce Department constructed the building.
    (B) The building was commercially owned.
    (C) The builder erected the building in a business area.
    (D) The builder was instructed to achieve commercial success.

19. (A) They arrived too late to catch the plane.
    (B) They arrived just after the plane took off.
    (C) They weren't in time to catch the plane.
    (D) The plane took off just after they arrived.

20. (A) You can choose a card at the end of the aisle.
    (B) Your library card will be ready later.
    (C) At the end of the day you can pick out some books.
    (D) You can pick which day to get a library card.

GO ON TO THE NEXT PAGE ➤

Part B

Directions: In Part B you will hear short conversations between two speakers. At the end of each conversation, a third person will ask a question about what was said. You will hear each conversation and question about it just one time. Therefore, you must listen carefully to understand what each speaker says. After you hear a conversation and the question about it, read the four possible answers in your test book and decide which one is the best answer to the question you heard. Then, on your answer sheet, find the number of the question and fill in the space that corresponds to the letter of the answer you have chosen.

Look at the following example.

You will hear: Sample Answer

You will read: (A) The exam was really awful.   Ⓐ
                 (B) It was the worst exam she had   Ⓑ
                     ever seen.   Ⓒ
                 (C) It couldn't have been more   ●
                     difficult.
                 (D) It wasn't that hard.

From the conversation you learn that the man thought the exam was very difficult and that the woman disagreed with the man. The best answer to the question "What does the woman mean?" is (D), "It wasn't that hard." Therefore, you should choose answer (D).

21. (A) She needs to get a driver's
        license and a credit card.
    (B) Two pieces of identification are
        necessary.
    (C) He should check to see if he
        needs credit.
    (D) A credit card can be used to get
        a driver's license.

22. (A) It's not possible to pass the class.
    (B) She'll definitely fail.
    (C) It's always possible.
    (D) She shouldn't say anything about
        the class.

23. (A) Nothing went well today.
    (B) She has a terrible life.
    (C) The day wasn't particularly bad.
    (D) She only has one day left in her
        life.

24. (A) The headings for today's reading
        assignment.
    (B) The chance to make the
        headlines.
    (C) Her reading ability.
    (D) The daily newspaper.

25. (A) He hasn't felt like eating for
        weeks.
    (B) Because he's weak, he can't eat.
    (C) It's been weeks since he's had
        anything to eat.
    (D) He'd really like to have
        something to eat.

26. (A) She'd like more to drink.
    (B) The teapot only holds one cup.
    (C) She never has more than one cup.
    (D) She should put another cup into
        the teapot.

GO ON TO THE NEXT PAGE ▶

27. (A) He thinks he got a good grade.
    (B) The history grades were all C or above.
    (C) No one got history grades.
    (D) There were no high scores.

28. (A) Paul had improved.
    (B) This visit was better than the last.
    (C) Paul looked at him in the hospital.
    (D) Paul didn't seem to be doing very well.

29. (A) Sit down.
    (B) Talk to the woman.
    (C) Go to his appointment.
    (D) Notify Mr. Martin.

30. (A) She would be welcome in the desert.
    (B) He'd like to go to the desert.
    (C) It's all right if she takes some of his food.
    (D) She looks better than he does.

31. (A) He's found a new ring.
    (B) He needs to help her find something.
    (C) He's shopping for a carpet.
    (D) He's thankful she has a rag.

32. (A) He goes early because the food is so delicious.
    (B) The cafeteria closes at 7 o'clock.
    (C) The selection is better early.
    (D) It's hard to wait until 7 o'clock to eat.

33. (A) Food is already being served at that table.
    (B) They'll have to sit elsewhere.
    (C) They can have that table.
    (D) He's sorry the table is by the window.

34. (A) In a department store.
    (B) In a bank.
    (C) In an accounting firm.
    (D) In a checkout line.

35. (A) Martha's jobs are easy.
    (B) It's easy to hold two jobs.
    (C) It's better for Martha to have two jobs.
    (D) Martha should slow down.

Part C

Directions: In this part of the test, you will hear short talks and conversations. After each of them, you will be asked some questions. You will hear the talks and conversations and the questions about them just one time. They will not be written out for you. Therefore, you must listen carefully to understand what each speaker says.

After you hear a question, read the four possible answers in your test book and decide which one is the best answer to the question you heard. Then, on your answer sheet, find the number of the question and fill in the space that corresponds to the letter of the answer you have chosen.

Listen to this sample talk.

You will hear:

Now look at the following example.

GO ON TO THE NEXT PAGE ➡

You will hear:

You will read: (A) Art from America's inner cities.
(B) Art from the central region of the U.S.
(C) Art from various urban areas in the U.S.
(D) Art from rural sections of America.

The best answer to the question "What style of painting is known as American regionalist?" is (D), "Art from rural sections of America." Therefore, you should choose answer (D).

Now look at the next example.

You will hear:

You will read: (A) *American Regionalist.*
(B) *The Family Farm in Iowa.*
(C) *American Gothic.*
(D) *A Serious Couple.*

The best answer to the question "What is the name of Wood's most successful painting?" is (C), *"American Gothic."* Therefore, you should choose answer (C).

36. (A) Attend a football game alone.
(B) Go to a sporting event.
(C) Eat in the cafeteria and study.
(D) See a play.

37. (A) It's the final game of the season.
(B) It's better than the drama department's play.
(C) It's a very important game.
(D) It's close to the cafeteria.

38. (A) At 4 o'clock on Saturday.
(B) At 6 o'clock on Saturday.
(C) At 8 o'clock on Saturday.
(D) At 1 o'clock on Sunday.

39. (A) A play.
(B) A game.
(C) A study group meeting.
(D) Dinner in the cafeteria.

40. (A) Saturday night.
(B) After dinner in the cafeteria.
(C) Sunday afternoon.
(D) Maybe next weekend.

41. (A) Modern American Authors.
(B) United States History.
(C) American Democracy.
(D) Nineteenth Century American Literature.

42. (A) It's a poem about the author.
(B) It's a poem about Abraham Lincoln.
(C) It's a collection of twelve poems that remained unchanged.
(D) It's a volume of poetry that grew with its author.

43. (A) The death of Abraham Lincoln.
(B) The beauty of American democracy.
(C) The raising of plants.
(D) The maturity of poetry.

GO ON TO THE NEXT PAGE

44. (A) *Leaves of Grass.*
    (B) "Song of Myself."
    (C) "When Lilacs Last in the Dooryard Bloomed."
    (D) "American Democracy."

45. (A) The poem was too long for the first edition.
    (B) Whitman at first believed that a poem about Lincoln didn't fit with the other poems.
    (C) Lincoln had not yet died when the first edition appeared.
    (D) It took Whitman a long time to write the poem after Lincoln's death.

46. (A) Boring.
    (B) Fantastic.
    (C) Lengthy.
    (D) Faithful.

47. (A) By car.
    (B) By plane.
    (C) By train.
    (D) By bicycle.

48. (A) She went directly to Yellowstone.
    (B) She spent a few weeks in Laramie.
    (C) She stopped at the Devil's Tower National Monument.
    (D) She made a few stops before going on to Yellowstone.

49. (A) Laramie.
    (B) Devil's Tower National Monument.
    (C) Old Faithful.
    (D) Wyoming.

50. (A) Hear again about Yellowstone.
    (B) Take a trip to Yellowstone.
    (C) Get a job in a national park.
    (D) Move to Yellowstone.

THIS IS THE END OF THE LISTENING COMPREHENSION SECTION OF THE TEST

THE NEXT PART OF THE TEST IS SECTION 2. TURN TO THE
DIRECTIONS FOR SECTION 2 IN YOUR TEST BOOK.
READ THEM, AND BEGIN WORK.
DO NOT READ OR WORK ON ANY OTHER SECTION OF THE TEST.

STOP STOP STOP **STOP** STOP STOP STOP

SECTION TWO

STRUCTURE AND WRITTEN EXPRESSION

TOEFL PRE-TEST

SECTION 2
STRUCTURE AND WRITTEN EXPRESSION
Time—25 minutes

This section is designed to measure your ability to recognize language that is appropriate for standard written English. There are two types of questions in this section, with special directions for each type.

Directions: Questions 1–15 are incomplete sentences. Beneath each sentence you will see four words or phrases, marked (A), (B), (C), and (D). Choose the one word or phrase that best completes the sentence. Then, on your answer sheet, find the number of the question and fill in the space that corresponds to the letter of the answer you have chosen. Fill in the space so that the letter inside the oval cannot be seen.

Example I   Sample Answer

The president _____ the election   ● Ⓑ Ⓒ Ⓓ
by a landslide.

(A) won
(B) he won
(C) yesterday
(D) fortunately

The sentence should read, "The president won the election by a landslide." Therefore, you should choose answer (A).

Example II   Sample Answer

When _____ the conference?   Ⓐ ● Ⓒ Ⓓ

(A) the doctor attended
(B) did the doctor attend
(C) the doctor will attend
(D) the doctor's attendance

The sentence should read, "When did the doctor attend the conference?" Therefore, you should choose answer (B).

After you read the directions, begin work on the questions.

1. The North Pole _____ a latitude of ninety degrees north.

(A) it has
(B) is having
(C) which is having
(D) has

2. _____ of government results in a vertical distribution of power.

(A) A federal type
(B) A federal
(C) A federation is
(D) The type is federal

GO ON TO THE NEXT PAGE

3. The city of Beverly Hills _____ on all sides by the city of Los Angeles.

   (A) surrounds
   (B) is surrounding
   (C) has surrounded
   (D) is surrounded

4. _____ greyhound, can achieve speeds up to 36 miles per hour.

   (A) The
   (B) The fastest
   (C) The fastest dog
   (D) The fastest dog, the

5. Marmots spend their time foraging among meadow plants and flowers or _____ on rocky cliffs.

   (A) gets sun
   (B) sunning
   (C) the sun
   (D) sunny

6. _____ fourteen phalanges, three in each finger and two in the thumb.

   (A) That human hand
   (B) Every human hand
   (C) Each human hand has
   (D) The human hand which has

7. The greenhouse effect occurs _____ heat radiated from the sun.

   (A) when does the earth's atmosphere trap
   (B) does the earth's atmosphere trap
   (C) when the earth's atmosphere traps
   (D) the earth's atmosphere traps

8. It is possible for a microscope _____ one or more lenses.

   (A) has
   (B) have
   (C) to have
   (D) that has

9. According to the World Health Organization, outbreaks of any _____ can be cause for quarantine.

   (A) of six diseases
   (B) these six diseases
   (C) six diseases which
   (D) the six most dangerous diseases

10. _____ on New Year's Day, the Rose Bowl is the oldest post-season collegiate football game in the United States.

    (A) It is held
    (B) It holds
    (C) Holding
    (D) Held

11. The Hawaiian coastline is bordered by many coral reefs, some living but _____ dead.

    (A) most of them
    (B) most of their
    (C) others are
    (D) the rest are being

12. Some economists now suggest that home equity loans are merely a new trap to push consumers beyond _____.

    (A) they can afford
    (B) they can afford it
    (C) what they can afford
    (D) able to afford

13. Rubber _____ from vulcanized silicones with a high molecular weight is difficult to distinguish from natural rubber.

    (A) is produced
    (B) producing
    (C) that produces
    (D) produced

GO ON TO THE NEXT PAGE

STRUCTURE AND WRITTEN EXPRESSION PRE-TEST   79

14. Featured at the Henry Ford Museum _____ of antique cars dating from 1865.

    (A) is an exhibit
    (B) an exhibit
    (C) an exhibit is
    (D) which is an exhibit

15. _____ appears considerably larger at the horizon than it does overhead is merely an optical illusion.

    (A) The moon
    (B) That the moon
    (C) When the moon
    (D) The moon which

Directions: In questions 16–40 each sentence has four underlined words or phrases. The four underlined parts of the sentence are marked (A), (B), (C), and (D). Identify the one underlined word or phrase that must be changed in order for the sentence to be correct. Then, on your answer sheet, find the number of the question and fill in the space that corresponds to the letter of the answer you have chosen.

Example I   Sample Answer

The four <u>string</u> on a violin <u>are</u> <u>tuned</u>
A   B   C D
in fifths.

                              Ⓐ ● Ⓒ Ⓓ

The sentence should read, "The four strings on a violin are tuned in fifths." Therefore, you should choose answer (B).

Example II   Sample Answer

The <u>research</u> <u>for the</u> book *Roots* <u>taking</u>
A   B   C
Alex Haley <u>twelve years</u>.
             D

                              Ⓐ Ⓑ ● Ⓓ

The sentence should read, "The research for the book *Roots* took Alex Haley twelve years." Therefore, you should choose answer (C).

After you read the directions, begin work on the questions.

16. On <u>the floor of</u> the Pacific Ocean are <u>hundred</u> of <u>flat-topped</u> mountains <u>more than</u> a
      A   B   C   D
mile beneath sea level.

17. The state seal <u>still</u> <u>used</u> in Massachusetts was designed by Paul Revere, <u>which</u> also
               A   B   C
designed <u>the first</u> Continental currency.
         D

18. Segregation in <u>public</u> schools <u>was declare</u> <u>unconstitutional</u> by the Supreme Court
               A   B   C
<u>in 1954</u>.
 D

GO ON TO THE NEXT PAGE ➤

19. Sirius, the Dog Star, is the most brightest star in the sky with an absolute magnitude
          A   B
    about twenty-three times that of the sun.
          C   D

20. Killer whales tend to wander in family clusters that hunt, play, and resting together.
              A   B   C   D

21. Some of the most useful resistor material are carbon, metals, and metallic alloys.
    A   B   C   D

22. The community of Bethesda, Maryland, was previous known as Darcy's Store.
        A   B   C   D

23. Alloys of gold and copper has been widely used in various types of coins.
                          A   B   C   D

24. J. H. Pratt used group therapy early in this century when he brought tuberculosis
                   A   B   C
    patients together to discuss its disease.
                                D

25. Sapphires weighing very much as two pounds have on occasion been mined.
              A   B   C   D

26. Irving Berlin wrote "Oh How I Hate to Get Up in the Morning" while served in the
                 A   B   C
    U.S. Army during World War I.
              D

27. Nimbostratus clouds are thick, dark gray clouds what forebode rain.
                      A   B   C   D

28. That water has a very high specific heat means that without a large temperature
    A   B
    change water can add or lose a large amount of hot.
                       C   D

29. Temperatures that are to high to be measured on a mercury thermometer can be
    A   B   C   D
    measured on a pyrometer.

30. Alike snakes, lizards can be found on all continents except Antarctica.
    A   B   C   D

31. During the 1960s the Berkeley campus of the University of California came to
    A   B
    national attention as a result its radical political activity.
                              C   D

32. <u>Artist</u> Gutzon Borglum designed the Mount Rushmore Memorial and worked on
      A

    <u>project</u> from 1925 <u>until</u> <u>his</u> death in 1941.
      B   C   D

33. Because of the flourish with <u>which</u> John Hancock signed the Declaration of
                          A

    Independence, <u>his</u> name <u>become</u> <u>synonymous</u> with *signature*.
             B   C   D

34. Benny Goodman was <u>equally</u> talented as both a jazz <u>performer</u> <u>as well as</u> a
                  A   B   C

    <u>classical musician</u>.
         D

35. Quarter horses were developed in eighteenth-century Virginia <u>to race</u> on
                                        A

    <u>courses short</u> of about a quarter <u>of a mile</u> <u>in length</u>.
        B   C   D

36. <u>No longer</u> <u>satisfied</u> with <u>the emphasis</u> of the Denisham school, Martha Graham
       A   B   C

    <u>has moved</u> to the staff of the Eastman School in 1925.
       D

37. The United States <u>imports</u> <u>all</u> carpet wools <u>because of</u> domestic wools are <u>too fine</u>
             A   B   C   D

    and soft for carpets.

38. General Ambrose Burnside shaved his chin <u>but</u> allowed hair to <u>grow</u> on the sides of
                                 A   B

    <u>the</u> face in a style <u>that became</u> known as *sideburns*.
     C   D

39. William Hart was an <u>an act</u> <u>best known</u> for <u>his</u> roles <u>as</u> Western heroes in silent films.
             A   B   C   D

40. Banks, savings and loans, and finance companies <u>have recently</u> been <u>doing</u> home
                                    A   B

    equity loans with <u>greater frequency</u> than <u>ever before</u>.
                C   D

THIS IS THE END OF SECTION 2

IF YOU FINISH BEFORE TIME IS CALLED, CHECK YOUR WORK
ON SECTION 2 ONLY.
DO NOT READ OR WORK ON ANY OTHER SECTION OF THE TEST.
THE SUPERVISOR WILL TELL YOU WHEN TO BEGIN
WORK ON SECTION 3.

STRUCTURE AND WRITTEN EXPRESSION

The second section of the TOEFL is the Structure and Written Expression Section. This section consists of 40 questions (some tests may be longer). You have 25 minutes to complete the 40 questions in this section.

There are two types of questions in the Structure and Written Expression Section of the TOEFL:

1. **Structure** (questions 1–15) consists of 15 sentences in which part has been replaced with a blank. Each sentence is followed by four answer choices. You must choose the answer that completes the sentence in a grammatically correct way.
2. **Written Expression** (questions 16–40) consists of 25 sentences in which four words or groups of words have been underlined. You must choose the underlined word or group of words that is **not** correct.

GENERAL STRATEGIES

1. **Make the best use of your time.** Because you must complete 40 questions in 25 minutes (on a standard test), you have only slightly more than 30 seconds per question. You must therefore work quickly and efficiently through this section of the test.

2. **Begin with questions 1 through 15.** Anticipate that questions 1 through 5 will be rather easy. Anticipate that questions 11 through 15 will be rather difficult. Do not spend too much time on questions 11 through 15. There will be easier questions that come later.

3. **Continue with questions 16 through 40.** Anticipate that questions 16 through 20 will be rather easy. Anticipate that questions 36 through 40 will be rather difficult. Do not spend too much time on questions 36 through 40.

4. **If you have time, return to questions 11 through 15.** You should spend extra time on questions 11 through 15 only after you spend all the time you want on the easier questions.

5. **Do not leave any questions blank on your answer sheet.** Even if a question is very difficult, you should answer the question. There is no penalty for guessing.

INTRODUCTION TO THE STRUCTURE QUESTIONS _____

Questions 1 through 15 test your knowledge of the correct structure of English sentences. They are multiple choice questions in which you must choose the letter of the answer that best completes the sentence.

Example

_____ is taking a trip to New York.

(A) They
(B) When
(C) The woman
(D) Her

In this example, you should notice immediately that the sentence has a verb (*is taking*), and that the verb needs a subject. Answers (B) and (D) are incorrect because *when* and *her* are not subjects. In answer (A) *they* is a subject, but *they* is plural and the verb *is taking* is singular. The correct answer is answer (C); *the woman* can be a singular subject. You should therefore choose answer (C).

STRATEGIES FOR THE STRUCTURE QUESTIONS

1. **First study the sentence.** Your purpose is to determine what is needed to complete the sentence correctly.

2. **Then study each answer based on how well it completes the sentence.** Eliminate answers that do not complete the sentence correctly.

3. **Do not try to eliminate incorrect answers by looking only at the answers.** The incorrect answers are generally correct by themselves. The incorrect answers are generally incorrect only when used to complete the sentence.

4. **Never leave any answers blank.** Be sure to answer each question even if you are unsure of the correct response.

5. **Do not spend too much time on the Structure questions.** Be sure to leave adequate time for the Written Expression questions.

INTRODUCTION TO THE WRITTEN EXPRESSION QUESTIONS ____

Questions 16 through 40 test your knowledge of the correct way to express yourself in English writing. Each question in this section consists of one sentence in which four words or groups of words have been underlined. You must choose the letter of the word or group of words that is **not** correct.

Example I

> The <u>final</u> delivery of <u>the day</u> <u>is</u> the <u>importantest</u>.
>   A   B   C   D

If you look at the underlined words in this example, you should notice immediately that *importantest* is not correct. The correct superlative form of *important* is *the most important*. Therefore, you should choose answer (D) because (D) is not correct.

Example II

> The books <u>that</u> I <u>read</u> <u>was</u> <u>interesting</u>.
>   A   B   C   D

If you look at the underlined words in this example, each word by itself appears to be correct. However, the singular verb *was* is incorrect because it does not agree with the plural subject *books*. Therefore, you should choose answer (C) because (C) is not correct.

STRATEGIES FOR THE WRITTEN EXPRESSION QUESTIONS

1. **First look at each of the four underlined words or groups of words.** You want to see if you can spot which of the four answer choices is **not** correct.

2. **If you have been unable to find the error by looking only at the four underlined expressions, then read the complete sentence.** Some underlined expressions are incorrect because of something in another part of the sentence.

3. **Never leave any answers blank.** Be sure to answer each question even if you are unsure of the correct response.

The following skills will help to prepare you for the Structure and Written Expression Section of the TOEFL. The Structure and Written Expression skills have been included together because many grammatical points are tested in both the Structure section and the Written Expression section of the TOEFL.

Skills 1–13 generally help to prepare for the Structure section of the TOEFL, and Skills 14–48 generally help to prepare for the Written Expression section. However, certain points within Skills 1–13 can also be tested in the Written Expression section of the test, and certain points within Skills 14–48 can also be tested in the Structure section. The TOEFL exercises at the end of each skill reflect the emphasis that is given to this skill in each part of the Structure and Written Expression Section of the TOEFL. For example, if the TOEFL exercise at the end of a particular skill contains eight Structure questions and two Written Expression questions, this means that this particular skill is tested mostly in the Structure section of the test but it may occasionally be tested in the Written Expression section.

PROBLEMS IN SENTENCES WITH ONE SUBJECT AND VERB _____

Some sentences in English have just one subject and verb, and it is very important for you to find the subject and verb. In some sentences it is easy to find the subject and verb. However, certain structures such as objects of prepositions, appositives, and participles can cause confusion in locating the subject and verb because each of these structures can look like a subject or verb. The object of the preposition can be mistaken for the subject; an appositive can also be mistaken for the subject; a participle can be mistaken for a verb.

Therefore, you should be able to do the following in sentences with one subject and verb: (1) be sure the sentence has a subject and a verb, (2) be careful of objects of prepositions, (3) be careful of appositives, and (4) be careful of participles.

SKILL I: BE SURE THE SENTENCE HAS A SUBJECT AND A VERB

You know that a sentence in English should have a subject and a verb. The most common problem that you will encounter in the Structure section of the TOEFL is that the sentence is missing either the subject or the verb or both, or has an extra subject or verb.

_____ was backed up for miles on the freeway.

(A) Yesterday
(B) In the morning
(C) Traffic
(D) Cars

In this example you should notice immediately that there is a verb (*was*), but there is no subject. Answer (C) is the best answer because it is a singular subject that agrees with the singular verb *was*. Answer (A) *yesterday* and answer (B) *in the morning* are not subjects, so they are not correct. Although answer (D) *cars* could be a subject, it is not correct because *cars* is plural and it does not agree with the singular verb *was*.

Engineers _____ for work on the new space project.

(A) necessary
(B) are needed
(C) hopefully
(D) next month

In this example you should notice immediately that the sentence has a subject (*engineers*), and that there is no verb. Because answer (B) *are needed* is a verb, it is the best answer. Answers (A), (C), and (D) are not verbs, so they are not correct.

The boy _____ going to the movies with a friend.

(A) he is
(B) he always was
(C) is relaxing
(D) will be

This sentence has a subject (*boy*) and has part of a verb (*going*); to be correct, some form of the verb *be* is needed to make the verb complete. Answers (A) and (B) are incorrect because the sentence already has a subject (*boy*) and does not need the extra subject *he*. Answer (C) is incorrect because *relaxing* is an extra verb that is unnecessary because of *going*. Answer (D) is the best answer; *will be* together with *going* is a complete verb.

EXERCISE I: Underline the subjects once and the verbs twice in each of the following sentences. Then indicate if the sentences are correct (C) or incorrect (I).

_I_   1. Last weekend <u>went</u> fishing for trout at the nearby mountain lake.

_C_   2. A <u>schedule</u> of the day's events <u>can be obtained</u> at the front desk.

_____   3. A job on the day shift or the night shift at the plant available.

_____   4. The new computer program has provides a variety of helpful applications.

_____   5. The box can be opened only with a special screwdriver.

_____   6. The assigned text for history class it contains more than twenty chapters.

_____   7. The papers in the wastebasket should be emptied into the trash can outside.

_____   8. Departure before dawn on a boat in the middle of the harbor.

_____   9. Yesterday found an interesting article on pollution.

_____   10. The new machine is processes 50 percent more than the previous machine.

SKILL 2:   BE CAREFUL OF OBJECTS OF PREPOSITIONS

An object of a preposition is a noun or a pronoun that comes after a preposition such as *in, at, of, to, by, behind, on,* and so on to form a prepositional phrase.

(After his exams) Tom will take a trip (by boat).

This example contains two objects of prepositions. *Exams* is the object of the preposition *after* and *boat* is the object of the preposition *by.*

An object of a preposition can cause confusion in the Structure section of the TOEFL because it can be mistaken for the subject of a sentence.

With his friend _____ found the movie theater.

(A) has
(B) he
(C) later
(D) when

In this example you should look first for the subject and the verb. You should notice the verb *found* and should also notice that there is no subject. Do not think that *friend* is the subject; *friend* is the object of the preposition *with,* and one noun cannot be both a subject and an object at the same time. Because a subject is needed in this sentence, answer (B) *he* is the best answer. Answers (A), (C), and (D) are not correct because they cannot be subjects.

EXERCISE 2:   Each of the following sentences contains one or more prepositional phrases. Underline the subjects once and the verbs twice. Circle the prepositional phrases that come before the verb. Then indicate if the sentences are correct (C) or incorrect (I).

_C_   1. The interviews (by radio broadcasters) were carried live by the station.

_I_   2. (In the last possible moment) (before takeoff) took his seat in the airplane.

_____   3. At the neighborhood flower shop, flowers in quantities of a dozen or a half dozen can be delivered for free.

_____   4. The progressive reading methods at this school are given credit for the improved test scores.

_____   5. For the last three years at various hospitals in the county has been practicing medicine.

_____   6. In the past a career in politics was not considered acceptable in some circles.

_____   7. Shopping in the downtown area of the city it has improved a lot in recent years.

_____   8. At the building site the carpenters with the most experience were given the most intricate work.

_____   9. For the fever and headache took two aspirin tablets.

_____   10. The report with complete documentation was delivered at the conference.

SKILL 3: BE CAREFUL OF APPOSITIVES

Appositives can cause confusion in the Structure section of the TOEFL because an appositive can be mistaken for the subject of a sentence. An appositive is a noun that comes before or after another noun and has the same meaning.

Sally, the best student in the class, got an A on the exam.

In this example *Sally* is the subject of the sentence and *the best student in the class* can easily be recognized as an appositive phrase because of the noun *student* and because of the commas. The sentence says that *Sally* and *the best student in the class* are the same thing. Note that if you leave out the appositive phrase, the sentence still makes sense (*Sally got an A on the exam*).

The following example shows how an appositive can be confused with the subject of a sentence in the Structure section of the TOEFL.

_____, George, is attending the lecture.

(A) Right now
(B) Happily
(C) Because of the time
(D) My friend

In this example you should recognize from the commas that *George* is not the subject of the sentence. *George* is an appositive. Because this sentence still needs a subject, the best answer is answer (D) *my friend*. Answers (A), (B), and (C) are incorrect because they are not subjects.

EXERCISE 3: Each of the following sentences contains an appositive. Underline the subjects once and the verbs twice. Circle the appositive phrases. Then indicate if the sentences are correct (C) or incorrect (I).

__C__   1. (The son of the previous owner,) the new owner is undertaking some fairly broad changes in management policy.

__I__   2. Last semester, (a friend,) graduated *cum laude* from the university.

_____   3. Valentine's Day, February 14, is a special holiday for sweethearts.

_____   4. At long last, the chief executive officer, has decided to step down.

_____   5. Tonight's supper, leftovers from last night, did not taste any better tonight than last night.

_____   6. The new bathroom tile pattern, yellow flowers on a white background, really brightens up that room.

_____   7. The door to the left, the only entrance to the closet, was kept locked at all times.

_____   8. In the cold of winter, the wall heating unit, would not turn on.

_____   9.   The high-powered computer, the most powerful machine of its type, was finally readied for use.

_____   10.   A longtime friend and confident, the psychologist was often invited over for Sunday dinner.

SKILL 4:   BE CAREFUL OF PRESENT PARTICIPLES

Present participles can cause confusion in the Structure section of the TOEFL because a present participle can be mistaken for a part of the verb. A present participle is the *-ing* form of the verb. It is part of the verb when it is accompanied by some form of the verb *be*.

VERB
The man is talking to his friend.

In this sentence *talking* is part of the verb because it is accompanied by *is*.

The present participle *-ing* is an adjective when it is not accompanied by some form of the verb *be*.

ADJ
The man talking to his friend has a beard.

In this sentence *talking* is an adjective and not part of the verb because it is not accompanied by some form of *be*. The verb in this sentence is *has*.

The following example shows how a present participle can be confused with the verb in the Structure section of the TOEFL.

The child _____ playing in the yard is my son.

(A)   now
(B)   is
(C)   he
(D)   was

In this example, if you look at only the first words of the sentence, it appears that *child* is the subject and *playing* is part of the verb. If you think that *playing* is part of the verb, you might choose answer (B) *is* or answer (D) *was* to complete the verb. However, these two answers are incorrect because *playing* is not part of the verb. You should recognize that *playing* is a participial adjective rather than a verb because there is another verb in the sentence (*is*). In this sentence there is a complete subject (*child*) and a complete verb (*is*), so this sentence does not need another subject or verb. The best answer to this question is answer (A).

EXERCISE 4: Each of the following sentences contains one or more present participles. Underline the subjects once and the verbs twice. Circle the present participles and label them as adjectives or verbs. Then indicate if the sentences are correct (C) or incorrect (I).

__C__   1. The companies (offering) [Adj] the lowest prices will have the worst business.

__I__   2. Those travelers are (completing) [V] their trip on TWA should report to Gate Three.

_____   3. The artisans were demonstrating various handicrafts at booths throughout the fair.

_____   4. The fraternities are giving the wildest parties attract the most new pledges.

_____   5. The first team winning four games is awarded the championship.

_____   6. The speaker was trying to make his point was often interrupted vociferously.

_____   7. The fruits were rotting because of the moisture in the crates carrying them to market.

_____   8. Any students desiring official transcripts should complete the appropriate form.

_____   9. The advertisements were announcing the half-day sale received a lot of attention.

_____   10. The spices flavoring the meal were quite distinctive.

SKILL 5: BE CAREFUL OF PAST PARTICIPLES

Past participles can cause confusion in the Structure section of the TOEFL because a past participle can be part of a main verb or it can be an adjective. The past participle is the form of the verb that appears with *have* or *be*. It often ends in *-ed*, but there are also many irregular past participles in English.

VERB
The family has purchased a television.

VERB
The poem was written by Paul.

In the first sentence the past participle *purchased* is part of the verb because it is accompanied by *has*. In the second sentence the past participle *written* is part of the verb because it is accompanied by *was*.

The past participle is an adjective when it is not accompanied by some form of *be* or *have*.

ADJ
The television purchased yesterday was expensive.

ADJ
The poem written by Paul appeared in the magazine.

In the first sentence *purchased* is an adjective rather than a verb because it is not accompanied by a form of *be* or *have* (and there is a verb *was* later in the sentence). In the second sentence *written* is an adjective rather than a verb because it is not accompanied by a form of *be* or *have* (and there is a verb *appeared* later in the sentence).

The following example shows how a past participle can be confused with the verb in the Structure section of the TOEFL.

The packages _____ mailed at the post office will arrive Monday.

(A) have
(B) were
(C) them
(D) just

In this example, if you look only at the first few words of the sentence, it appears that *packages* is the subject and *mailed* is either a complete verb or a past participle that needs a helping verb. But if you look further in the sentence, you will see that the verb is *will arrive*. You will then recognize that *mailed* is a participial adjective and is therefore not part of the verb. Answers (A) and (B) are incorrect because *mailed* is an adjective and does not need a helping verb such as *have* or *were*. Answer (C) is incorrect because there is no need for the object *them*. Answer (D) is the best answer to this question.

EXERCISE 5:   Each of the following sentences contains one or more past participles. Underline the subjects once and the verbs twice. Circle the past participles and label them as adjectives or verbs. Then indicate if the sentences are correct (C) or incorrect (I).

__I__   1. The money was (offered) by the client was not (accepted.)

__C__   2. The car (listed) in the advertisement had already (stalled.)

_____   3. The chapters were taught by the professor this morning will be on next week's exam.

_____   4. The loaves of bread were baked in a brick oven at a low temperature for several hours.

_____   5. The ports reached by the sailors were under the control of a foreign nation.

_____   6. Those suspected in the string of robberies were arrested by the police.

_____   7. The pizza is served in this restaurant is the tastiest in the county.

_____   8. The courses are listed on the second page of the brochure have several prerequisites.

_____   9. All the tenants were invited to the Independence Day barbeque at the apartment complex.

_____   10. Any bills paid by the first of the month will be credited to your account by the next day.

REVIEW EXERCISE (SKILLS 1–5): Underline the subjects once and the verbs twice in each of the following sentences. Then indicate if the sentences are correct (C) or incorrect (I).

_____ 1. For three weeks at the beginning of the semester students with fewer than the maximum number of units can add additional courses.

_____ 2. On her lunch hour went to a nearby department store to purchase a wedding gift.

_____ 3. The fir trees were grown for the holiday season were harvested in November.

_____ 4. In the grove the overripe oranges were falling on the ground.

_____ 5. The newspapers being delivered at 4:00 will contain the announcement of the president's resignation.

_____ 6. A specialty coffee shop with various blends from around the world in the shopping mall.

_____ 7. The portraits exhibited in the Los Angeles museum last month are now on display in San Francisco.

_____ 8. With a sudden jerk of his hand threw the ball across the field to one of the other players.

_____ 9. Construction of the housing development it will be underway by the first of the month.

_____ 10. Those applicants returning their completed forms at the earliest date have the highest priority.

TOEFL EXERCISE (SKILLS 1–5): Choose the letter of the word or group of words that best completes the sentence.

1. The North Platte River _____ from Wyoming into Nebraska.
   (A) it flowed
   (B) flows
   (C) flowing
   (D) with flowing water

2. _____ Biloxi, Mississippi, received its name from a Sioux word meaning "first people."
   (A) The city of
   (B) Located in
   (C) It is in
   (D) The tour included

3. A pride of lions _____ up to thirty-five lions, including one to three male lions, several female lions, and cubs.
   (A) can contain
   (B) it contains
   (C) contain
   (D) containing

4. _____ tea plant are small and white.
   (A) The
   (B) On the
   (C) Having flowers the
   (D) The flowers of the

5. The tetracyclines, _____ antibiotics, are used to treat infections.

   (A) are a family of
   (B) being a family
   (C) a family of
   (D) their family is

6. Any possible academic assistance from taking stimulants _____ marginal at best.

   (A) it is
   (B) there is
   (C) is
   (D) as

7. Henry Adams, born in Boston, _____ famous as a historian and novelist.

   (A) became
   (B) and became
   (C) he was
   (D) and he became

8. The major cause _____ the pull of the moon on the earth.

   (A) the ocean tides are
   (B) of ocean tides is
   (C) of the tides in the ocean
   (D) the oceans' tides

Choose the letter of the underlined word or group of words that is not correct.

_____ 9. The University of Florida it has made the only controlled comparison of
                                 A   B   C
interactive teaching.
            D

_____ 10. Parts of the region having an annual rainfall of less than ten inches,
          A   B
compared to the national average of thirty inches.
          C   D

PROBLEMS IN SENTENCES WITH MORE THAN ONE SUBJECT AND VERB _____

Many sentences in English have more than one clause. (A clause is a group of words containing a subject and a verb.) Whenever you find a sentence on the TOEFL with more than one clause, you first need to make sure that every subject has a verb and every verb has a subject. Next you need to check that the various clauses in the sentence are correctly joined. There are various ways to join clauses in English. Certain patterns appear frequently in English and on the TOEFL. You should be very familiar with these patterns.

SKILL 6: USE SENTENCE CONNECTORS CORRECTLY (PATTERN ONE)

When you have two clauses in an English sentence, you must connect the two clauses correctly. One way to connect two clauses is to use *and, but, or,* or *so* between the clauses.

Tom is singing, *and* Paul is dancing.

Tom is tall, *but* Paul is short.

Tom told a joke, *so* Paul laughed.

Tom must write the letter, *or* Paul will do it.

In each of these examples, there are two clauses that are correctly joined. In the first example the clauses *Tom is singing* and *Paul is dancing* are joined with the connector *and*. In the second example the two clauses *Tom is tall* and *Paul is short* are joined with the connector *but*. In the third example the two clauses *Tom told a joke* and *Paul laughed* are joined with the connector *so*. In the last example the two clauses *Tom must write the letter* and *Paul will do it* are joined with the connector *or*.

The following example shows how this sentence pattern could be tested in the Structure section of the TOEFL:

A power failure occurred, _____ the lamps went out.

(A) then
(B) so
(C) later
(D) next

In this example you should notice quickly that there are two clauses: *a power failure occurred* and *the lamps went out*. What this sentence needs is a connector to join the two clauses. *Then, later,* and *next* are not connectors, so answers (A), (C), and (D) are not correct. The best answer is answer (B) because *so* can connect two clauses.

EXERCISE 6:   Each of the following sentences contains more than one clause. Underline the subjects once and the verbs twice. Circle the connectors. Then indicate if the sentences are correct (C) or incorrect (I).

  __C__   1. The software should be used on an IBM computer, and that is the kind of computer in the office.

  __I__   2. The rain clouds can be seen in the distance, but no has fallen yet.

  _____   3. They are trying to sell their house, it has been on the market for two months.

  _____   4. So the quality of the print was not good, I changed the typewriter ribbon.

  _____   5. The lifeguard will warn you about the riptides, or she may require you to get out of the water.

  _____   6. Yesterday you could have cashed that check, but is impossible today.

  _____   7. The phone rang again and again, so the receptionist was not able to get much work done.

  _____   8. The missing wallet was found, but the cash and credit cards had been removed.

  _____   9. Or you can drive your car for another two thousand miles, you can get it fixed.

  _____   10. The chemist was awarded the Nobel Prize, he flew to Europe to accept it.

SKILL 7:   USE SENTENCE CONNECTORS CORRECTLY (PATTERN TWO)

Study the clauses and the connectors in the following sentences. The following patterns are very common in the Structure section of the TOEFL.

> I will sign the check *before* you leave.
>
> *Before* you leave, I will sign the check.

In each of these sentences there are two clauses: *you leave* and *I will sign the check*. These two clauses are joined with the connector *before*. In the first sentence the connector *before* comes in the middle of the sentence. In the second sentence the connector *before* comes at the beginning of the sentence. In this pattern, when the connector comes at the beginning of the sentence, a comma (,) is required in the middle of the sentence.

The following words can be used as connectors in this type of sentence pattern:

after	if	unless	where
although	provided	until	wherever
because	since	when	whether
before	though	whenever	while

Here is an example of how this sentence pattern can be tested on the TOEFL.

> _____ was late, I missed the appointment.
>
> (A) I
> (B) Because
> (C) The train
> (D) Since he

In this example you should recognize easily that there is a verb *was* that needs a subject. There is also another clause *I missed the appointment*. If you choose answer (A) or answer (C), you will have a subject for the verb *was*, but you will not have a connector to join the two clauses. Because you need a connector to join two clauses, answers (A) and (C) are incorrect. Answer (B) is incorrect because there is no subject for the verb *was*. Answer (D) is the best answer because there is a subject *he* for the verb *was*, and there is a connector *since* to join the two clauses.

EXERCISE 7:   Each of the following sentences contains more than one clause. Underline the subjects once and the verbs twice. Circle the connectors. Then indicate if the sentences are correct (C) or incorrect (I).

__C__   1. It is impossible to enter the doctoral program in education (if) you lack experience as a teacher.

__I__   2. The commandant left strict orders about weekend passes, several soldiers left the post anyway.

____   3. The citizens become more and more incensed about traffic accidents whenever occur at that intersection.

_____ 4. After the ground had been prepared, the seedlings were carefully planted.

_____ 5. Before are admitted to the organization, their backgrounds are thoroughly investigated.

_____ 6. No one can be admitted to the police academy unless he or she the age, size, and education requirements.

_____ 7. You should park your car it is legal to park.

_____ 8. Because the recent change in work shifts was not posted, several workers missed their shifts.

_____ 9. I will wait here in the airport with you whether the plane leaves on time or not.

_____ 10. Provided the envelope is postmarked by this Friday, your application still acceptable.

SKILL 8: USE SENTENCE CONNECTORS CORRECTLY (PATTERN THREE)

Study the clauses and connectors in the following sentences. These patterns are also found in the Structure section of the TOEFL.

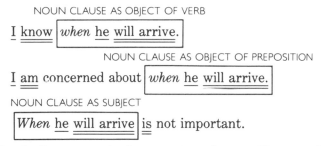

NOUN CLAUSE AS OBJECT OF VERB

I know | *when* he will arrive. |

NOUN CLAUSE AS OBJECT OF PREPOSITION

I am concerned about | *when* he will arrive. |

NOUN CLAUSE AS SUBJECT

| *When* he will arrive | is not important.

In the first example there are two clauses, *I know* and *he will arrive*. These two clauses are joined with the connector *when*. *When* changes the clause *he will arrive* into a noun clause which functions as the object of the verb *know*.

In the second example the two clauses *I am concerned* and *he will arrive* are also joined by the connector *when*. *When* changes the clause *he will arrive* into a noun clause which functions as the object of the preposition *about*.

The third example is more difficult. In this example there are also two clauses, but they are a little harder to recognize. *He will arrive* is one of the clauses, and the connector *when* changes it into a noun clause which functions as the subject of the sentence. The other clause has the noun clause *when he will arrive* as its subject and *is* as its verb.

The following connectors can be used in the sentence patterns above:

how	what	whether
if	when	which
that	where	while

The following example shows how these sentence patterns can be tested in the Structure section of the TOEFL.

_____ was late caused many problems.

(A) That he
(B) The driver
(C) There
(D) Because

In this example there are two verbs (*was* and *caused*), and each of these verbs needs a subject. Answer (B) is wrong because *the driver* is one subject, and two subjects are needed. Answers (C) and (D) are incorrect because *there* and *because* are not subjects.

The best answer is answer (A). If you choose answer (A), the completed sentence would be: *That he was late caused many problems.* In this correct sentence *he* is the subject of the verb *was,* and the noun clause *that he was late* is the subject of the verb *caused.*

EXERCISE 8: Each of the following sentences contains more than one clause. Underline the subjects once and the verbs twice. Circle the connectors and put boxes around the noun clauses. Label the noun clauses as subjects or objects. Then indicate if the sentences are correct (C) or incorrect (I).

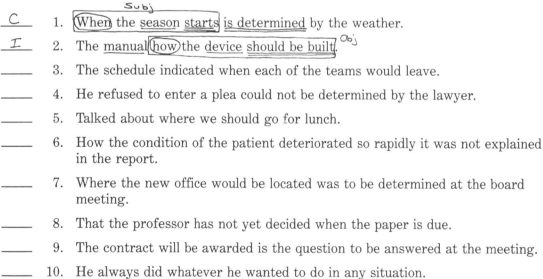

<u>C</u> 1. When the season starts is determined by the weather.

<u>I</u> 2. The manual how the device should be built.

_____ 3. The schedule indicated when each of the teams would leave.

_____ 4. He refused to enter a plea could not be determined by the lawyer.

_____ 5. Talked about where we should go for lunch.

_____ 6. How the condition of the patient deteriorated so rapidly it was not explained in the report.

_____ 7. Where the new office would be located was to be determined at the board meeting.

_____ 8. That the professor has not yet decided when the paper is due.

_____ 9. The contract will be awarded is the question to be answered at the meeting.

_____ 10. He always did whatever he wanted to do in any situation.

Skill 9:   Use Sentence Connectors Correctly (Pattern Four)

It is important for you to be able to use the following sentence patterns correctly, because they often appear on the TOEFL.

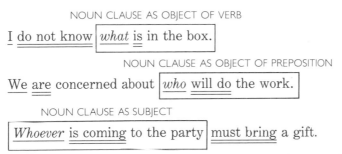

NOUN CLAUSE AS OBJECT OF VERB

I do not know *what* is in the box.

NOUN CLAUSE AS OBJECT OF PREPOSITION

We are concerned about *who* will do the work.

NOUN CLAUSE AS SUBJECT

Whoever is coming to the party must bring a gift.

In the first example there are two clauses: *I do not know* and *what is in the box.* These two clauses are joined by the connector *what.* It is important to understand that in this sentence the word *what* serves two functions. It is both the subject of the verb *is* and the connector that joins the two clauses.

In the second example there are two clauses. In the first clause *we* is the subject of *are.* In the second clause *who* is the subject of *will do. Who* also serves as the connector that joins the two clauses. The noun clause *who will do the work* functions as the object of the preposition *about.*

In the last example there are also two clauses: *whoever* is the subject of the verb *is coming,* and the noun clause *whoever is coming to the party* is the subject of *must bring.* The word *whoever* serves two functions in this sentence: it is the subject of the verb *is coming,* and it is the connector that joins the two clauses.

The following words can be used as connectors in this sentence pattern:

what	which	who
whatever	whichever	whoever

Here is an example of how this pattern can be tested in the Structure section of the TOEFL.

_____ was on television made me angry.

(A) It
(B) The story
(C) What
(D) When

In this example you should notice immediately that there are two verbs, *was* and *made,* and each of those verbs needs a subject. Answers (A) or (B) are incorrect because *it* and *the story* are each subjects, but two subjects are needed. Answer (D) is incorrect because *when* is not a subject.

The best answer to this question is (C): *What was on television made me angry.* In this correct sentence, *what* is the subject of the verb *was,* and the noun clause *what was on television* is the subject of the verb *made. What* is also the connector that joins these two clauses.

EXERCISE 9: Each of the following sentences contains more than one clause. Underline the subjects once and the verbs twice. Circle the connectors and put boxes around the noun clauses. Label the noun clauses as subjects or objects. Then indicate if the sentences are correct (C) or incorrect (I).

_C_   1. The game show contestant was able to respond to (whatever) was asked.

_I_   2. You should buy (whatever) the cheapest and most durable.

____ 3. The employee was unhappy about what was added to his job description.

____ 4. Whoever wants to take the desert tour during spring break signing up at the office.

____ 5. The motorist was unable to discover who he had struck his car.

____ 6. It is not yet known who will be elected president next year.

____ 7. Before you decide on a university, you should find out which the best engineering department.

____ 8. It was difficult to distinguish what was on sale and what was merely on display.

____ 9. What was written in the letter angered him beyond belief.

____ 10. You can decide whatever important to you.

SKILL 10: USE SENTENCE CONNECTORS CORRECTLY (PATTERN FIVE)

You should also review the following sentence patterns, because they are very common on the TOEFL.

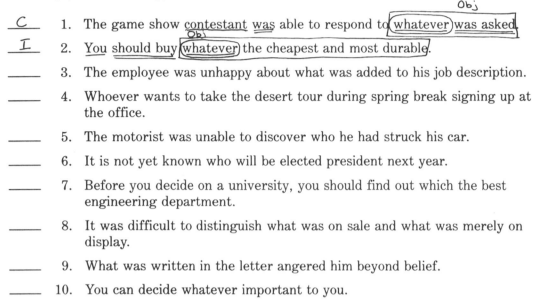

In the first example there are two clauses: in one clause *woman* is the subject of the verb *is filling,* and in the other clause *that* is the subject of the verb *is.* These two clauses are joined with the connector *that.* Notice that in this example the word *that* serves two functions at the same time: it is the subject of the verb *is* and it is the connector that joins the two clauses. Notice also that the connector *that* has the same meaning as *glass* and that the clause *that is on the table* is an adjective clause describing the noun *glass.*

In the second example there are also two clauses: in one clause *glass* is the subject of the verb *contains,* and in the other clause *that* is the subject of the verb *is.* In this example *that* also serves two functions: it is the subject of the verb *is* and it is the connector that joins the two clauses. Because *that is on the table* is an adjective clause describing the noun *glass,* it directly follows *glass.*

In the third example there are also two clauses: *woman* is the subject of the verb *is filling,* and *she* is the subject of the verb *put.* Notice in this example, however, that *that* serves only one function. It is the connector that joins the two clauses.

Finally, in the last example there are also two clauses: *glass* is the subject of *contains,* and *she* is the subject of *put. That* is the connector that joins the two clauses.

The following words can be used as connectors with adjective clauses:

that   which   who

However, *who* can be used only in the patterns shown in the first two examples.

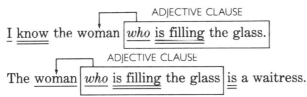

Who must serve as both a subject and a connector. It cannot serve as only a connector as in the next two incorrect examples.

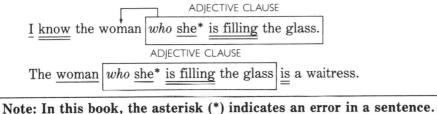

> **Note: In this book, the asterisk (*) indicates an error in a sentence.**

Here is an example of how this sentence pattern can be tested on the TOEFL.

_____ is on the desk has four sections.

- (A) The notebook
- (B) The notebook which
- (C) Because the notebook
- (D) In the notebook

In this example you should notice immediately that the sentence has two verbs, *is* and *has,* and each of them needs a subject. (You should know that *desk* is not a subject because it follows the preposition *on; desk* is the object of the preposition.) The only answer that has two subjects is answer (B), so answer (B) is the correct answer. The correct sentence should say: *The notebook which is on the desk has four sections.* In this sentence *notebook* is the subject of the verb *has,* and *which* is the subject of the verb *is. Which* is also the connector that joins the two clauses.

EXERCISE 10: Each of the following sentences contains more than one clause. Underline the subjects once and the verbs twice. Circle the connectors and put boxes around the adjective clauses. Indicate if the sentences are correct (C) or incorrect (I).

 C   1. The ice cream (that) is served in the restaurant has a smooth, creamy texture.

 I   2. The cars are trying to enter the freeway system are lined up for blocks.

____ 3. It is important to fill out the form in the way that you have been instructed.

____ 4. The plane that he was scheduled to take to Hawaii was delayed.

____ 5. The door that leads to the vault it was tightly locked.

____ 6. The neighbors reported the man who was trying to break into the car to the police.

____ 7. The boss would like to meet with any production workers who they have surpassed their quotas.

____ 8. These plants can only survive in an environment is extremely humid.

____ 9. The sales clerk ran after the woman who had left her credit card in the store.

____ 10. The newspapers that were piled up on the front porch were an indication that the residents had not been home in some time.

REVIEW EXERCISE (SKILLS 6–10): Underline the subjects once and the verbs twice in each of the following sentences. Circle the connectors. Then indicate if the sentences are correct (C) or incorrect (I).

____ 1. Until the registrar makes a final decision about your status, you must remain in an unclassified category.

____ 2. Or the bills can be paid by mail by the first of the month.

____ 3. The part of the structure that has already been built needs to be torn down.

____ 4. Whenever you want to hold the meeting is the time that it will be held.

____ 5. The king has not returned to his homeland, the government was overthrown in a revolution.

____ 6. What was most important was to finish in time.

____ 7. Trash will be collected in the morning, so you should put the trash cans out tonight.

____ 8. He was still sick was obvious to the entire medical staff.

____ 9. It is impossible for the airplane to take off while is snowing so hard.

____ 10. The fire did not damage any homes, but it several trees.

TOEFL EXERCISE (SKILLS 6–10): Choose the letter of the word or group of words that best completes the sentence.

1. The President of the U.S. appoints the cabinet members, _____ their appointments are subject to Senate approval.

    (A) however
    (B) that
    (C) which
    (D) but

2. The prisoners were prevented from speaking to reporters because _____.

    (A) not wanting the story in the papers
    (B) the story in the papers the superintendent did not want
    (C) the public to hear the story
    (D) the superintendent did not want the story in the papers

3. During free fall, _____ to a full minute, a skydiver will fall at a constant speed of 120 mph.

    (A) it is up
    (B) which is up
    (C) being up
    (D) that it is up

4. _____ contained in the chromosomes, and they are thought of as the units of heredity.

    (A) Genes which are
    (B) Genes are
    (C) When genes
    (D) Because of genes

5. The fact _____ the most important ratings period is about to begin has caused all three networks to shore up their schedules.

    (A) is that
    (B) of
    (C) that
    (D) which is

6. _____ will be carried in the next Space Shuttle payload has not yet been announced to the public.

    (A) It
    (B) What
    (C) That
    (D) Whenever

7. _____ show the relations among neurons, they do not preclude the possibility that other aspects are important.

    (A) Neural theories
    (B) A neural theory
    (C) Although neural theories
    (D) Theories

8. The report on the nuclear power plant indicated that when the plant had gone on line _____ unsafe.

    (A) and it had been
    (B) it had been
    (C) had been
    (D) that it had been

Choose the letter of the underlined word or group of words that is not correct.

_____ 9. The production <u>manager was</u> directed to do <u>whom</u> <u>was</u> necessary <u>to reach</u>
                       A   B   C   D
the quota.

_____ 10. The <u>same symptoms</u> that <u>occur</u> with amphetamines <u>which</u> occur with
                    A   B   C
<u>cocaine</u>.
    D

TOEFL REVIEW EXERCISE (SKILLS 1–10): Choose the letter of the word or group of words that best completes the sentence.

1. The three basic chords in _____ the tonic, the dominant, and the subdominant.

    (A) functional harmony
    (B) functional harmony is
    (C) functional harmony are
    (D) functional harmony which are

2. _____ Hale Telescope, at the Palomar Observatory in Southern California, can photograph objects several billion light years away.

    (A) Through the
    (B) With the
    (C) Using the
    (D) The

3. Without the proper card installed inside the computer, _____ impossible to run a graphical program.

    (A) is definitely
    (B) because of
    (C) it is
    (D) is

4. At the end of the nineteenth century, Alfred Binet developed a test for measuring intelligence _____ served as the basis of modern IQ tests.

    (A) has
    (B) it has
    (C) whose
    (D) which has

5. If a food label indicates that a food is mostly carbohydrate, it does not mean _____ is a good food to eat.

    (A) and it
    (B) and
    (C) that it
    (D) for it

6. Period VI extended from about 3000 B.C. until 2700 B.C., _____ began.

    (A) Period VII
    (B) when Period VII it
    (C) when Period VII was
    (D) when Period VII

7. The benefit _____ the study is that it provides necessary information to anyone who needs it.

    (A) of
    (B) which
    (C) that
    (D) because

8. _____ creation of such a community was a desirable step, the requisite political upheaval had to be accepted.

    (A) Since the
    (B) The
    (C) Later, the
    (D) It was the

Choose the letter of the underlined word or group of words that is not correct.

_____ 9. When appears in the first draft of the budget will not necessarily be in the
           ‾‾‾‾A‾‾‾   ‾‾‾B‾‾ ‾‾‾‾C‾‾‾‾‾ ‾D‾
           final draft.

_____ 10. The television, it has so long been a part of our culture, has an enormous
                          ‾‾A‾ ‾‾B‾‾ ‾C‾   ‾D‾
            influence.

PROBLEMS WITH INVERTED SUBJECTS AND VERBS _____

Subjects and verbs are inverted in a variety of situations in English. The most common time to invert the subject and verb is when forming a question. To form a question with a helping verb (*be, have, can, could, would, will,* etc.), the subject and helping verb are inverted.

> He <u>can go</u> to the movies.
> <u>Can he go</u> to the movies?
>
> You <u>would tell</u> me the truth.
> <u>Would you tell</u> me the truth?
>
> She <u>was</u> sick yesterday.
> <u>Was she</u> sick yesterday?

To form a question when there is no helping verb in the sentence, the helping verb *do* is used.

> He <u>goes</u> to the movies.
> <u>Does he go</u> to the movies?
>
> You <u>told</u> me the truth.
> <u>Did you tell</u> me the truth?

There are many other situations in English when subjects and verbs are inverted, but if you just remember this method of inverting subjects and verbs, you will be able to handle the other situations. The most common problems with inverted subjects and verbs on the TOEFL occur in the following situations: (1) with question words such as *when, where,* and *how,* (2) after place expressions, and (3) after negatives.

SKILL 11: INVERT THE SUBJECT AND VERB WITH QUESTION WORDS

There is sometimes confusion about when to invert the subject and verb after question words such as *when, where, why, what,* and *how.* These words can have two very different functions in a sentence. First, they can be at the beginning of a question, and in this case the subject and verb that follow are inverted.

> *What* <u>is</u> the homework?
> *When* <u>can I</u> leave?
> *Where* <u>are you</u> going?

Also, these words can join together two clauses, and in this case the subject and verb that follow are not inverted.

I do not know *what* the homework is.

When I can leave, I will take the first train.

Do you know *where* you are going?

In each of these examples there are two clauses joined by a question word. Notice that the subjects and verbs that follow the question words *what, when,* and *where* are not inverted in this case.

EXERCISE 11:   Each of the following sentences contains a question word. Circle the question word. Look at the clause that follows the question word, and underline the subject once and the verb twice. Then indicate if the sentences are correct (C) or incorrect (I).

<u>I</u>   1. The phone company is not certain (when) will the new directories be ready.

<u>C</u>   2. The professor does not understand (why) so many students did poorly on the exam.

_____   3. How new students can get information about parking?

_____   4. Where is it cheapest to get typeset copies printed?

_____   5. Only the pilot can tell you how far can the plane go on one tank of fuel.

_____   6. What type of security does he prefer for his investments?

_____   7. Not even the bank president knows when the vault will be opened.

_____   8. How long it has been since you arrived in the United States?

_____   9. The jury doubts what the witness said under cross-examination.

_____   10. Do you know why he wants to take an extended leave of absence?

SKILL 12:   INVERT THE SUBJECT AND VERB AFTER PLACE EXPRESSIONS

After ideas expressing place, the subject and verb sometimes invert in English. This can happen with single words expressing place, such as *here, there,* or *nowhere.*

Here is the book that you lent me.

There are the keys that I thought I lost.

Nowhere have I seen such beautiful weather.

In the first example the place word *here* causes the subject *book* (and its modifiers) to come after the verb *is.* In the second example the place word *there* causes the subject *keys* (and its modifiers) to come after the verb *are.* In the last example the place word *nowhere* causes the subject *I* to come after the verb *have.*

The subject and verb can also be inverted after prepositional phrases expressing place.

In the closet are the clothes that you want.

Around the corner is Sam's house.

Beyond the mountains lies the town where you will live.

In the first example the prepositional phrase of place *in the closet* causes the subject *clothes* (and its modifiers) to come after the verb *are*. In the second example the prepositional phrase of place *around the corner* causes the subject *house* (and its modifier) to come after the verb *is*. In the last example the prepositional phrase of place *beyond the mountains* causes the subject *town* (and its modifiers) to come after the verb *lies*.

EXERCISE 12: Each of the following sentences contains an expression of place at the beginning of the sentence. Circle the expression of place. Look at the clause that immediately follows and underline the subject once and the verb twice. Then indicate if the sentences are correct (C) or incorrect (I).

__C__ 1. (In front of the house) stood some giant trees.

__I__ 2. (There) a big house is on the corner.

_____ 3. In the cave was a vast treasure of gems and jewels.

_____ 4. To the north the stream is that the settlers will have to ford.

_____ 5. Around the corner are the offices that you are trying to find.

_____ 6. Nowhere I can find the book I need for that course.

_____ 7. There were some very personal letters sitting out on the desk.

_____ 8. In the backyard the two trees are that need to be pruned.

_____ 9. Around the recreation hall and down the path are the tents where we will be staying this weekend.

_____ 10. Nowhere in the world can farmers grow such delicious fruit.

SKILL 13:   INVERT THE SUBJECT AND VERB AFTER NEGATIVES

The subject and verb can also be inverted after certain negatives and related expressions. When negative expressions such as *no, not,* or *never* come at the beginning of a sentence, the subject and verb are inverted.

> Not once did I miss a question.
>
> Never has Mr. Jones taken a vacation.
>
> At no time can the woman talk on the telephone.

In the first example the negative expression *not once* causes the subject *I* to come after the helping verb *did*. In the second example the negative word *never* causes the subject *Mr. Jones* to come after the helping verb *has*. In the last example the negative expression *at no time* causes the subject *woman* (and its modifier) to come after the helping verb *can*.

Certain words in English, such as *hardly, barely, scarcely,* and *only*, act like negatives when they refer to time. If one of these words comes at the beginning of a sentence, the subject and verb are also inverted.

Hardly ever <u>does</u> he <u><u>take</u></u> time off.

(This means that he *almost never* takes time off.)

Only once <u>did</u> the manager <u><u>issue</u></u> overtime paychecks.

(This means that the mangager *almost never* issued overtime paychecks).

In the first example the almost negative expression *hardly ever* causes the subject *he* to come after the helping verb *does*. In the second example the almost negative expression *only once* causes the subject *manager* (and its modifier) to come after the helping verb *did*.

Two other negative words that cause the subject and verb to invert are *neither* and *nor*. When these two words are found in the middle of a sentence, the subject and verb that follow them are inverted.

I do not want to go, and neither <u><u>does</u></u> <u>Tom</u>.

The secretary is not attending the meeting, nor <u><u>is</u></u> her <u>boss</u>.

In the first example the negative *neither* causes the subject *Tom* to come after the helping verb *does*. In the second sentence the negative *nor* causes the subject *boss* (and its modifier) to come after the verb *is*.

EXERCISE 13: Each of the following sentences contains a negative or almost negative expression. Circle the negative expressions. Look at the clauses that follow and underline the subjects once and the verbs twice. Then indicate if the sentences are correct (C) or incorrect (I).

<u>I</u> 1. (Never) the <u>boy</u> <u><u>wrote</u></u> to his sisters.

<u>C</u> 2. (On no occasion) <u>did</u> <u>they</u> <u><u>say</u></u> that to me.

_____ 3. Steve did not win the prize, nor did he expect to do so.

_____ 4. Only once in my life gone I have to New York City.

_____ 5. Did he go out of the house at no time.

_____ 6. Seldom their secretary has made such mistakes.

_____ 7. No sooner had she hung up the phone than it rang again.

_____ 8. Sheila did not arrive late for work, nor she left early.

_____ 9. Barely had he finished the exam when the graduate assistant collected the papers.

_____ 10. The police did not arrive in time to save the girl, and neither did the paramedics.

REVIEW EXERCISE (SKILLS 11–13): Underline the subjects once and the verbs twice in each of the following sentences. Then indicate if the sentences are correct (C) or incorrect (I).

_____ 1. Not once did the judge listen to what the lawyers were suggesting.

_____ 2. On the island in the middle of the stream is the house that I want to buy.

_____ 3. The town council is not sure why have the land developers changed their plans.

_____ 4. Never in the world I believed that this would happen.

_____ 5. Nowhere in the county can you purchase that magazine.

_____ 6. Where can I find the nearest bus stop?

_____ 7. It is impossible to know how the fire got started.

_____ 8. Hardly ever it snows in this section of the country.

_____ 9. Did the scientist explain what he put in the beaker?

_____ 10. Down the hall to the left the offices are that need to be painted.

TOEFL EXERCISE (SKILLS 11–13): Choose the letter of the word or group of words that best completes the sentence.

1. Rarely _____ located near city lights or at lower elevations.
   (A) observatories are
   (B) are
   (C) in the observatories
   (D) are observatories

2. There are geographic, economic, and cultural reasons why _____ around the world.
   (A) diets differ
   (B) do diets differ
   (C) are diets different
   (D) to differ a diet

3. Located behind _____ the two lacrimal glands.
   (A) each eyelid
   (B) is each eyelid
   (C) each eyelid are
   (D) each eyelid which is

4. Nowhere _____ more skewed than in the auto industry.
   (A) that retail trade figures
   (B) retail trade figures
   (C) are retail trade figures
   (D) retail trade figures are

5. In the U.S. _____ approximately 4 million miles of roads, streets, and highways.
   (A) there
   (B) is
   (C) because of
   (D) there are

6. Potassium has a valence of positive one because it usually loses one electron when _____ with other elements.
   (A) does it combine
   (B) it combines
   (C) in combining
   (D) combination

7. The economic background of labor legislation will not be mentioned in this course, _____ be treated.
   (A) trade unionism will not
   (B) nor trade unionism will
   (C) nor will trade unionism
   (D) neither trade unionism will

8. In the Morgan Library in New York City _____ of Medieval and Renaissance manuscripts.
   (A) a collection is
   (B) in a collection
   (C) is a collection
   (D) which is a collection

Choose the letter of the underlined word or group of words that is not correct.

_____ 9. Only <u>for a</u> short period of time <u>a cheetah will</u> <u>run</u> at <u>top</u> speed.
              A   B   C   D

_____ 10. The <u>Kern River flows</u> from the high Sierras into the San Joaquin valley,
                 A

where <u>is the water</u> <u>diverted</u> into an <u>irrigation system</u>.
      B   C   D

TOEFL REVIEW EXERCISE (SKILLS 1–13): Choose the letter of the word or group of words that best completes the sentence.

1. As an emergency measure, _____ by the Governor to curtail railway expenditure.
   (A) because it proposed
   (B) was proposed
   (C) because of the proposal
   (D) it was proposed

2. _____ twelve million immigrants entered the U.S. via Ellis Island.
   (A) More than
   (B) There were more than
   (C) Of more than
   (D) The report

3. _____ variety of flowers in the show, from simple carnations to the most exquisite roses.
   (A) A wide
   (B) There was a wide
   (C) Was there
   (D) Many

4. _____ that Emily Dickinson wrote, only twenty-four were given titles and only seven were published during her lifetime.
   (A) Of the 1,800 poems
   (B) There were 1,800 poems
   (C) Because the 1,800 poems
   (D) The 1,800 poems

5. The wedges _____ dart board are worth from one to twenty points each.
   (A) they are on a
   (B) are on a
   (C) are they on a
   (D) on a

6. Alpha Centauri appears to the naked eye to be a single star, _____ in reality a triple star system.
   (A) it is
   (B) when it is
   (C) while is
   (D) when is it

7. _____ producing many new movies for release after the new season begins.
   (A) His company is
   (B) His companies
   (C) The company
   (D) Why the company is

8. The Dewey Decimal System, currently used in libraries throughout the world, _____ all written works into ten classes according to subject.
   (A) dividing
   (B) divides
   (C) it would divide
   (D) was divided

Choose the letter of the underlined word or group of words that is not correct.

_____ 9. <u>Based on</u> recommendations proposed in the annual report, the board
    A

   <u>does not want</u> to delay its judgment, nor <u>it wants</u> to report <u>its findings</u>
     B   C   D
   publicly.

_____ 10. Because <u>the project depends</u> on <u>what happens</u> at the federal level, <u>so</u> the
       A   B   C

   city and the county <u>may have</u> to wait until the budget cutting ends.
           D

PROBLEMS WITH SUBJECT/VERB AGREEMENT _____

Subject/verb agreement is simple: if the subject of a sentence is singular, then the verb must be singular, and if the subject of the sentence is plural then the verb must be plural. An *s* on a verb usually indicates that a verb is singular, while an *s* on a noun usually indicates that the noun is plural. (Do not forget irregular plurals of nouns, such as *women, children,* and *people.*)

   The <u>boy</u> <u>walks</u> to school.

   The <u>boys</u> <u>walk</u> to school.

In the first example the singular subject *boy* requires a singular verb *walks*. In the second example the plural subject *boys* requires a plural verb *walk*.

  Although this might seem quite simple, there are a few situations on the TOEFL when subject/verb agreement can be a little tricky. You should be careful of subject/verb agreement in the following situations: (1) after prepositional phrases, (2) after inverted verbs, and (3) after certain words such as *anybody, everything, no one, something, each,* and *every.*

SKILL 14: MAKE VERBS AGREE AFTER PREPOSITIONAL PHRASES

Sometimes prepositional phrases can come between the subject and the verb. If the object of the preposition is singular and the subject is plural, or if the object of the preposition is plural and the subject is singular, there can be confusion in making the subject and verb agree.

    SING   PL
   The <u>key</u> (to the doors) <u>are</u>* in the drawer.

     PL   SING
   The <u>keys</u> (to the door) <u>is</u>* in the drawer.
   (Remember, in this book an asterisk (*) shows an incorrect word.)

In the first example you might think that *doors* is the subject because it comes directly in front of the verb *are*. However, *doors* is not the subject, because it is the object of the preposition *to*. The subject of the sentence is *key*, so the verb should be *is*.

In the second example you might think that *door* is the subject because it comes directly in front of the verb *is*. You should recognize in this example that *door* is not the subject, because it is the object of the preposition *to*. Because the subject of the sentence is *keys,* the verb should be *are.*

A particular agreement problem occurs when the subject of a sentence is a word like *all, most, some,* or *part* followed by the preposition *of.* In this situation, the subject (*all, most, some,* or *part*) can be singular or plural, depending on what follows the preposition *of.*

SING   SING
All (of the *book*) was interesting.

PL   PL
All (of the *books*) were interesting.

In the first example the subject *all* is singular because it is all of one thing (*book*). The correct verb is therefore the singular *was.* In the second example the subject *all* is plural because it is all of several things (*books*). The correct verb is therefore the plural *were.*

EXERCISE 14: Each of the following sentences has one or more prepositional phrases between the subject and the verb. Circle the prepositional phrases. Underline the subjects one time and the verbs two times. Then indiciate if the sentences are correct (C) or incorrect (I).

_C_ 1. The climbers (on the sheer face)(of the mountain) need to be rescued.

_I_ 2. The interrogation, conducted (by three police officers) have lasted for several hours.

_____ 3. All of the students in the class taught by Professor Roberts is required to turn in their term papers next Monday.

_____ 4. The tenants in the apartment next to mine is giving a party this evening.

_____ 5. The President, surrounded by Secret Service Agents, is trying to make his way to the podium.

_____ 6. All of the witnesses in the jury trial, which lasted more than two weeks, have indicated that they believed the defendant was guilty.

_____ 7. Some of the animals from the zoo was released into the animal preserve.

_____ 8. The buildings destroyed during the fire are being rebuilt at the taxpayers' expense.

_____ 9. Because of the seriousness of the company's financial problems, the board of directors have called an emergency meeting.

_____ 10. Manufacture of the items you requested have been discontinued because of lack of profit on those items.

Skill 15: Make Inverted Verbs Agree

We have seen that sometimes in English the subject comes after the verb. This can occur after question words (Skill 11), after place expressions (Skill 12) and after negative expressions (Skill 13). When the subject and verb are inverted, it can be difficult to find them, and it can therefore be a problem to make them agree.

(Behind the house) <u>was</u>* the <u>bicycles</u> I wanted.

(Behind the houses) <u>were</u>* the <u>bicycle</u> I wanted.

In the first example it is easy to think that *house* is the subject, because it comes directly in front of the verb *was. House* is not the subject, however, because it is the object of the preposition *behind.* The subject of the sentence is *bicycles,* and the subject *bicycles* comes after the verb because of the place expression *behind the house.* Because the subject *bicycles* is plural, the verb should be changed to the plural *were.*

In the second example the subject *bicycle* comes after the verb *were* because of the place expression *behind the houses.* Because the subject *bicycle* is singular, the verb should be changed to the singular *was.*

EXERCISE 15: Each of the following sentences contains an inverted subject and verb. Circle the word or group of words that causes the subject and verb to invert. Then find the subject and verb which follow these words. Underline the subject once and the verb twice. Then indicate if the sentences are correct (C) or incorrect (I).

__C__   1. (Only once) this morning <u>were</u> the <u>letters</u> <u>delivered</u> by the campus mail service.

__I__   2. The computer programmer was unaware that (there) <u>was</u> so many <u>mistakes</u> in the program he had written.

_____   3. South of the town is some tall trees and a pleasant picnic area.

_____   4. Seldom in the history of television has two new comedies been so successful in one season.

_____   5. Around the corner and to the right are the rooms that have been assigned to that program.

_____   6. Here is all the facts that you asked me to collect from various sources.

_____   7. In the plant located across the street was the missing parts needed since yesterday.

_____   8. It is unbelievable that there have been so many murders in such a peaceful neighborhood.

_____   9. Nowhere else in the country are water skiers able to spend so many months in the water.

_____   10. In the parking lot south of the stadium was the cars that were about to be towed.

Skill 16: Make Verbs Agree after Certain Words

Certain words in English are always grammatically singular, even though they might have plural meanings. You should be very careful of subject/verb agreement with the following words:

anybody	everybody	nobody	somebody	each
anyone	everyone	no one	someone	every [+ noun]
anything	everything	nothing	something	

These words can have a plural meaning, but they are grammatically singular and they must have singular verbs.

> Everybody are going* to the theater.

Even though we understand from this example that a lot of people are going to the theater, *everybody* is singular and requires a singular verb. The plural verb *are going* should be changed to the singular verb *is going*.

EXERCISE 16:   Each of the following sentences contains one of the words listed above in Skill 16. Circle these words. Underline twice the verbs that follow. Then indicate if the sentences are correct (C) or incorrect (I).

_I_   1. It is impossible to believe that (somebody) actually admire that man.

_C_   2. (Each) of the doctors in the building needs to have a separate reception area.

_____   3. The president felt that no one were better suited for the position of chief staff advisor.

_____   4. Everybody participating in the fund raiser are to turn in the tickets by 8:00.

_____   5. Because of the low number of orders, nothing has to be done now.

_____   6. Every time someone take unnecessary breaks, precious moments of production time are lost.

_____   7. Anybody who goes to the top of the Empire State Building is impressed with the view.

_____   8. Every man, woman, and child in this line are required to sign the forms in order to complete the registration process.

_____   9. It is nice to believe that anything is possible if a person tries hard enough.

_____   10. The company reiterated to reporters that nobody have been dismissed because of the incident.

STRUCTURE AND WRITTEN EXPRESSION   115

REVIEW EXERCISE (SKILLS 14–16):   Underline the subjects once and the verbs twice in each of the following sentences. Then indicate if the sentences are correct (C) or incorrect (I).

_____   1. The contracts signed by the company has been voided because a number of stipulations were not met.

_____   2. Ten miles beyond the river was the farmlands they had purchased with their life savings.

_____   3. Only the most expensive jewels in the safe were taken by the thief.

_____   4. Each package that is not properly wrapped have to be returned to the sender.

_____   5. The proposal brought so much new work to the partnership that there was not enough hours to complete all of it.

_____   6. The box of ribbons for the IBM computer have been misplaced.

_____   7. It is disconcerting to believe that every possible candidate has been rejected for one reason or another.

_____   8. The advice offered by the team of lawyers was that he should turn himself in.

_____   9. Only once have there been more excitement in this city about a sporting event.

_____   10. If nobody have bought that car from the dealer, then you should return and make another offer.

TOEFL EXERCISE (SKILLS 14–16):   Choose the letter of the word or group of words that best completes the sentence.

1. Among bees _____ a highly elaborate form of communication.
   - (A) occur
   - (B) occurs
   - (C) it occurs
   - (D) they occur

2. _____ heated by solar energy have special collectors on the roofs to trap sunlight.
   - (A) A home is
   - (B) Homes are
   - (C) A home
   - (D) Homes

Choose the letter of the underlined word or group of words that is not correct.

_____   3. Each number in a binary system are formed from only two symbols.
                        A   B   C   D

_____   4. Scientists at the medical center is trying to determine if there is a
                                            A   B   C
   relationship between saccharine and cancer.
                                D

_____ 5. On the rim of the Kilauea volcano in the Hawaiian Islands are a hotel called
           ___A___   _____B_____ _C_   _D_
           the Volcano House.

_____ 6. The great digital advances of the electronic age, such as integrated
               _____A_____
           circuitry and a microcomputer, has been planted in tiny chips.
           _____B_____   _C_   ___D___

_____ 7. There are many frequently mentioned reasons why one out of four arrests
                          _____ _____   _____
                              A   B   C
           involve a juvenile.
           ___D___

_____ 8. Kepler's Laws, principles outlining planetary movement, was formulated
                                                                    ___ _____
                                                                     A   B
           based on observations made without a telescope.
           _____   ____
             C   D

_____ 9. Only with a two-thirds vote by both houses are the U.S. Congress able to
                     _____   ___   _____
                           A   B   C
           override a Presidential veto.
                                   ____
                                    D

_____ 10. Of all the evidence that has piled up since Webster's paper was published,
                                    _____   _____
                                        A   B
           there is no new ideas to contradict his original theory.
                 _____ _____
                      C   D

TOEFL Review Exercise (Skills 1–16): Choose the letter of the word or group of words that best completes the sentence.

1. _____ several unsuccessful attempts, Robert Peary reached the North Pole on April 6, 1909.
    (A) After
    (B) He made
    (C) When
    (D) His

2. The musical instrument _____ is six feet long.
    (A) is called the bass
    (B) it is called the bass
    (C) called the bass
    (D) calls the bass

3. One problem with all languages _____ they are full of irregularities.
    (A) when
    (B) so
    (C) is that
    (D) and

4. Seldom _____ of economic cycles been helpful in predicting turning points in cycles.
   (A) psychological theories
   (B) psychological theories have
   (C) have psychological theories
   (D) psychologists have theories

5. Hospital committees _____ spent weeks agonizing over which artificial kidney candidate would receive the treatments now find that the decision is out of their hands.
   (A) once
   (B) that once
   (C) have
   (D) once had

Choose the letter of the underlined word or group of words that is not correct.

_____ 6. A quantitative analysis, <u>using</u> both the computer and quantitative
                                      A

techniques, <u>are used</u> <u>to optimize</u> financial decisions.
              B   C   D

_____ 7. The worker <u>was</u> told <u>to replace</u> the ribbon <u>when was</u> <u>used</u> up.
                      A   B   C   D

_____ 8. Five miles beyond <u>the hills</u> <u>were</u> a fire with <u>its</u> flames <u>reaching</u> up to the
                             A   B   C   D
sky.

_____ 9. Kettledrums, <u>what</u> were first <u>played</u> on horseback, <u>were</u> incorporated
                       A   B   C
<u>into the</u> orchestra in the eighteenth century.
   D

_____ 10. When <u>is a flag</u> <u>hung</u> upside down, <u>it is</u> an <u>internationally</u> recognized symbol
                A   B   C   D
of distress.

PROBLEMS WITH THE COMPARATIVE AND SUPERLATIVE _____

Sentences with incorrect comparatives and superlatives can appear in the TOEFL. It is therefore important for you to know how to do the following: (1) form the comparative and the superlative correctly, and (2) use the comparative and superlative correctly.

SKILL 17: FORM THE COMPARATIVE AND SUPERLATIVE CORRECTLY

The problem with some of the comparative and superlative sentences on the TOEFL is that the comparative or superlative is formed incorrectly. You should therefore understand how to form the comparative and superlative to answer such questions correctly.

The comparative is formed with either *-er* or *more* and *than*. In the comparative, *-er* is used with short adjectives such as *tall,* and *more* is used with longer adjectives such as *beautiful.*

Bob is <u>taller than</u> Ron.

Sally is <u>more beautiful than</u> Sharon.

The superlative is formed with *the,* either *-est* or *most,* and sometimes *in* or *of.* In the superlative, *-est* is used with short adjectives such as *tall,* and *most* is used with longer adjectives such as beautiful.

Bob is <u>the tallest man in</u> the room.

Sally is <u>the most beautiful of</u> all the women at the party.

The <u>fastest runner</u> wins the race. (no *in* or *of*)

EXERCISE 17:   Each of the following sentences contains a comparative or superlative. Circle the comparative or superlative. Then indicate if the sentences are correct (C) or incorrect (I).

_I_   1. Oxygen is (abundanter than) nitrogen.

_C_   2. The directions to the exercise say to choose (the most appropriate) response.

_____ 3. The lesson you are studying now is the most importantest lesson you will have.

_____ 4. Fashions this year are shorter and more colorful than they were last year.

_____ 5. The professor indicated that Anthony's research paper was more long than the other students' papers.

_____ 6. Alaska is the coldest than all the states in the United States.

_____ 7. The workers on the day shift are more rested than the workers on the night shift.

_____ 8. She was more happier this morning than she had been yesterday.

_____ 9. The quarterback on this year's football team is more versatile than the quarterback on last year's team.

_____ 10. I prefer to live in the dormitory that is the closest to the school.

SKILL 18: USE THE COMPARATIVE AND SUPERLATIVE CORRECTLY

Another problem with the comparative and superlative on the TOEFL is that they can be used incorrectly. The comparative and superlative have different uses, and you should understand these different uses to answer such questions correctly. The comparative is used to compare two things.

> The history class is <u>larger than</u> the math class.

> Mary is <u>more intelligent than</u> Sue.

In the first example *the history class* is being compared with *the math class*. In the second example *Mary* is being compared with *Sue*.

The superlative is used when there are more than two items to compare and you want to show the one that is the best, the biggest, or in some way the most outstanding.

> The history class is <u>the largest</u> in the school.

> Mary is <u>the most intelligent</u> in the class.

In the first example *the history class* is compared with all the other classes in the school, and the history class is larger than each of the other classes. In the second example, *Mary* is compared with all the other students in the class, and Mary is more intelligent than each of the other students.

EXERCISE 18:   Each of the following sentences contains a comparative or superlative. Circle the comparative or superlative. Then indicate if the sentences are correct (C) or incorrect (I).

__C__   1.   Harvard is probably (the most prestigious university) in the United States.

__I__   2.   Mary is (more intelligent) of the class.

_____   3.   The engineers hired this year have more experience than those hired last year.

_____   4.   The graduate assistant informed us that the first exam is the most difficult of the two.

_____   5.   He bought the more powerful stereo speakers that he could find.

_____   6.   The afternoon seminar was much more interesting than the morning lecture.

_____   7.   The food in this restaurant is the best of the restaurant we visited last week.

_____   8.   The plants that have been sitting in the sunny window are far healthier than the other plants.

_____   9.   The photocopies are the darkest that they have ever been.

_____   10.   The first journal article is the longest of the second article.

REVIEW EXERCISE (SKILLS 17–18):   Circle the comparatives and superlatives in the following sentences. Then indicate if the sentences are correct (C) or incorrect (I).

_____   1.   The coffee is more stronger today than it was yesterday.

_____   2.   The tree that was struck by lightning had been the tallest of the two trees we had in the yard.

_____   3.   He will buy the most fuel-efficient car that he can afford.

_____   4.   The business department is bigger of the departments in the university.

_____   5.   The Bijoux Theater is better than the Fox because the seats at the Bijoux are larger and more comfortable.

_____   6.   I really do not want to live in the southeast because it is one of the most hot areas in the United States.

_____   7.   Tonight's dinner was more filling than last night's.

_____   8.   It is preferable to use the most efficient and most effective method that you can.

_____   9.   The janitor was asked if he could make the building a little more warm.

_____   10. The house is now the cleanest it has ever been.

TOEFL EXERCISE (SKILLS 17–18):   Choose the letter of the word or group of words that best completes the sentence.

1.   The speed of light is _____ the speed of sound.
   (A) faster
   (B) much faster than
   (C) the fastest
   (D) as fast

2.   The use of detail is _____ method of developing a controlling idea, and almost all students employ this method.
   (A) more common
   (B) common
   (C) most common
   (D) the most common

Choose the letter of the underlined word or group of words that is not correct.

_____   3.   Certain types of snakes have been known to survive fasts more as a year
                     A   B   C   D
            long.

_____ 4. The widely used natural fiber of all is cotton.
             A   B   C   D

_____ 5. Climate, soil type, and availability of water are the most critical factors than
                                 A   B   C

   selecting the best type of grass for a lawn.
            D

_____ 6. The leek, a member of the lily family, has a mildest taste than the onion.
              A   B   C   D

_____ 7. The Monarch butterfly migrates from Canada and the northern U.S. to
                             A   B

   warmest areas in California, Florida, and Mexico.
      C   D

_____ 8. Peter Abelard, a logician and theologian, was the controversialest teacher
                       A   B   C

   of his age.
     D

_____ 9. Protein molecules are the most complex than the molecules of
                      A   B   C

   carbohydrates and lipids.
         D

_____ 10. The grizzly bear, which can grow up to eight feet tall, has been called
                        A   B   C

   a more dangerous animal of North America.
     D

TOEFL REVIEW EXERCISE (SKILLS 1–18): Choose the letter of the word or group of words that best completes the sentence.

1. _____, a liberal arts college specifically for deaf people, is located in Washington, D.C.
   - (A) Gallaudet College
   - (B) Gallaudet College is
   - (C) About Gallaudet College
   - (D) Because of Gallaudet

2. _____ varieties of dogs at the show, including spaniels, poodles, and collies.
   - (A) The several
   - (B) Those
   - (C) Several
   - (D) There were several

3. William Sydney Porter _____ O'Henry in his 250 works of fiction.
   - (A) using the pen name
   - (B) a useful pen name
   - (C) who used the pen name
   - (D) used the pen name

4. _____ a long-term loan in which the borrower agrees to pay a fixed rate of interest over the life of the debt.
   - (A) There are
   - (B) Although a bond is
   - (C) Because a bond is
   - (D) A bond is

Choose the letter of the underlined word or group of words that is not correct.

_____ 5. The coyote is <u>somewhat</u> <u>smaller</u> in <u>size</u> <u>that</u> a timber wolf.
                              A   B   C D

_____ 6. The weather <u>reports all</u> <u>showed</u> that there <u>were</u> a tremendous storm front
                           A   B   C

           <u>moving</u> in.
             D

_____ 7. Seldom <u>cactus plants are</u> <u>found</u> <u>outside</u> <u>of</u> North America.
                     A   B   C   D

_____ 8. In a basketball game a player <u>what</u> <u>is fouled</u> <u>receives</u> one or two
                                   A   B   C

           <u>free throws</u>.
             D

_____ 9. <u>Until</u> <u>recently</u>, California was <u>largest</u> <u>producer</u> of oranges in the U.S.
             A   B   C   D

_____ 10. An understanding of <u>engineering theories</u> and problems <u>are</u> impossible until
                                A   B

           basic arithmetic <u>is</u> fully <u>mastered</u>.
                    C   D

PROBLEMS WITH PARALLEL STRUCTURE

In good English an attempt should be made to make the language as even and balanced as possible. This balance is called parallel structure. You can achieve parallel structure by making the forms of words as similar as possible. The following is an example of a sentence that is not parallel:

I like <u>to sing</u> and <u>dancing</u>.*

The problem in this sentence is not the expression *to sing,* and the problem is not the word *dancing.* The expression *to sing* is correct by itself, and the word *dancing* is correct by itself. Both of the following sentences are correct:

I like <u>to sing</u>.

I like <u>dancing</u>.

The problem in the incorrect example is that *to sing* and *dancing* are joined together in one sentence with *and.* They are different forms where it is possible to have similar forms; therefore the example is not parallel. It can be corrected in two different ways: we can make the first expression like the second, or we can make the second expression like the first.

I like to sing and to dance.

I like singing and dancing.

There are several situations in which you should be particularly careful of parallel structure. Parallel structures are required with coordinate conjunctions (*and, but, or*), with comparisons, and with certain special expressions (*both . . . and, either . . . or, neither . . . nor, not only . . . but also*).

SKILL 19: USE PARALLEL STRUCTURE WITH COORDINATE CONJUNCTIONS

The job of the coordinate conjunctions (*and, but, or*) is to join together equal expressions. In other words, what is on one side of these words must be parallel to what is on the other side. These conjunctions can join nouns, or verbs, or adjectives, or phrases, or subordinate clauses, or main clauses; they just must join together two of the same thing. Here are examples of two nouns joined by a coordinate conjunction:

I need to talk to the manager *or* the assistant manager.

She is not a teacher *but* a lawyer.

You can choose from activities such as hiking *and* kayaking.

Here are examples of two verbs joined by a coordinate conjunction:

He eats *and* sleeps only when he takes a vacation.

She invites us to her home *but* never talks with us.

You can stay home *or* go to the movies with us.

Here are examples of two adjectives joined by a coordinate conjunction:

My boss is sincere *and* nice.

The exam that he gave was short *but* difficult.

Class can be interesting *or* boring.

Here are examples of two phrases joined by a coordinate conjunction:

There are students in the classroom *and* in front of the building.

The papers are on my desk *or* in the drawer.

The checks will be ready not at noon *but* at 1:00.

Here are examples of two clauses joined by a coordinate conjunction:

They are not interested in what you say or what you do.

I am here because I want to be *and* because I have to be.

Mr. Brown likes to go home early, *but* his wife prefers to stay late.

EXERCISE 19: Each of the following sentences contains words or groups of words that should be parallel. Circle the word or words that indicate that the sentence should have parallel parts. Underline the parts that should be parallel. Then indicate if each sentence is correct (C) or incorrect (I).

__I__   1. She held jobs as a typist, a housekeeper, (and) in a restaurant.

__C__   2. The report you are looking for could be in the file (or) on the desk.

_____   3. He was angry not at what you said but your manner.

_____   4. The speaker introduced himself, told several interesting anecdotes, and he finished with an emotional plea.

_____   5. You should know when the program starts and how many units you must complete to finish it.

_____   6. The term paper he wrote was rather short but very impressive.

_____   7. She suggested taking the plane this evening or that we go by train tomorrow.

_____   8. The dean or the assistant dean will inform you of when and where you should apply for your diploma.

_____   9. There are papers to file, reports to type, and those letters should be answered.

_____   10. The manager needed a quick but thorough response.

SKILL 20: USE PARALLEL STRUCTURE WITH COMPARISONS

When you make a comparison, you point out the similarities or differences between two things, and those similarities or differences must be in parallel form. You can recognize a comparison showing how two things are different from the *-er . . . than* or the *more . . . than*.

> My school is farth*er than* your school.

> To be rich is bett*er than* to be poor.

> A house in the suburbs is *more* expensive *than* a house in town.

> What is written is *more* easily understood *than* what is spoken.

A comparison showing how two things are the same might contain *as . . . as* or expressions such as *the same as* or *similar to*.

> Their car is *as* big *as* a small house.

> Renting those apartments costs about *the same as* leasing them.

> The work that I did is *similar to* the work that you did.

EXERCISE 20: Each of the following sentences contains words or groups of words that should be parallel. Circle the word or words that indicate that the sentence should have parallel parts. Underline the parts that should be parallel. Then indicate if each sentence is correct (C) or incorrect (I).

__C__   1. His research for the thesis was (more useful than) hers.

__I__   2. Dining in a restaurant is (more fun than) to eat at home.

_____   3. I want a new secretary who is as efficient as the previous one.

_____   4. What you do today should be the same as did yesterday.

_____   5. This lesson is more difficult than we had before.

_____   6. You have less homework than they do.

_____   7. What you do has more effect than what you say.

_____   8. Music in your country is quite similar to my country.

_____   9. The collection of foreign journals in the university library is more extensive than the high school library.

_____   10. How to buy a used car can be as difficult as buying a new car.

SKILL 21:   USE PARALLEL STRUCTURE WITH SPECIAL EXPRESSIONS

The expressions *both . . . and, either . . . or, neither . . . nor,* and *not only . . . but also* require parallel structure.

> I know *both* where you went *and* what you did.
>
> *Either* Mark *or* Sue has the book.
>
> The tickets are *neither* in my pocket *nor* in my purse.
>
> He is *not only* an excellent student *but also* an outstanding athlete.

The following is not parallel and must be corrected:

> He wants *either* to go by train *or* by plane*.

It is not correct because *to go by train* is not parallel to *by plane*. It can be corrected in several ways.

> He wants *either* to go by train *or* to go by plane.
>
> He wants to go *either* by train *or* by plane.
>
> He wants to go by *either* train *or* plane.

When you are using these special expressions, be sure that the correct parts are used together. The following are incorrect.

> I want *both* this book *or** that one.
>
> *Either* Sam *nor** Sue is taking the course.

In the first example *or* cannot be used with *both*; *or* should be changed to *and*. In the second example, *nor* cannot be used with *either*; *nor* should be changed to *or*.

EXERCISE 21: Each of the following sentences contains words or groups of words that should be parallel. Circle the word or words that indicate that the sentence should have parallel parts. Underline the parts that should be parallel. Then indicate if each sentence is correct (C) or incorrect (I).

__I__ 1. According to the syllabus, you can (either) write a paper (or) you can take an exam.

__C__ 2. It would be (both) noticed (and) appreciated if you could finish the work before you leave.

_____ 3. She would like neither to see a movie or to go bowling.

_____ 4. Either the manager or her assistant can help you with your refund.

_____ 5. She wants not only to take a trip to Europe but she also would like to travel to Asia.

_____ 6. He could correct neither what you said nor you wrote.

_____ 7. Both the tailor or the laundress could fix the damage to the dress.

_____ 8. He not only called the police department but also called the fire department.

_____ 9. You can graduate either at the end of the fall semester or you can graudate at the end of the spring semester.

_____ 10. The movie was neither amusing nor was it interesting.

REVIEW EXERCISE (SKILLS 19–21): Circle the word or words that indicate that the sentence should have parallel parts. Underline the parts that should be parallel. Then indicate if the sentences are correct (C) or incorrect (I).

_____ 1. After retirement he plans on traveling and playing a lot of golf.

_____ 2. She was both surprised by and pleased with the seminar.

_____ 3. Sam is always good-natured, generous, and helps you.

_____ 4. When we arrived, when we left, and on our return, we were cheered by the crowds.

_____ 5. I searched in the closet, under the bed, and behind the sofa.

_____ 6. He exercised not only in the morning, but he also exercised every afternoon.

_____ 7. Working four days per week is much more relaxing than working five days per week.

_____ 8. He indicated when to leave and that I should take the car.

_____ 9. Either you have to finish the project, or the contract will be cancelled.

_____ 10. The courses that you are required to take are more important than the courses that you choose.

TOEFL Exercise (Skills 19–21): Choose the letter of the word or group of words that best completes the sentence.

1. Truman Capote's *In Cold Blood* is neither journalistically accurate _____.
   - (A) a piece of fiction
   - (B) nor a fictitious work
   - (C) or written in a fictitious way
   - (D) nor completely fictitious

2. Vitamin C is necessary for the prevention and _____ of scurvy.
   - (A) it cures
   - (B) cures
   - (C) cure
   - (D) for curing

3. A baby's development is influenced by both heredity and _____.
   - (A) by environmental factors
   - (B) environmentally
   - (C) the influence of the environment
   - (D) environment

4. Because bone loss occurs earlier in women than _____, the effects of osteoporosis are more apparent in women.
   - (A) men do
   - (B) in men
   - (C) as men
   - (D) similar to men

Choose the letter of the underlined word or group of words that is not correct.

_____ 5. Fire <u>extinguishers</u> <u>can contain</u> liquified gas, dry chemicals, <u>or</u> <u>watery</u>.
             A   B   C   D

_____ 6. The U.S. Congress <u>consists</u> <u>of</u> both <u>the Senate</u> <u>as well as</u> the House of
                       A B   C   D
Representatives.

_____ 7. The prison <u>population</u>, now <u>at an all-time high</u>, <u>is higher</u> than <u>any state</u>.
                  A   B   C   D

_____ 8. When the Liberty Bell <u>cracked</u> in 1846, there was <u>far more</u> damage <u>than it</u>
                            A   B   C
had cracked <u>the first</u> time in 1835.
            D

_____ 9. Manufacturers <u>may use</u> food additives <u>for preserving</u>, to color, to flavor, or
                     A   B
to <u>fortify</u> <u>foods</u>.
     C   D

_____ 10. A bankruptcy <u>may be</u> either <u>voluntary</u> <u>nor</u> involuntary.
          A   B   C   D

TOEFL REVIEW EXERCISE (SKILLS 1–21): Choose the letter of the word or group of words that best completes the sentence.

1. The growth of hair _____ cyclical process, with phases of activity and inactivity.
   (A) it is
   (B) is a
   (C) which is
   (D) a regular

2. The fire _____ to have started in the furnace under the house.
   (A) is believed
   (B) that is believed
   (C) they believe
   (D) that they believe

3. In roman numerals, _____ symbols for numeric values.
   (A) are letters of the alphabet
   (B) letters of the alphabet are
   (C) which uses letters of the alphabet
   (D) in which letters of the alphabet are

4. The legal systems of most countries can be classified _____ common law or civil law.
   (A) as either
   (B) either as
   (C) either to
   (D) to either

5. One difference between mathematics and language is that mathematics is precise _____.
   (A) language is not
   (B) while language is not
   (C) but language not
   (D) while is language

6. Your criticism of the three short stories should not be less than 2,000 words, nor _____ more than 3,000.
   (A) should it be
   (B) it should be
   (C) it is
   (D) should be it

Choose the letter of the underlined word or group of words that is not correct.

_____ 7. The General Sherman Tree, the largest of all the giant sequoias, are reputed
                                     A   B   C
to be the world's largest living thing.
                            D

_____ 8. The most largest single use of lead is in the plates of
              A   B   C
electrical storage batteries.
          D

_____ 9. The skeleton of a shark is made of cartilage rather than having bone.
                      A   B   C   D

_____ 10. At least one sample of each of the brands contains measurable amounts of
                             A   B
aflatoxin, and there is three which exceed the maximum.
                  C   D

PROBLEMS WITH THE FORM OF THE VERB _____

It is common in the Written Expression part of the TOEFL for the verbs to be formed incorrectly. Therefore, you should check the form of each verb carefully. You should be familiar with the following verb forms: the main verb, the present tense, the present participle, the past, and the past participle. The following are examples of each of these verb forms as they are used in this text.

MAIN VERB	PRESENT	PRESENT PARTICIPLE	PAST	PAST PARTICIPLE
walk	walk(s)	walking	walked	walked
hear	hear(s)	hearing	heard	heard
cook	cook(s)	cooking	cooked	cooked
sing	sing(s)	singing	sang	sung
come	come(s)	coming	came	come
begin	begin(s)	beginning	began	begun
go	go(es)	going	went	gone
have	have (has)	having	had	had
be	am/is/are	being	was/were	been

You should be particularly aware of the following three problematic situations with verbs because they are the most common and the easiest to correct: (1) check what comes after *have,* (2) check what comes after *be,* and (3) check what comes after *will, would,* and other modals.

SKILL 22:   AFTER *HAVE,* USE THE PAST PARTICIPLE

Whenever you see the verb *have* in any of its forms (*have, has, having, had*), be sure that a verb that follows it is the past participle.

They had walk* to school.	(should be had walked)
We have see* the show.	(should be have seen)
He has took* the test.	(should be has taken)
Having ate*, he went to school.	(should be Having eaten)
She should have did* the work.	(should be should have done)

Also you should be sure that if you have a subject and a past participle, you also have the verb *have.* This problem is particularly common with those verbs (such as *sing, sang, sung*) that change from present to past to past participle by changing only the vowel.

My friend sung* in the choir.	(should be sang or has sung)
He become* angry at this friend.	(should be became or has become)
The boat sunk* in the ocean.	(should be sank or has sunk)

EXERCISE 22: Each of the following sentences contains a verb in the past or a past participle. Underline the verbs twice. Indicate if the sentences are correct (C) or incorrect (I).

_I_   1. The young girl <u>drunk</u> a glass of milk.

_C_   2. Before she <u>left</u>, she <u>had asked</u> her mother for permission.

_____ 3. Having finished the term paper, he began studying for the exam.

_____ 4. The secretary has broke her typewriter.

_____ 5. The installer should have completes the task more quickly.

_____ 6. He has often become angry during meetings.

_____ 7. She has rarely rode her horse in the park.

_____ 8. Having saw the film, he was quite disappointed.

_____ 9. Tom has thought about taking that job.

_____ 10. You might have respond more effectively.

SKILL 23: AFTER *BE*, USE THE PRESENT OR THE PAST PARTICIPLE

The verb *be* in any of its forms (*am, is, are, was, were, be, been, being*) can be followed by either the present participle or the past participle. The verb *be* is not correct if it is followed by the main verb.

We <u>are do</u>* our homework.	(should be <u>are doing</u>)
The homework <u>was do</u>* early.	(should be <u>was done</u>)
Tom <u>is take</u>* the book.	(should be <u>is taking</u>)
The book <u>was take</u>* by Tom.	(should be <u>was taken</u>)

EXERCISE 23: Each of the following sentences contains a verb formed with *be*. Underline the verbs twice. Then indicate if the sentences are correct (C) or incorrect (I).

_I_   1. At 12:00 Sam <u>is eat</u> his lunch.

_C_   2. We <u>are meeting</u> them later today.

_____ 3. The message was took by the receptionist.

_____ 4. Being heard was extremely important to him.

_____ 5. The Smiths are build their own house on some property they own in the desert.

_____ 6. It had been noticed that some staff members were late.

_____   7. The report should have been submit by noon.

_____   8. Are the two companies merge into one?

_____   9. He could be taking four courses this semester.

_____   10. The score information has been duplicates on the back-up disk.

Skill 24: After *Will, Would,* or Other Modals, Use the Main Verb

Whenever you see a modal such as *will, would, should, could, may, might,* or *must,* you should be sure that the verb that follows it is in the main form.

The boat <u>will leaving</u>* at 3:00.	(should be <u>will leave</u>)
The doctor <u>may arrives</u>* soon.	(should be <u>may arrive</u>)
The student <u>must taken</u>* the exam.	(should be <u>must take</u>)

Exercise 24: Each of the following sentences contains a verb formed with a modal. Underline the verbs twice. Then indicate if the sentences are correct (C) or incorrect (I).

__C__   1. The salesman <u>might lower</u> the price.

__I__   2. The television movie <u>will finishes</u> in a few minutes.

_____   3. Should everyone arrive by 8 o'clock?

_____   4. The method for organizing files can be improved.

_____   5. The machine may clicks off if it is overused.

_____   6. Every morning the plants must be watered.

_____   7. The houses with ocean views could sell for considerably more.

_____   8. Would anyone liked to see that movie?

_____   9. I do not know when it will depart.

_____   10. She will work on the project only if she can has a full-time secretary.

Review Exercise (Skills 22–24): Underline the verbs twice in each of the following sentences. Then indicate if the sentences are correct (C) or incorrect (I).

_____   1. I have gave you all the money I have.

_____   2. The articles were put in the newspaper before he was able to stop production.

_____ 3. All the tickets for the concert might already be sold.

_____ 4. He was so thirsty that he drunk several large glasses of water.

_____ 5. The deposit will has to be paid before the apartment can be rented.

_____ 6. He objects to being held without bail.

_____ 7. Having completed the first chapter of the manuscript, she decided to take a break.

_____ 8. If Steve had really wanted to pass his exam, he would has studied much more.

_____ 9. He thought that he should have be invited to attend the conference.

_____ 10. Before the speaker finished, many guests had rose from their seats and started for the door.

TOEFL EXERCISE (SKILLS 22–24):   Choose the letter of the underlined word or group of words that is not correct.

_____ 1. *Alice in Wonderland,* first published in 1865, has since being translated into
                              A   B   C   D
30 languages.

_____ 2. The Peace Corps was establish on March 1, 1961, by then President John F.
          A   B   C   D
Kennedy.

_____ 3. The advisor told himself, while listening to the speech, that a dozen other
                    A   B
reporters would had already asked that question.
          C   D

_____ 4. At the start of the American Revolution, lanterns were hung in the Old
          A   B   C
North Church as a signal that the British were came.
                                              D

_____ 5. Linus Pauling has wins two Nobel Prizes: the 1954 Noble Prize
                       A   B   C
in Chemistry and the 1962 Nobel Peace Prize.
   D

_____ 6. On the huge ferris wheel constructed for a world exhibition in Chicago in
               A   B
1893, each of the 36 cabs could held 60 people.
      C   D

_____ 7. To overcome rejection of a skin graft, a system for <u>matching</u> donor and
A

recipient tissues <u>has</u> <u>be</u> developed.
B   C D

_____ 8. Nails <u>are</u> commonly <u>make</u> of steel but also <u>can</u> <u>contain</u> substances such as
A   B   C   D
aluminum or brass.

_____ 9. A patient <u>suffering</u> from amnesia <u>may</u> <u>had</u> partial or total <u>loss</u> of memory.
A   B   C   D

_____ 10. The financial officer is <u>conduct</u> a <u>study</u> <u>to find</u> new ways to <u>reduce</u> costs.
A   B   C   D

TOEFL REVIEW EXERCISE (SKILLS 1–24): Choose the letter of the word or group of words that best completes the sentence.

1. _____ separates Manhattan's Upper East Side from the Upper West Side.
   - (A) Central Park
   - (B) Where Central Park
   - (C) Where is Central Park
   - (D) Central Park which

2. Bioluminescent animals _____ the water or on land.
   - (A) live
   - (B) are living either
   - (C) they are found in
   - (D) can be found in

3. The government says _____ were only 69 cases of major water pollution.
   - (A) that in 1964
   - (B) there in 1964 that
   - (C) in 1964 that
   - (D) that in 1964 there

4. The purpose of a labor union is to improve the working conditions, _____, and pay of its members.
   - (A) jobs are secure
   - (B) to be secure
   - (C) job security
   - (D) the job's security

5. Seldom _____ pushed for such a reduction.
   - (A) would the Office of Management
   - (B) has the Office of Management
   - (C) the Office of Management
   - (D) the Office of Management has

Choose the letter of the underlined word or group of words that is not correct.

_____ 6. Helium <u>has</u> the <u>most low</u> <u>boiling</u> point of <u>all substances</u>.
A   B   C   D

_____ 7. There <u>is</u> twenty-six bones in <u>the human foot</u>, fourteen of <u>them</u> in <u>the toes</u>.
A   B   C   D

_____ 8. Extension of the countdown <u>hold</u> to fourteen <u>was order</u> to give crews
                                         A   B
more <u>time</u> to repair <u>wiring and clear</u> away equipment.
      C   D

_____ 9. The study <u>demonstrates</u> <u>that</u> neither the experience <u>or</u> the awareness is able
                    A   B   C
to improve <u>chances</u> of success.
           D

_____ 10. Some of the eye movements <u>used</u> in <u>reading</u> <u>is</u> <u>actually</u> unnecessary.
                                     A   B   C   D

PROBLEMS WITH THE MEANING OF THE VERB _____

Many different problems with the meaning of the verb are possible in English. However, three specific problems occur on the TOEFL, so you need to pay careful attention to these three: (1) knowing when to use the past with the present, (2) using *had* and *have* correctly, and (3) using the correct tense with *will* and *would*.

SKILL 25:   KNOW WHEN TO USE THE PAST WITH THE PRESENT

One verb tense problem that is very common both in student writing and on the TOEFL is the switch from the past tense to the present tense for no particular reason. Often when a sentence has both a past tense and a present tense, the sentence is incorrect.

> He <u>took</u> the money when he <u>wants</u>* it.

This sentence says that *he took the money* (in the past) *when he wants it* (in the present). This meaning does not make any sense; it is impossible to do something in the past as a result of something you want in the present. This sentence can be corrected in several ways, depending on the desired meaning.

> He <u>took</u> the money when he <u>wanted</u> it.

> He <u>takes</u> the money when he <u>wants</u> it.

The first example means that *he took the money* (in the past) *when he wanted it* (in the past). This meaning is logical and the sentence is correct. The second example means that *he takes the money* (habitually) *when he wants it* (habitually). This meaning is also logical, and the second example is also correct.

It is necessary to point out, however, that it is possible for a logical sentence in English to have both the past and the present tense.

> I <u>know</u> that he <u>took</u> the money yesterday.

The meaning of this sentence is logical: *I know* (right now, in the present) that *he took the money* (yesterday, in the past). You can see from this example that it is possible for an English sentence to have both the past and the present tense. The error you need to avoid is the switch from the past to the present for no particular reason. Therefore, when you see a sentence on the TOEFL with both the past and the present tense, you must check the meaning of the sentence carefully to see if it is logical in English.

EXERCISE 25: Each of the following sentences has at least one verb in the past and one verb in the present. Underline the verbs twice and decide if the meanings are logical. Then indicate if the sentences are correct (C) or incorrect (I).

_I_ 1. I <u>tell</u> him the truth when he <u>asked</u> me the question.

_C_ 2. I <u>understand</u> that you <u>were</u> angry.

_____ 3. When he was a child, he always goes to the circus.

_____ 4. Last semester he reads seven books and wrote five papers.

_____ 5. Steve wakes up early every morning because he went to work early.

_____ 6. Mark studied at the American University when he is in Washington, D.C.

_____ 7. He is telling the teacher that he did not have time to finish.

_____ 8. He put some money in his account when he goes to the bank.

_____ 9. Tom keeps studying hard because he intended to go to dental school.

_____ 10. She is where she is today because she worked hard when she was a student.

SKILL 26:   USE *HAVE* AND *HAD* CORRECTLY

Two tenses that are often confused are the present perfect (*have* + past participle) and the past perfect (*had* + past participle). These two tenses have completely different uses, and you should understand how to differentiate them.

  The present perfect (*have* + past participle) refers to the period of time **from the past until the present.**

   Sue <u>has lived</u> in Los Angeles for ten years.

This sentence means that Sue has lived in Los Angeles for the ten years until now. According to this sentence, Sue is still living in Los Angeles.

  Because the present perfect refers to a period of time from the past until the present, it is not correct in a sentence that indicates past only.

   In 1800 Thomas Jefferson <u>has become</u>* President of the U.S.

   Every time Jim <u>worked</u> on his car, he <u>has improved</u>* it.

In the first example, the phrase *in 1800* indicates that the action of the verb was in the past only, but the verb indicates the period of time from the past until the present. Since this is not logical, the sentence is not correct. The verb in the first example should be *became.* The second example indicates that Jim *worked* on his car in the past, but he improved it in the period from the past until the present. This idea also is not logical. The verb in the second example should be the simple past *improved.*

The past perfect (*had* + past participle) refers to a period of time **that started in the past and ended in the past, before something else happened in the past.**

Sue <u>had lived</u> in Los Angeles for ten years when she <u>moved</u> to San Diego.

This sentence means that Sue lived in Los Angeles for ten years in the past before she moved to San Diego in the past. According to this sentence, she no longer lives in Los Angeles.

Because the past perfect begins in the past and ends in the past, it is generally not correct in the same sentence with a present tense.

Tom <u>had finished</u> the exam when the teacher <u>collects</u>* the papers.

This sentence indicates that *Tom finished the exam* (in the past) and that action ended *when the professor collects the papers* (in the present). This is not logical, so the sentence is not correct. Tom finished the exam (in the past), and the action of finishing the exam ended when the teacher collected the papers. Therefore, the second verb in this example should be the past tense *collected*.

EXERCISE 26:   Each of the following sentences contains *had* or *have*. Underline the verbs twice and decide if the meanings are logical. Then indicate if the sentences are correct (C) or incorrect (I).

<u> C </u>   1. I <u>have</u> always <u>liked</u> the designs that <u>are</u> on the cover.

<u> I </u>   2. Because her proposal <u>had been rejected</u>, she <u>is</u> depressed.

_____   3. The students have registered for classes before the semester started.

_____   4. When she had purchased the car, she contacted the insurance agent.

_____   5. He said that he had finished the typing when you finish the reports.

_____   6. The Pilgrims have just arrived in the New World in 1612.

_____   7. He drove directly to the post office after he had finished preparing the package for mailing.

_____   8. Since the new law was passed, it has been difficult to estimate taxes.

_____   9. Last night all the waiters and waitresses have worked overtime.

_____   10. He had fastened his seat belt before the airplane took off.

SKILL 27: USE THE CORRECT TENSE WITH *WILL* AND *WOULD*

Certain combinations of verbs are very common in English. One is the combination of the simple present and *will*.

I <u>know</u> that they <u>will arrive</u> soon.

It <u>is</u> certain that he <u>will graduate</u>.

Another combination that is quite common is the combination of the simple past and *would*.

> I <u>knew</u> that he <u>would arrive</u>.

> It <u>was</u> certain that he <u>would graduate</u>.

It is important to stress that in the combinations discussed here, the present should be used with *will* and the past should be used with *would;* they generally should not be mixed. The common errors that must generally be avoided are the combination of the past with *will* and the combination of the present with *would*.

> I <u>know</u> that he <u>would* arrive</u> soon.

> It <u>was</u> certain that he <u>will* graduate</u>.

In the first example, the present *know* is illogical with *would*. It can be corrected in two different ways.

> I <u>knew</u> that he <u>would arrive</u> soon.

> I <u>know</u> that he <u>will arrive</u> soon.

In the second example, the past *was* is illogical with *will*. It can also be corrected in two different ways.

> It <u>was</u> certain that he <u>would graduate</u>.

> It <u>is</u> certain that he <u>will graduate</u>.

EXERCISE 27:   Each of the following sentences contains *will* or *would*. Underline the verbs twice and decide if the meanings are logical. Then indicate if the sentences are correct (C) or incorrect (I).

_I_   1.   He <u>knew</u> that he <u>will be able</u> to pass the exam.

_C_   2.   I <u>think</u> that I <u>will leave</u> tomorrow.

_____   3.   Paul did not say when he will finish the project.

_____   4.   Jake doubts that he would have time to finish the project.

_____   5.   I know that I will go if I can afford it.

_____   6.   The police officer indicated that he would write a ticket if he has the time.

_____   7.   Students will often study in the library before they go to classes or before they go home.

_____   8.   He told me that he thought he will get the job in spite of his lack of education.

_____   9.   The executive vice-president emphasizes at the conferences that the board would not change its position.

_____   10.   Students will register for classes according to who has the highest number of units.

REVIEW EXERCISE (SKILLS 25–27):   Underline the verbs twice in each of the following sentences. Then indicate if the sentences are correct (C) or incorrect (I).

_____   1.   When he receives the money from the insurance company, he had rebuilt the house.

_____   2.   The position on the city council will be filled next week when the electorate votes.

_____   3.   The dentist fills the cavities every time the X-rays show that it was necessary.

_____   4.   When the bell rang, the students have left the class.

_____   5.   The space shuttle would be launched next month if the weather is good.

_____   6.   It is probable that the students who were tested yesterday were quite successful.

_____   7.   After forty-five students had signed up for the class, the class was closed.

_____   8.   The parking at the arena was inadequate for the tremendous number of drivers who will want to park there.

_____   9.   Because the copies were not clear, he is not able to understand the report.

_____   10.   They have not returned to Rhode Island since they left in 1970.

TOEFL EXERCISE (SKILLS 25–27):   Study the verbs in the following sentences. Choose the letter of the underlined word or group of words that is not correct.

_____   1.   In several of his paintings, Edward Hicks depicted the Quaker farm in
                    A
            Pennsylvania where he spends his youth.
                            B   C   D

_____   2.   Florida has become the twenty-seventh state in the U.S. on March 3, 1845.
                    A   B   C   D

_____   3.   After last week's meeting, the advertising department quickly realized that
                    A   B
            the product will need a new slogan.
                        C   D

_____   4.   John F. Kennedy's grandfather, John F. Fitzgerald, serves two terms as the
                        A   B   C
            mayor of Boston in the beginning of the twentieth century.
                                    D

_____   5.   Fort Ticonderoga, a strategically important fortification during the
            Revolution, had since been reconstructed and turned into a museum.
                        A   B   C   D

_____   6. In <u>making</u> their calculations, Institute researchers assume that
           A

the least costly form of energy <u>would</u> <u>be</u> used.
<u>   B</u>   C   D

_____   7. A 21-year-old man became <u>the second casualty</u> yesterday <u>when</u> he <u>loses</u>
                              A   B   C

<u>control</u> of his truck.
  D

_____   8. Most people <u>had</u> <u>written</u> with quill <u>pens until pens</u> with metal points <u>become</u>
                A   B   C   D

popular in the middle of the nineteenth century.

_____   9. <u>After</u> the chemist <u>put</u> the liquid in the test tube, he <u>will mix</u> it and then
   A   B   C

<u>will study</u> it.
  D

_____   10. The formula <u>used</u> in the study calls <u>for either</u> peroxide or metaldehyde, <u>but</u>
               A   B   C

metaldehyde <u>was</u> not always available.
        D

TOEFL REVIEW EXERCISE (SKILLS 1–27): Choose the letter of the word or group of words that best completes the sentence.

1. _____ in the U.S. declined from 20 million in 1910 to 9 million in the 1970's.
   - (A) For number of horses
   - (B) The number of horses
   - (C) When the number of horses
   - (D) That the number of horses

2. Because of his reservations about the issue, _____ refused to vote for it.
   - (A) who
   - (B) and
   - (C) which the senator
   - (D) the senator

3. Bats avoid running into objects by _____ high-frequency sounds and listening for echoes.
   - (A) the emission
   - (B) emitted
   - (C) emitting
   - (D) they emit

4. It has been estimated that if we intend to stay above the starvation level _____ the world's food supply.
   - (A) so we will have to double
   - (B) and it must double
   - (C) which it must be doubled
   - (D) we must double

5. Barley generally grows best where _____ cool.
   - (A) is it
   - (B) the climate is
   - (C) its
   - (D) is the climate

Choose the letter of the underlined word or group of words that is not correct.

_____   6. <u>To determine</u> the force of an object, the <u>mass and</u> acceleration of <u>the</u> object
                   A   B   C
       should be <u>measure</u>.
                           D

_____   7. The <u>most common</u> time for <u>tornados</u> to occur <u>are</u> in the afternoon or
                        A   B   C
       evening on a <u>hot, humid spring day</u>.
                                 D

_____   8. When a <u>country in</u> an early stage of economic development, <u>investments</u> in
                        A   B
       <u>fixed</u> capital are <u>vital</u>.
          C   D

_____   9. John Chapman became <u>famous</u> in American folklore as "Johnny Appleseed"
                                      A
       after he <u>plants</u> apple trees <u>throughout</u> the northeastern <u>part of</u> the U.S.
                    B   C   D

_____   10. <u>More</u> serious <u>plant diseases</u> are caused by fungi <u>as</u> by <u>other</u> parasites.
           A   B   C D

PROBLEMS WITH PASSIVE VERBS

Sentences in which the error is an incorrect passive are common in the Written Expression section of the TOEFL. You therefore need to recognize the correct form of the passive and to determine when a passive verb rather than an active verb is needed in a sentence.

    The difference between an active and a passive verb is that the subject in an active sentence *does* the action of the verb, and the subject in a passive sentence *receives* the action of the verb. To convert a sentence from active to passive, two changes must be made: (1) The subject of the active sentence becomes the object of the passive sentence, while the object of the active sentence becomes the subject of the passive sentence. (2) The verb in the passive sentence is formed by putting the helping verb *be* in the same form as the verb in the active sentence and then adding the past participle of this main verb.

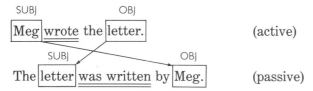

The first example is an active sentence. To convert this active sentence to a passive sentence, you must first make the subject of the active sentence *Meg* the object of the passive sentence with *by*. The object of the active sentence *letter* becomes the subject of the passive sentence. Next, the passive verb can be formed. Because *wrote* is in the past tense in the active sentence, the past tense of *be* (*was*) is used in the passive sentence. Then the main verb *wrote* in the active sentence is changed to the past participle *written* in the passive sentence.

It should be noted that in a passive sentence, the *by + object* does not need to be included to have a complete sentence. The following are both examples of correct sentences.

The letter was written yesterday <u>by Meg</u>.

The letter was written yesterday.

Notice that these passive sentences are correct if *by Meg* is included (as in the first example) or if *by Meg* is omitted (as in the second example).

SKILL 28:   USE THE CORRECT FORM OF THE PASSIVE

One way that the passive can be tested on the TOEFL is simply with an incorrect form of the passive. The following are examples of passive errors that might appear on the TOEFL.

The portrait <u>was painting</u>* by a famous artist.

The project <u>will finished</u>* by Tom.

In the first example, the passive is formed incorrectly because the past participle *painted* should be used rather than the present participle *painting*. In the second example, the verb *be* has not been included, and some form of *be* is necessary for a passive verb. The verb in the second sentence should be *will be finished*.

EXERCISE 28:   Each of the following sentences has a passive meaning. Underline twice the verbs that should be passive. Then indicate if the sentences are correct (C) or incorrect (I).

_I_   1. The boy <u>had never be stung</u> by a bee.

_C_   2. The suits <u>were hung</u> in the closet when they <u>were returned</u> from the cleaners.

_____   3. Money is lending by the credit union to those who want to buy homes.

_____   4. The record had been chose by dancers near the jukebox.

_____   5. The topic for your research paper should have been approved by Professor Thomas.

_____   6. That song has been playing over and over again by Steve.

_____   7. Their utility bills have been increased again and again.

_____   8. The patients who are too sick to sit up are being assisted by the orderlies.

_____   9. The offices were thoroughly clean last evening by the night crew.

_____   10. The car that was struck in the intersection yesterday is being repaired today.

SKILL 29:   RECOGNIZE ACTIVE AND PASSIVE MEANINGS

The second type of passive problem on the TOEFL is a little more difficult to recognize. In this case, an incorrect passive verb is given, but it is not easy to recognize because the incorrect passive verb looks just like a correct active verb.

> Eli Whitney <u>invented</u> the cotton gin.
>
> The phonograph <u>invented</u>* by Thomas Edison.

In the first example, the verb *invented* is correctly used in its active form. However, in the second sentence the verb *invented* is incorrect. The verb in the second sentence looks just like the correct active verb, but it is incorrect in the second sentence because the passive verb *was invented* is needed.

The need for the passive verb is fairly easy to recognize in the second sentence because of the expression *by Thomas Edison.* As we have seen, however, the *by* + *object* does not always appear in passive sentences. Sentences with an incorrect passive verb and no *by* + *object* to tell you that the verb should be passive are the most difficult passive errors to recognize on the TOEFL. Study the following examples:

> We <u>mailed</u> the package at the post office.
>
> The letter <u>was mailed</u> <u>by us</u> today before noon.
>
> The letter <u>was mailed</u> today before noon.
>
> The letter <u>mailed</u>* today before noon.

The first three examples above are correct. The first example is a correct active sentence; the second example is a correct passive sentence with *by us;* the third sentence is a correct passive sentence in which *by us* has been omitted.

The fourth example is the type of passive error that appears most often on the TOEFL. This type of sentence has the following characteristics: (1) an incorrect passive verb that looks like a correct active verb, and (2) no *by* + *object* to tell you that a passive is needed. To correct the fourth example, the active verb needs to be changed to the passive *was mailed.*

To determine that such a sentence is incorrect, you must study the meaning of the subject and the verb. You must ask yourself if the subject *does* the action of the verb (and so an active verb is needed) or if the subject *receives* the action of the verb (and so a passive verb is needed). In the incorrect example, you should study the meaning of the subject and verb *the letter mailed.* You should ask yourself if *a letter mails itself* (the letter *does* the action) or if *someone mails a letter* (the letter receives the action of being mailed). Since a letter does not mail itself, the passive is required in this sentence.

EXERCISE 29:   Each of the following sentences contains at least one active verb; however, some of the verbs should be passive. Underline the verbs twice. Then indicate if the sentences are correct (C) or incorrect (I).

___I___   1. The car <u><u>parked</u></u> in a no-parking zone.

___C___   2. The coffee <u><u>turned</u></u> bitter when it <u><u>was left</u></u> on the stove for so long.

_____   3. Everything to organize the picnic has already done.

_____   4. The police investigated him because of his unusual actions.

_____   5. The package containing the necessary samples has just sent.

_____   6. The vacation to Europe will carefully plan before the scheduled departure date.

_____   7. The physics exam began just a few minutes ago.

_____   8. The soccer game won in the closing minutes.

_____   9. The clothes made to rival the latest fashions of the season.

_____   10. When the roads are icy, the buses do not drive.

REVIEW EXERCISE (SKILLS 28–29): Underline the verbs twice in the following sentences. Then indicate if the sentences are correct (C) or incorrect (I).

_____   1. After the old radiator hoses had be replaced, the travelers continued their cross-country trip.

_____   2. During the lightning storm, he struck in the head by a falling tree.

_____   3. While I am on vacation, the pets should be feeds every morning and evening.

_____   4. It was announced by a presidential aide that the President would be gone from the White House for a week.

_____   5. A book being written now by a team of writers will be published in the fall.

_____   6. The appliance company has said that the refrigerator will deliver next week.

_____   7. The house that Mrs. Martin has always wanted to buy has just been placed on the market.

_____   8. The foundation should have been finishing by the construction workers before they quit for the day.

_____   9. We must leave that money in the checking account because the bills pay on the first of the month.

_____   10. The horses can't be taken out now because they have been rode for the past few hours.

TOEFL EXERCISE (SKILLS 28–29): Choose the letter of the word or group of words that best completes the sentence.

1. Much of the carnage of elephants, giraffes, and big cats _____ uncaring hunters.
   (A) must commit by
   (B) must be committed
   (C) must have committed
   (D) must have been committed by

2. _____ discussed by the board of directors when it was proposed again by the supervisors.
   (A) The problem had already
   (B) The problem is already
   (C) The problem had already been
   (D) The problem has already

3. The X-ray treatments _____ up to the time that he was dismissed from the hospital.
   (A) gave daily
   (B) were given on a daily basis
   (C) basically have given
   (D) daily had been given

Choose the letter of the underlined word or group of words that is not correct.

_____ 4. Particular <u>issues</u> that <u>concern</u> teenagers <u>were</u> <u>covering</u> in the half-hour
                   A   B   C   D

   program.

_____ 5. Electrical <u>impulses</u> <u>may</u> also <u>picked</u> up <u>by the optic</u> nerve.
                     A   B   C   D

_____ 6. Workers <u>training</u> for a specific job <u>have</u> a strong possibility of <u>being</u> <u>replace</u>
                    A   B   C   D

   by a machine.

_____ 7. The salient feature of medicine today <u>is</u> that these factors <u>are</u> no longer
                                           A   B

   <u>allow</u> <u>to play</u> their part.
     C   D

_____ 8. The report <u>could not be</u> <u>turned</u> in on time because all the <u>needed</u> work <u>lost</u>.
                        A   B   C   D

_____ 9. In English these questions <u>have be</u> <u>formed</u> by <u>changing</u> the word order of a
                                        A   B   C

   statement, whereas in other languages the word order <u>remains</u> the same.
                                                       D

_____ 10. He <u>was not</u> able <u>to define</u> the process <u>by which</u> the body <u>had protected</u> by
                   A   B   C   D

   the immunologic system.

TOEFL REVIEW EXERCISE (SKILLS 1–29): Choose the letter of the word or group of words that best completes the sentence.

1. _____ Big Dipper, a seven-star constellation in the shape of a cup, is part of Ursa Major.
   - (A) The
   - (B) It is the
   - (C) With the
   - (D) That the

2. The Military Academy at West Point _____ on the west bank of the Hudson River, north of New York City.
   - (A) located
   - (B) is located
   - (C) which is located
   - (D) whose location is

3. _____ is necessary for any project that is undertaken in this program.
   - (A) Although a word processor
   - (B) For a word processor
   - (C) A word processor
   - (D) Because a word processor

4. _____ impressive chapter in the book was the chapter on Stuart's scientific theories.
   - (A) It was the most
   - (B) The most
   - (C) Most
   - (D) Most of the

Choose the letter of the underlined word or group of words that is not correct.

_____ 5. The first fish have appeared on the earth approximately 500 million years
              A   B   C   D
         ago.

_____ 6. Only rarely sound waves are of a single frequency encountered in practice.
          A   B   C   D

_____ 7. Cameos can be carved not only from onyx and sardonx or from agate.
          A   B   C   D

_____ 8. During this period, $206 was spend annually on food by families in the
                            A   B   C
         lower third income bracket.
             D

_____ 9. In the appendix at the end of the chapter is the instructions to be used for
                          A   B   C
         the correct completion of the form.
             D

_____ 10. In a recent survey of Americans, more than 75 percent expressed the view
                A   B
          that the government it should take a more active role in health care.
                          C   D

PROBLEMS WITH NOUNS _____

The same types of problems with nouns appear often in the Written Expression section of the TOEFL. You should be familiar with these problems so that you will recognize them easily. You should be able to do the following: (1) use the correct singular or plural noun, (2) distinguish countable and uncountable nouns, and (3) distinguish "person-nouns" from "thing-nouns."

SKILL 30: USE THE CORRECT SINGULAR OR PLURAL NOUN

A problem that is common in the Written Expression section of the TOEFL is a singular noun used where a plural noun is needed, or a plural noun used where a singular noun is needed.

> On the table there were many dish*.
>
> The lab assistant finished every tests*.

In the first example, *many* indicates that the plural *dishes* is needed. In the second example, *every* indicates that the singular *test* is needed.

In the Written Expression section of the TOEFL you should watch very carefully for quantifying words such as *each, every, a,* and *single* that indicate that a noun should be singular. You should also watch very carefully for quantifying words such as *many, several,* and *three* that indicate that a noun should be plural.

EXERCISE 30: Each of the following sentences contains at least one quantifying word describing a noun. Circle the quantifying words. Draw arrows to the nouns they describe. Then indicate if the sentences are correct (C) or incorrect (I).

__I__ 1. The automotive shop stocked (many) part for the various types of Hondas.

__C__ 2. There were (several) boxes in the cupboard, and each box contained a dozen glasses.

_____ 3. Every receipts must be removed from the cashier's drawer and tallied.

_____ 4. We will stop for dinner after we cover a few more mile.

_____ 5. The busboy cleared the only other table and took the dirty dishes to the kitchen.

_____ 6. He became more and more discouraged with each passing days.

_____ 7. An extended cruise would be a nice way to spend a vacation one days.

_____ 8. She was surprised that not a single worker was available on Tuesday.

_____ 9. The housekeeper cleaned the room and took two of the occupant's dress to the laundry.

_____ 10. When the first bill was defeated, the Senate immediately began work on a different bills.

SKILL 31: DISTINGUISH COUNTABLE AND UNCOUNTABLE NOUNS

In English, nouns are classified as countable or uncountable. For certain questions on the TOEFL, it is necessary to distinguish countable and uncountable nouns in order to use the correct modifiers with them.

As the name implies, countable nouns are nouns that can be counted. Countable nouns can come in quantities of one, or two, or a hundred. The noun *book* is countable because you can have one book or several books.

Uncountable nouns, on the other hand, are nouns that cannot be counted because they come in some indeterminant quantity or mass. A noun such as *milk* or *happiness* cannot be counted; you cannot have one milk or two milks, and you cannot find one happiness or two happinesses. Uncountable nouns are often liquid items such as *water, oil* or *shampoo*. Uncountable nouns can also refer to abstract ideas such as *security, friendship,* or *hope*.

It is important for you to recognize the difference between countable and uncountable nouns when you come across such quantifying words as *much* and *many, amount* and *number, less* and *fewer, little* and *few*.

COUNTABLE	UNCOUNTABLE
many	much
number	amount
few	little
fewer	less

Much and *many* have similar meanings, but they are different grammatically: *much* is used with uncountable nouns and *many* is used with countable nouns.

He has seen <u>much</u>* foreign films.

He didn't have <u>many</u>* fun at the movies.

In the first example, *much* is incorrect because *films* is countable. This sentence should say *many foreign films*. In the second example, *many* is incorrect because *fun* is uncountable. This sentence should say *much fun*.

The difference between the quantifying words *amount* and *number* also lies in the type of noun they accompany. *Amount* is used with uncountable nouns, and *number* is used with countable nouns.

The professor assigned a large <u>number</u>* of homework.

The professor gave a large <u>amount</u>* of assignments.

In the first example, *number* is incorrect because *homework* is an uncountable noun. The sentence should say *a large amount of homework*. In the second example, *amount* is incorrect because *assignments* is a countable noun. The sentence should say *a large number of assignments*.

Less and *fewer* are also quantifying words that are differentiated by the countable and uncountable nouns they accompany. *Less* is used with uncountable nouns, and *fewer* is used with countable nouns.

This job pays <u>fewer</u>* money than I thought.

It will take <u>less</u>* dollars this way.

In the first example, *fewer* is incorrect because *money* is uncountable (you cannot say *one money, two moneys, three moneys*). This sentence should say *less money*. In the second example, *less* is incorrect because *dollars* is countable. This sentence should say *fewer dollars*.

There is a similar difference between the quantifying words *few* and *little*. *Few* is used with countable nouns, and *little* is used with uncountable nouns.

The plane leaves in a <u>little</u>* hours.

There is only a <u>few</u>* time before the plane leaves.

In the first example, *little* is incorrect because *hours* is countable. This sentence should say *a few hours*. In the second example, *few* is incorrect because *time* is uncountable. This sentence should say *a little time*.

EXERCISE 31:   Each of the following sentences contains at least one quantifying word describing a noun. Circle the quantifying words. Draw arrows to the nouns they describe. Then indicate if the sentences are correct (C) or incorrect (I).

___C___   1.   He received (little) notice that the bill would have to be paid in full.

___I___   2.   The police had (few) opportunities to catch the thief who had committed a large (amount) of crimes.

_____   3.   It is better to go shopping in the late evening because there are less people in the market, and you can accomplish a number of tasks in a short period of time.

_____   4.   You will have fewer problems with your income taxes if you get professional assistance.

_____   5.   After the strike, the company dismissed many employees.

_____   6.   Because the bottom corner of the pocket was torn, much coins fell out.

_____   7.   Since he bought the new adapter, he has had less trouble with the machine.

_____   8.   There are much new items to purchase before leaving, and there is such a short amount of time.

_____   9.   The less time you take on the assignment, the less pages you will complete.

_____   10.   A few soldiers who had been in heavy combat were brought back for a little rest.

SKILL 32:   DISTINGUISH THE "PERSON-NOUN" FROM THE "THING-NOUN"

Nouns in English can refer to persons or things. Sometimes in the Written Expression section of the TOEFL the "person-noun" is used in place of the "thing-noun," or the "thing-noun" is used in place of the "person-noun."

Ralph Nader is an <u>authorization</u>* in the field of consumer affairs.

There are many job opportunities in <u>accountant</u>*.

In the first example, *authorization* is incorrect because *authorization* is a thing and Ralph Nader is a person. The "person-noun" *authority* should be used in this sentence. In the second example, *accountant* is incorrect because an *accountant* is a person and the field in which an accountant works is *accounting*. The "thing-noun" *accounting* should be used in this sentence.

EXERCISE 32: Some of the following sentences contain incorrectly used "person-nouns" or "thing-nouns." Circle the incorrectly used words. Then indicate if the sentences are correct (C) or incorrect (I).

__I__ 1. In the evening he relaxes in front of the fire and writes long (poets)

__C__ 2. Service in the restaurant was slow because one cook had called in sick.

_____ 3. The sculpture worked from sunrise until sunset on his new project.

_____ 4. She has received several awards for her research in engineer.

_____ 5. The economist's radical views were printed in a column in the Sunday newspaper.

_____ 6. You must have remarkable looks to work as a model for *Vogue*.

_____ 7. He had several critics to offer about the new play.

_____ 8. The gardener worked feverishly after the frost to save as many plants as possible.

_____ 9. The company hired a statistic to prepare marketing studies for the new product.

_____ 10. That famous acting has appeared in more than fifty Broadway plays.

REVIEW EXERCISE (SKILLS 30–32): Circle the quantifying words. Beware of incorrectly used "person-nouns" and "thing-nouns." Then indicate if the sentences are correct (C) or incorrect (I).

_____ 1. The professor does not give many exam in chemistry class, but the ones she gives are difficult.

_____ 2. The hilltop location gives the house a view interrupted by only a few trees.

_____ 3. It was his dream to be a musical in the New York Philharmonic.

_____ 4. For the reception, the caterers are preparing a large amount of food to serve a large number of people.

_____ 5. There are not much neighbors who would put up with such loud music.

_____ 6. Many job opportunities exist in the field of nurse if you are willing to accept a low-paying position.

_____ 7. For each business trip you make, you can choose from many different airlines.

_____ 8. She would like to undergo the series of treatments, but she thinks it costs a little too much money.

_____ 9. The television producer that was shown last night on the CBS network from 9:00 until 11:00 was one of the best shows of the season.

_____ 10. Various sightseeing excursion were available from the tourist agency.

TOEFL EXERCISE (SKILLS 30–32): Choose the letter of the word or group of words that best completes the sentence.

1. Cauliflower provides _____ of vitamin C and a smaller amount of vitamin A.
   (A) a large amount
   (B) a large quantity of
   (C) a tremendous number of
   (D) a tremendous number

2. It takes _____ time to read an abstract of an article than to read the article itself.
   (A) considerably fewer
   (B) considerably less
   (C) considerable amount
   (D) considerable number

Choose the letter of the underlined word or group of words that is not correct.

_____ 3. As a compilation of <u>useful details</u>, a <u>weekly</u> magazine commends <u>itself</u> in
                     A   B   C

   several <u>respect</u>.
          D

_____ 4. Through aquaculture, or fish farming, <u>more than</u> 500 million <u>tons of fish</u>
                                         A   B

   <u>are produced</u> each <u>years</u>.
      C   D

_____ 5. The legal system has <u>much</u> safeguards to protect <u>the right</u> of a <u>defendant</u> to
                                A   B   C

   an <u>impartial jury</u>.
        D

_____ 6. The *Song of Hiawatha,* by Longfellow, <u>tells</u> the story of the Indian <u>heroic</u>
                                                    A   B
<u>who</u> <u>married</u> Minehaha.
 C   D

_____ 7. Uranus <u>is</u> <u>the</u> seventh <u>planets</u> from <u>the sun</u>.
                  A   B   C   D

_____ 8. The sycamore has <u>broad</u> <u>leaves</u> with a large <u>amount</u> of <u>pointed</u> teeth.
                           A   B   C   D

_____ 9. The first of two such <u>investigation</u> <u>requires</u> the students to read
                                A   B
continuously over a <u>period</u> of <u>four hours</u>.
                     C   D

_____ 10. <u>To enter</u> the FBI National <u>Academy</u>, an <u>application</u> must be between
          A   B   C
<u>the ages</u> of 23 and 34.
 D

TOEFL REVIEW EXERCISE (SKILLS 1–32): Choose the letter of the word or group of words that best completes the sentence.

1. Presidential _____ held every four years on the first Tuesday after the first Monday in November.
   (A) electing
   (B) elections are
   (C) is elected
   (D) elected and

2. Studies of carcinogenesis in animals can provide data on _____ in human susceptibility.
   (A) differences are
   (B) that differences are
   (C) differences have
   (D) differences

3. Those who favor the new law say that the present law does not set spending limits on lobbyists' gifts to politicians, nor _____ statewide funds.
   (A) it limits
   (B) limits it
   (C) does it limit
   (D) does it

4. The population of the earth is increasing at a tremendous rate and _____ out of control.
   (A) they have become
   (B) are soon going to be
   (C) soon will be
   (D) why it will be

Choose the letter of the underlined word or group of words that is not correct.

_____ 5. Temperature is <u>indicates</u> on <u>a</u> bimetallic thermometer by the <u>amount</u> <u>that</u>
                         A   B   C   D
the bimetallic strip bends.

_____ 6. <u>Many</u> of the food <u>consumed</u> by penguins <u>consists of</u> fish <u>obtained from</u> the
      A   B   C   D
ocean.

_____ 7. Before the newspaper became <u>widespread</u>, a town crier <u>has walked</u>
                                  A   B
throughout a <u>village or town</u> <u>singing out</u> the news.
                C   D

_____ 8. A group <u>is creating</u> by communication, <u>not by</u> the mere fact of spatial
             A   B
<u>proximity</u> <u>or</u> physical contact.
    C   D

_____ 9. Linseed oil, used <u>primarily</u> in paints and <u>varnishes</u>, <u>are</u> derived from
                      A   B   C
<u>flax seeds</u>.
   D

_____ 10. <u>All of</u> NASA's <u>manned</u> spacecraft <u>project</u> are <u>headquartered</u> at the
     A   B   C   D
Lyndon B. Johnson Space Center in Houston.

PROBLEMS WITH PRONOUNS

Pronouns are words such as *he, she,* or *it* that take the place of nouns. When you see a pronoun in the Written Expression section of the TOEFL, you need to check that it serves the correct function in the sentence (as a subject or object, for example) and that it agrees with the noun it is replacing. The following pronoun problems are the most common on the TOEFL: (1) distinguishing subject and object pronouns, (2) distinguishing possessive pronouns and possessive adjectives, and (3) checking pronoun reference for agreement.

SKILL 33: DISTINGUISH SUBJECT AND OBJECT PRONOUNS

Subject and object pronouns can be confused on the TOEFL, so you should be able to recognize these two types of pronouns.

SUBJECT	*OBJECT*
I	me
you	you
he	him
she	her
it	it
we	us
they	them

A subject pronoun is used as the subject of a verb. An object pronoun can be used as the object of a verb or the object of a preposition. Compare the following two sentences.

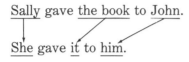

Sally gave the book to John.

She gave it to him.

In the second sentence the subject pronoun *she* is replacing the noun *Sally.* The object of the verb *it* is replacing the noun *the book,* and the object of the preposition *him* is replacing the noun *John.*

The following are examples of the types of subject or object pronoun errors that you might see on the TOEFL.

Him* and the girl are going shopping.

The gift was intended for you and I*.

In the first example, the object pronoun *him* is incorrect because this pronoun serves as the subject of the sentence. The object pronoun *him* should be changed to the subject pronoun *he.* It can be difficult to recognize that *him* is the subject because the verb *are* has a double subject *him* and *girl.* In the second example, the subject pronoun *I* is incorrect because this pronoun serves as the object of the preposition *for.* The subject pronoun *I* should be changed to the object pronoun *me.* It can be difficult to recognize that *I* is the object of the preposition *for* because the preposition *for* has two objects *you* and *I.*

EXERCISE 33:   Each of the following sentences contains at least one subject or object pronoun. Circle the pronouns. Then indicate if the sentences are correct (C) or incorrect (I).

__C__   1. The worst problem with (it) is that (he) cannot afford (it.)

__I__   2. (They) saw Steve and (I) at the movies last night after class.

_____   3. Perhaps you would like to go to the seminar with they and their friends.

_____   4. The mother took her son to the doctor's office because he was feeling sick.

_____   5. I did not know that you and her were working together on the project.

_____   6. She did not buy the sweater because it had a small hole in it.

_____   7. The man leading the conference gave me all the information I needed to make a decision.

_____   8. The cards attaching the computer to its printer need to be replaced before them wear down any further.

_____   9. He is going to the party with you and me, if you do not mind.

_____   10. You and her ought to return the books to the library because they are already overdue.

SKILL 34:   DISTINGUISH POSSESSIVE ADJECTIVES AND PRONOUNS

Possessive adjectives and possessive pronouns both show who or what "owns" a noun.

POSSESSIVE ADJECTIVES	POSSESSIVE PRONOUNS
my	mine
your	yours
his	his
her	hers
its	——
our	ours
their	theirs

However, possessive adjectives have a different function from that of possessive pronouns, and these two kinds of possessives can be confused on the TOEFL. A possessive adjective describes a noun: it must be accompanied by a noun. A possessive pronoun takes the place of a noun: it cannot be accompanied by a noun.

> They lent me their book.
>   ADJ

> They lent me theirs.
>   PRON

Notice that in the first example the possessive adjective *their* is accompanied by the noun *book*. In the second example the possessive pronoun *theirs* is not accompanied by a noun.

The following examples show the types of errors that are possible with possessive adjectives and possessive pronouns on the TOEFL.

> Each morning they read theirs* newspapers.

> Could you give me your*?

In the first example, the possessive pronoun *theirs* is incorrect because it is accompanied by the noun *newspapers,* and a possessive pronoun cannot be accompanied by a noun. The possessive adjective *their* is needed in the first example. In the second example, the possessive adjective *your* is incorrect because it is not accompanied by a noun, and a possessive adjective must be accompanied by a noun. The possessive pronoun *yours* is needed in the second example.

EXERCISE 34:   Each of the following sentences contains at least one possessive pronoun or adjective. Circle the possessives in these sentences. Then indicate if the sentences are correct (C) or incorrect (I).

I   1. If she borrows your coat, then you should be able to borrow her.

C   2. Each pot and pan in her kitchen has its own place on the shelf.

____ 3. Mary and Mark invited theirs parents to see their new apartment.

_____ 4. When my roommate paid her half of the rent, I paid mine.

_____ 5. All students need to bring theirs own pencils and answer sheets to the exam.

_____ 6. All of her secretaries are working late tonight to finish her report.

_____ 7. The horse trotting around the track won it's race a few minutes ago.

_____ 8. Before the report is finalized, the information in their notes and our must be proofed.

_____ 9. She worked all day cooking food and making decorations for her son's birthday party.

_____ 10. The weather in the mountains this weekend will be extremely cold, so please take yours heavy jackets.

SKILL 35:   CHECK PRONOUN REFERENCE FOR AGREEMENT

After you have checked that the subject and object pronouns and the possessives are used correctly, you should also check that each of these pronouns and possessives for agreement. The following are examples of errors of this type that you might find on the TOEFL.

The boys will cause trouble if you let <u>him</u>*.

Everyone must give <u>their</u>* name.

In the first example, the singular pronoun _him_ is incorrect because it refers to the plural noun _boys_. This pronoun should be replaced with the plural pronoun _them_. In the second example, the plural possessive adjective _their_ is incorrect because it refers to the singular _everyone_. This adjective should be replaced with the singular _his_ or _his or her_.

EXERCISE 35:   Each of the following sentences contains at least one pronoun or possessive. Circle the pronouns and possessives. Then indicate if the sentences are correct (C) or incorrect (I).

_I_ 1. If a person really wants to succeed, (they) must always work hard.

_C_ 2. If you see the students from the math class, could you return (their) exam papers to (them)?

_____ 3. Some friends and I went to see a movie, and afterwards we wrote a critique about them.

_____ 4. If you have a problem, you are welcome to discuss it with me before you try to resolve them.

_____ 5. I know you had a terrible time last week, but you must try to forget about it.

_____ 6. At the start of the program, each student needs to see his advisor about his schedule.

_____ 7. In spite of its small size, these video recorders produce excellent tapes.

_____ 8. Whatever the situation, you should reflect profoundly about them before coming to a decision.

_____ 9. The people I admire most are those who manage to solve their own problems.

_____ 10. If anyone stops by while I am at the meeting, please take a message from them.

REVIEW EXERCISE (SKILLS 33–35):   Circle the pronouns and possessives in the following sentences. Then indicate if the sentences are correct (C) or incorrect (I).

_____ 1. Helicopters are being used more and more in emergency situations because of its ability to reach out-of-the-way places.

_____ 2. The worker was fired by the chemical company because his refused to work with certain dangerous chemicals.

_____ 3. If you have car trouble while driving on the freeway, you should pull your car over to the side of the freeway and wait for help.

_____ 4. The administration is not in favor of installing the new security system because they cost so much.

_____ 5. Some parents prefer to send their children to private schools because they believe the children will be better educated.

_____ 6. The air traffic controller was not blamed for the accident because he had strictly followed the correct procedures.

_____ 7. The new student has been assigned to work on the group research project with you and I.

_____ 8. There are many different kinds of aspirin on the market, but theirs effectiveness seems to be equal.

_____ 9. You must bring a tent, a sleeping bag, and cooking utensils for your trip to the Sierras.

_____ 10. Each of the team members had their new uniform.

TOEFL EXERCISE (SKILLS 33–35):   Choose the letter of the underlined word or group of words that is not correct.

_____ 1. Superman made their comic strip debut in 1938 in *Action Comics.*
                  A   B   C   D

_____ 2. Commercial letters of credit are often used to finance export trade, but
                                 A   B

   them can have other uses.
    C   D

_____ 3. When adult children experience too much frustration, its behavior ceases to
                                    A   B   C   D
be integrated.

_____ 4. On March 30, 1981, President Reagan was shot as his was leaving
                                                          A   B   C
a Washington hotel.
     D

_____ 5. Although the destruction that it causes is often terrible, cyclones benefit a
                                         A   B
much wider belt than they devastate.
     C   D

_____ 6. President Andrew Jackson had an official Cabinet, but him preferred the
                                       A   B   C
advice of his informal advisors, the Kitchen Cabinet.
          D

_____ 7. After Clarence Day's book *Life with Father* was rewritten as a play, they
                               Λ   B   C
ran for six years on Broadway.
         D

_____ 8. Almost half of the Pilgrims did not survive theirs first winter in the New
             A   B   C   D
World.

_____ 9. There was no indication from the Senate that he would agree with the
             A   B   C
decision made in the House.
         D

_____ 10. A baby starts learning the meanings of words as they are spoken by others
                                                        A   B
and later uses they in sentences.
    C   D

TOEFL Review Exercise (Skills 1–35): Choose the letter of the word or group of words
that best completes the sentence.

1. _____ worst phase of the Depression,
   more than 13 million Americans had
   no jobs.
   (A) It was in the
   (B) During the
   (C) While the
   (D) The

2. When reading a book, you must keep
   your point of view separate from the
   point of view in _____ you are studying.
   (A) that
   (B) the material and
   (C) the material that
   (D) the material that is

3. Speech consists not merely of
   sounds but _____ that follow various
   structural patterns.
   (A) of organized sound patterns
   (B) organized sound patterns
   (C) that sound patterns are
       organized
   (D) in organizing sound patterns

Choose the letter of the underlined word or group of words that is not correct.

_____ 4. The latest medical report indicated that the patient's temperature was
           A
         near normal and their lungs were partially cleared.
             B   C   D

_____ 5. Most oxygen atoms have eight neutrons, but a small amount have
         A   B   C
         nine or ten.
             D

_____ 6. When Paine expressed his belief in independence, he praised by the public.
                              A   B   C   D

_____ 7. A vast quantity of radioactive material is produced when
         A   B   C
         does a hydrogen bomb explode.
                D

_____ 8. Genes have several alternative form, or alleles, which are produced
                            A   B   C
         by mutations.
             D

_____ 9. A star that has used up its energy and has lost its heat became a black
                 A   B   C   D
         dwarf.

_____ 10. Each lines of poetry written in blank verse has ten syllables which are
               A   B   C
          alternately stressed and unstressed.
              D

PROBLEMS WITH ADJECTIVES AND ADVERBS _____

Many different problems with adjectives and adverbs are possible in the Written Expression section of the TOEFL. To identify these problems, you must first be able to recognize adjectives and adverbs.

Adverbs are words that give information about *when, how,* or *where* something happens. Often adverbs are formed by adding *-ly* to adjectives, and these *-ly* adverbs are very easy to recognize. The following examples show adverbs that are formed by adding *-ly* to adjectives:

ADJECTIVE	*ADVERB*
recent	recently
public	publicly
evident	evidently

However, there are many adverbs in English that do not end in *-ly.* These adverbs can be recognized from their meaings. They can describe *when* something happens (*often, soon, later*); *how* something happens (*fast, hard, well*); or *where* something happens (*here, there, nowhere*).

There are four skills involving adjectives and adverbs that will help you on the Written Expression section of the TOEFL: (1) knowing when to use adjectives and adverbs, (2) using adjectives after linking verbs, (3) positioning adjectives and adverbs correctly, and (4) using *-ed* and *-ing* verbal adjectives correctly.

SKILL 36:   USE BASIC ADJECTIVES AND ADVERBS CORRECTLY

Sometimes in the Written Expression section of the TOEFL, adjectives are used in place of adverbs, or adverbs are used in place of adjectives. Adjectives and adverbs have very different uses in sentences. Adjectives have only one job: they describe nouns or pronouns:

She is a <u>beautiful</u> woman.
        ADJ   NOUN

She is <u>beautiful</u>.
PRON   ADJ

Adverbs can do three different things. They can describe verbs, adjectives, or other adverbs.

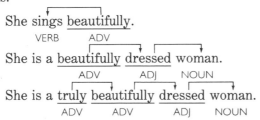

She sings <u>beautifully</u>.
   VERB   ADV

She is a <u>beautifully</u> <u>dressed</u> woman.
      ADV   ADJ   NOUN

She is a <u>truly</u> <u>beautifully</u> <u>dressed</u> woman.
    ADV   ADV   ADJ   NOUN

The following are examples of incorrect sentences as they might appear on the TOEFL.

They were seated at a largely* table .
                          ADV   NOUN

The child talked quick* to her mother.
              VERB   ADJ

We read an extreme* long story.
           ADJ   ADJ

In the first example, the adverb *largely* is incorrect because the adjective *large* is needed to describe the noun *table*. In the second example, the adjective *quick* is incorrect because the adverb *quickly* is needed to describe the verb *talked*. In the last example, the adjective *extreme* is incorrect because the adverb *extremely* is needed to describe the adjective *long*.

EXERCISE 36:   Each of the following sentences has at least one adjective or adverb. Circle the adjectives and adverbs and label them. Draw arrows to the words they describe. Then indicate if the sentences are correct (C) or incorrect (I).

_I_   1.   The mother was (pleasant)(surprised) when her daughter came to visit.
                              Adj   Adj

_C_   2.   The salespeople (frequently) visit the East Coast for trade shows.
                             Adv

____   3.   He was driving an expensively sports car.

____   4.   There is a special program on television this evening.

____   5.   She was chosen for the lead part because she sings so well.

____   6.   The car was not complete ready at 3:00.

____   7.   It was difficult to believe that what we read in the newspaper was a truly story.

____   8.   Points will be subtracted for each incorrect answered question.

____   9.   The production manager quietly requested a completely report of the incident.

____   10. The children finished their homework quickly so they could watch television.

SKILL 37:   USE ADJECTIVES AFTER LINKING VERBS

Generally an adverb rather than an adjective will come directly after a verb because the adverb is describing the verb.

She spoke nicely.
     VERB   ADV

She responded nicely.
     VERB   ADV

She answered nicely.
     VERB   ADV

However, you must be very careful with the following *linking verbs:*

appear	feel	smell
be	look	taste
become	seem	

After a linking verb there will be an adjective describing the subject rather than an adverb describing the verb.

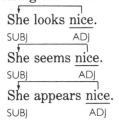

She looks nice.
SUBJ   ADJ

She seems nice.
SUBJ   ADJ

She appears nice.
SUBJ   ADJ

Be sure to use an adjective rather than an adverb after a linking verb. Be careful, however, because the adjective that goes with the linking verb does not always directly follow the linking verb.

He seems unusually nice.
SUBJ   ADV   ADJ

In this example the adjective *nice,* which describes the subject *he,* is itself described by the adverb *unusually.* From this example, you should notice that it is possible to have an adverb directly after a linking verb, but only if the adverb describes an adjective that follows.

EXERCISE 37:   Each of the following sentences has at least one adjective or adverb. Circle the adjectives and adverbs and label them. Draw arrows to the words they describe. Then indicate if the sentences are correct (C) or incorrect (I).

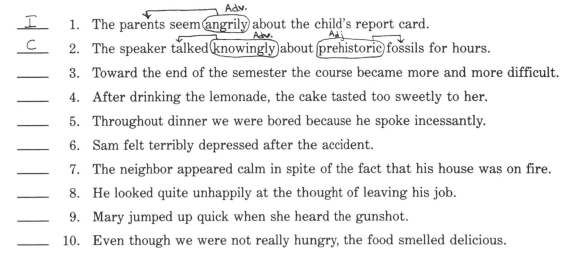

_I_   1. The parents seem (angrily) about the child's report card.

_C_   2. The speaker talked (knowingly) about (prehistoric) fossils for hours.

_____ 3. Toward the end of the semester the course became more and more difficult.

_____ 4. After drinking the lemonade, the cake tasted too sweetly to her.

_____ 5. Throughout dinner we were bored because he spoke incessantly.

_____ 6. Sam felt terribly depressed after the accident.

_____ 7. The neighbor appeared calm in spite of the fact that his house was on fire.

_____ 8. He looked quite unhappily at the thought of leaving his job.

_____ 9. Mary jumped up quick when she heard the gunshot.

_____ 10. Even though we were not really hungry, the food smelled delicious.

SKILL 38: POSITION ADJECTIVES AND ADVERBS CORRECTLY

Adjectives and adverbs can appear in an incorrect position in the Written Expression section of the TOEFL. There are two common errors of this type that you should beware of: (1) the position of adjectives with the nouns they describe, and (2) the position of adverbs with past participles.

In English it is correct to place a one-word adjective in front of the noun it describes. On the TOEFL, however, an incorrect sentence might have an adjective after the noun it describes. The following is an example of an incorrect sentence you might see on the TOEFL:

> The information important* is on the first page.

In this example the adjective *important* should come before the noun *information,* because *important* describes *information.*

A second problem you should beware of is the position of adverbs with past participles. When the verb is in the form *have + past participle,* an adverb describing the verb should not come immediately after the past participle. The following is an example of an incorrect sentence you might see on the TOEFL:

> He has taken recently* an English course.

This sentence is incorrect because the adverb *recently* immediately follows the past participle *taken* that it describes. There are many possible corrections for this sentence. The following sentences are all correct:

> Recently he has taken an English course.
>
> He recently has taken an English course.
>
> He has recently taken an English course.
>
> He has taken an English course recently.

You can see from these examples that there are many possible correct positions for the adverb. What is important for you to remember is that an adverb that describes a verb cannot come directly after the past participle when the verb is in the *have + past participle* form.

EXERCISE 38: Each of the following sentences has at least one adjective or adverb. Circle the adjectives and adverbs and label them. Draw arrows to the words they describe. Then indicate if the sentences are correct (C) or incorrect (I).

  I   1. The store opened with a sale (fantastic.) *Adj*

  C   2. The pharmacist has (always) filled our order (quickly.) *Adv Adv*

  _____   3. The political candidates expressed their opposing views.

  _____   4. The lawyer has selected carefully a new case.

  _____   5. The coffee has tasted frequently bitter.

  _____   6. The wedding reception was held at a restaurant expensive.

_____ 7. The salesman has often traveled to New York.

_____ 8. Following the failure of the first set of plans, the manager has altered subsequently them.

_____ 9. The students had to study many hours daily during the program intensive.

_____ 10. The naval officer was asked to transfer to a foreign country.

SKILL 39: USE *-ED* AND *-ING* ADJECTIVES CORRECTLY

Verb forms ending in *-ed* and *-ing* can be used as adjectives. For example, the verbal adjectives *cleaned* and *cleaning* come from the verb *to clean*.

The woman <u>cleans</u> the car.

The <u>cleaning</u> woman worked on the car.
    ADJ

The woman put the <u>cleaned</u> car back in the garage.
        ADJ

In the first example, *cleans* is the verb of the sentence. In the second example, *cleaning* is a verbal adjective describing *woman*. In the third example, *cleaned* is a verbal adjective describing *car*.

Verbal adjectives ending in *-ed* and *-ing* can be confused in the Written Expression section of the TOEFL. The following are examples of incorrect expressions that you might see on the TOEFL:

The <u>cleaning</u>* car . . .

The <u>cleaned</u>* woman . . .

The difference between an *-ed* and an *-ing* adjective is similar to the difference between the active and the passive (see Skills 28–29). An *-ing* adjective (like the active) means that the noun it describes is doing the action. The above example about *the cleaning car* is not correct because a car cannot do the action of cleaning: you cannot say that *a car cleans itself*. An *-ed* adjective (like the passive) means that the noun it describes is receiving the action from the verb. The above example about *the cleaned woman* is not correct because in this example a woman cannot receive the action of the verb *clean*: it is not possible to say that *someone cleaned the woman*.

EXERCISE 39: Each of the following sentences contains either an *-ed* or an *-ing* verbal adjective. Circle the verbal adjectives. Draw arrows to the words they describe. Then indicate if the sentences are correct (C) or incorrect (I).

_I_ 1. The teacher gave a quiz on the just (completing) lesson.

_C_ 2. There is a (fascinating) movie at the theater tonight.

_____ 3. They thought that it had been a very satisfied dinner.

_____ 4. The empty bottles are on the shelf to the left, and the filling bottles are to the right.

_____ 5. For lunch at the restaurant she ordered a mixed salad.

_____ 6. The students thought that it was an interesting assignment.

_____ 7. The shoppers were impressed by the reducing prices.

_____ 8. He can't afford to take long vacations to exotic places because he is a worked man.

_____ 9. The phone call from the insurance agent was annoying.

_____ 10. Today the bookkeeper is working on the unpaying bills.

REVIEW EXERCISE (SKILLS 36–39): Circle the adjectives and adverbs in the following sentences. Draw arrows to the words they describe. Then indicate if the sentences are correct (C) or incorrect (I).

_____ 1. After the earthquake, assistance was sent to the damaging areas.

_____ 2. They were unable to see where their friends were sitting in the theater because of the lights dim.

_____ 3. The thesis of your essay was not very well developed.

_____ 4. After the comprehensive exam, she looked exhaustedly by the experience.

_____ 5. His car was struck by an uninsured motorist.

_____ 6. Mark always does his homework careful.

_____ 7. The student had attended regularly all the lectures in the series.

_____ 8. The patient became healthy after the operation.

_____ 9. The grandparents speak proudly about all their successful offspring.

_____ 10. The manager seemed certainly that the project would be finished under budget.

TOEFL EXERCISE (SKILLS 36–39): Choose the letter of the word or group of words that best completes the sentence.

1. Modern art is on display at the Guggenheim Museum, a building with _____.
   (A) unusually designed
   (B) designed unusually
   (C) an unusual design
   (D) unusually designing

2. By the beginning of the 1980's, fifteen _____ no-fault insurance laws.
   (A) states had already adopted
   (B) had already adopted states
   (C) already adopted states
   (D) already states had adopted

Choose the letter of the underlined word or group of words that is not correct.

_____ 3. Heart attacks are fatally in 75 percent of occurrences.
          A   B   C   D

_____ 4. In spite of a tremendous amount of electronic gadgetry, air traffic control
                        A   B   C
          still depends heavy on people.
                        D

_____ 5. Signing at the outset of a business deal, a contract offers the participants
          A   B
          a certain degree of legal protection.
          C   D

_____ 6. A baboon's arms appear as lengthily as its legs.
          A   B   C   D

_____ 7. A serious problem is how to communicate reliable with a submerged
          A   B   C   D
          submarine.

_____ 8. Halley's comet, viewing through a telescope, was quite impressive.
                         A   B   C   D

_____ 9. The central banking system of the U.S. consists of twelve banks district.
          A   B   C   D

_____ 10. Telegraph service across the Atlantic was successful established in 1866.
                    A   B   C   D

TOEFL REVIEW EXERCISE (SKILLS 1–39): Choose the letter of the word or group of words that best completes the sentence.

1. Patty Berg, the top tournament winner in women's golf, _____ 83 golf tournaments from 1935 through 1964.
   (A) she won
   (B) winning
   (C) won
   (D) who won

2. _____ with about fifteen times its weight in air does gasoline allow the carburetor to run smoothly.
   (A) It is mixed
   (B) To mix it
   (C) When mixed
   (D) Only when mixed

3. _____ is used to discover how many abilities are involved in intelligence test performance.
   (A) After factor analysis
   (B) Factor analysis
   (C) With factor analysis
   (D) Factors

Choose the letter of the underlined word or group of words that is not correct.

_____ 4. The Colorado River <u>reaches</u> <u>their</u> maximum <u>height</u> <u>during</u> April and May,
$\qquad$ A $\qquad$ B $\qquad$ C $\qquad$ D
the springtime flood season.

_____ 5. Plant proteins <u>tend</u> to have <u>few</u> amino acids than proteins <u>from</u> animal
$\qquad$ A $\qquad$ B $\qquad$ C
<u>sources</u>.
D

_____ 6. <u>The</u> Viking Spacecraft <u>has landed</u> on Mars <u>in July</u> <u>of</u> 1976.
$\qquad$ A $\qquad$ B $\qquad$ C $\qquad$ D

_____ 7. Admiral Byrd <u>commanded</u> airplane <u>expeditions</u> <u>over</u> both the Arctic <u>or</u> the
$\qquad$ A $\qquad$ B $\qquad$ C $\qquad$ D
Antarctic.

_____ 8. The <u>advertising</u> campaign <u>will be</u> based on the <u>recent</u> <u>completed</u> study.
$\qquad$ A $\qquad$ B $\qquad$ C $\qquad$ D

_____ 9. Coronary occlusion <u>results from</u> a disease <u>in which</u> fatty substances with a
$\qquad$ A $\qquad$ B
large <u>amount</u> of cholesterol <u>is</u> deposited in the arteries.
$\qquad$ C $\qquad$ D

_____ 10. Her money <u>gave back</u> as soon as she <u>threatened</u> <u>to take</u> the matter <u>to court</u>.
$\qquad$ A $\qquad$ B $\qquad$ C $\qquad$ D

PROBLEMS WITH ARTICLES

Articles are very difficult to learn because there are many rules, many exceptions, and many special cases. It is possible, however, to learn a few rules that will help you to use articles correctly much of the time.

Nouns in English can be either countable or uncountable. If a noun is countable it must be either singular or plural. In addition to these different types of nouns, there are two types of articles: definite (specific) and indefinite (general).

ARTICLES	COUNTABLE SINGULAR NOUNS	COUNTABLE PLURAL	UNCOUNTABLE
Indefinite (General)	<u>a</u> dollar <u>an</u> apple	__ dollars __ apples	__ money __ juice
Definite (Specific)	<u>the</u> dollar <u>the</u> apple	<u>the</u> dollars <u>the</u> apples	<u>the</u> money <u>the</u> juice

SKILL 40: USE ARTICLES WITH SINGULAR NOUNS

You can see from the chart that if a noun is either countable plural or uncountable, it is possible to have either the definite article *the* or no article (indefinite). With **all** countable singular nouns, however, you must have an article (unless you have another determiner such as *my* or *each*).

> I have money.   (uncountable—no article needed)
>
> I have books.   (countable plural—no article needed)
>
> I have a book.   (countable singular—article needed)

EXERCISE 40: The following sentences contain different types of nouns. Circle only the countable singular nouns. Mark where articles (or determiners) have been omitted. Then indicate if the sentences are correct (C) or incorrect (I).

_I_   1. She is taking (trip) with friends.

_C_   2. In my (yard) there are flowers, trees, and grass.

____   3. The manager sent memo to his employees.

____   4. There is car in front of the building.

____   5. The child and his friends are having milk and cookies.

____   6. She is studying to be an actress in films.

____   7. My neighbor was arrested for throwing rocks through window.

____   8. We have machinery that prints ten pages each minute.

____   9. Teacher has many students during a semester.

____   10. Can you heat water for tea?

SKILL 41: DISTINGUISH *A* AND *AN*

The basic difference between *a* and *an* is that *a* is used in front of consonants and *an* is used in front of vowels (*a, e, i, o, u*):

a book	an orange
a man	an illness
a page	an automobile

There are two exceptions to this rule: *u* and *h*. When *u* is pronounced like the consonant *y* (as in *usual*), it is preceded by the article *a* rather than *an*. When *h* is not pronounced (as in *honor*), it is preceded by the article *an* rather than *a*. Pronounce the following examples:

a university	an unhappy man	a hospital	an honor
a unit	an understanding	a heart	an herb

EXERCISE 41:   Each of the following sentences contains *a* or *an*. Circle *a* or *an*. Draw an arrow to the word that directly follows. Pronounce the word. Then indicate if the sentences are correct (C) or incorrect (I).

__I__   1.   The dishwasher quit his job because he was making only four dollars (a) hour.

__C__   2.   It was (an) unexpected disappointment to receive (a) rejection letter from the university.

_____   3.   It is raining, so you should bring a umbrella.

_____   4.   He bought a half gallon of milk and a box of a hundred envelopes.

_____   5.   An objection was raised because it was such a unacceptable idea.

_____   6.   The workers at the plant do not belong to a union.

_____   7.   The police officer was not wearing an uniform when she arrested the suspect.

_____   8.   If you do not give me a hand, finishing the project on time will be an impossibility.

_____   9.   She was not upset when a honest mistake was made.

_____   10.   She opened a account at a local department store.

SKILL 42:   MAKE ARTICLES AGREE WITH NOUNS

The **definite** article (*the*) is used for both singular and plural nouns, so agreement is not a problem with the definite article. However, because use of the **indefinite** article is different for singular and plural nouns, you must be careful of agreement between the indefinite article and the noun. One very common agreement error is to use the singular indefinite article (*a* or *an*) with a plural noun.

> He saw <u>a</u>* new <u>movies</u>.
>
> They took a trip to <u>a</u>* nearby <u>mountains</u>.
>
> Do you have <u>another</u>* <u>books</u>?

In these examples, you should not have *a* or *an* because the nouns are plural. The following sentences are possible corrections of the sentences above.

He saw a new movie.	(singular)
He saw new movies.	(plural)
They took a trip to a nearby mountain.	(singular)
They took a trip to nearby mountains.	(plural)
Do you have another book?	(singular)
Do you have other books?	(plural)

EXERCISE 42:   Each of the following sentences contains *a* or *an*. Circle *a* or *an*. Draw arrows to the nouns they describe. Then indicate if the sentences are correct (C) or incorrect (I).

__C__   1.   She went to school in (a) local community.

__I__   2.   The doctor used (an)other pills.

_____   3.   It is necessary to have a farm or land of your own.

_____   4.   He must contact a members of the club.

_____   5.   You will need a pen or a pencil.

_____   6.   He is responsible for bringing a number of items.

_____   7.   You must write a report on a subjects of your choice.

_____   8.   They crossed through several forests and a stream.

_____   9.   There will be another important lessons tomorrow.

_____   10.   He could not give me a good reasons for what he did.

SKILL 43:   DISTINGUISH SPECIFIC AND GENERAL IDEAS

With countable singular nouns it is possible to use either the definite or the indefinite article, but they have different meanings. The definite article is used to refer to one specific noun.

> Tom will bring *the* book tomorrow.
> (There is one specific book that Tom will bring tomorrow.)
>
> He will arrive on *the* first Tuesday in July.
> (There is only one first Tuesday in July.)
>
> He sailed on *the* Pacific Ocean.
> (There is only one Pacific Ocean.)

The indefinite article is used when the noun could be one of the several different nouns.

> Tom will bring *a* book tomorrow.
> (Tom will bring any one book tomorrow.)
>
> He will arrive on *a* Tuesday in July.
> (He will arrive on one of four Tuesdays in July.)
>
> He sailed on *an* ocean.
> (He sailed on any one of the world's oceans.)

EXERCISE 43: Each of the following sentences contains one or more articles. Circle the articles. Draw arrows to the nouns they describe. Then indicate if the sentences are correct (C) or incorrect (I).

_I_   1. He took (a) trip on (a) Snake River.

_C_   2. I'll meet you at (the) library later.

_____   3. The ball hit a child on a head.

_____   4. He had a best grade in the class on the exam.

_____   5. The people who came here yesterday were here again today.

_____   6. She was a most beautiful girl in the room.

_____   7. The trip that I took last year to the Bahamas was the only vacation I had all year.

_____   8. I need a piece of paper so that I can finish the report that I am working on.

_____   9. A basketball player threw the ball to a center of the court.

_____   10. The sixth grade class went on a field trip to visit a Lincoln Memorial in Washington, D.C.

REVIEW EXERCISE (SKILLS 40–43): Circle the articles in the following sentences. Then indicate if the sentences are correct (C) or incorrect (I).

_____   1. He took a money from his wallet to pay for sweater.

_____   2. The notebook that he left had an important assignment in it.

_____   3. Because of previous disagreements, they are trying to arrive at an understanding.

_____   4. The appearance of room could be improved by adding a flourishing green plants.

_____   5. The Senate passed law banning smoking in public work places.

_____   6. Each chemistry student should bring laboratory manual to a next class.

_____   7. She admitted that she made mistake but said that she had made a honest effort.

_____   8. His absence from the board meeting was a strong indications of his desire to leave the company.

_____   9. The car needed gas, so she stopped at a service station.

_____   10. Anyone taking group tour to the Hawaiian Islands must pay fee before a first of the month.

TOEFL EXERCISE (SKILLS 40–43): Choose the letter of the underlined word or group of words that is not correct.

_____ 1. On <u>a trip</u> down to <u>the bottom</u> of <u>the</u> Grand Canyon, our equipment was
              A   B   C
          carried by <u>a burros</u>.
                    D

_____ 2. <u>The meaning</u> of <u>a great</u> painting increases with <u>time</u>, while the meaning of
              A   B   C
          <u>poor one</u> just disappears.
             D

_____ 3. <u>The</u> judge was in favor of having <u>a Federal government</u> take over <u>the</u>
           A   B   C
          prosecution of <u>the case</u>.
                  D

_____ 4. <u>The scholarship</u> that he received to study <u>history</u> at <u>Cambridge</u> presented
               A   B   C
          <u>an unique</u> opportunity.
             D

_____ 5. As <u>the hurricane</u> blew through <u>the town</u>, <u>tree</u> in front of <u>the</u> post office
              A   B   C   D
          came tumbling down.

_____ 6. <u>The professor</u> left <u>his</u> office, walked down <u>the</u> hall, went into <u>classroom</u>,
              A   B   C   D
          and began to lecture.

_____ 7. <u>Last weekend</u> we took <u>a trip</u> to <u>the</u> mountains and saw <u>a</u> most beautiful
              A   B   C   D
          waterfall that I have ever seen.

_____ 8. <u>The</u> person who is going to get <u>a promotion</u> is <u>the person</u> who comes up
           A   B   C
          with a new <u>ideas</u>.
                 D

_____ 9. <u>The legislator</u> believed that it was <u>a honor</u> to be named to <u>a</u> position on
              A   B   C
          <u>the council</u>.
             D

_____ 10. Because <u>the type</u> on <u>the typewriter</u> that <u>the</u> student is using is not very
                 A   B   C
          clear, he should find another <u>typewriters</u>.
                              D

TOEFL Review Exercise (Skills 1–43): Choose the letter of the word or group of words that best completes the sentence.

1. In economics, diminishing returns describes _____ resource inputs and production.
   - (A) among
   - (B) when it is
   - (C) among them
   - (D) the relationship between

2. When lava reaches the surface, its temperature can be ten times _____ boiling water.
   - (A) the temperature
   - (B) that of
   - (C) it is
   - (D) more

3. Rarely _____ remove the entire root of a dandelion because of its length and sturdiness.
   - (A) can the casual gardener
   - (B) the casual gardener
   - (C) the casual gardener will
   - (D) does the casual gardener's

Choose the letter of the underlined word or group of words that is not correct.

_____ 4. Operas can be <u>broadly</u> <u>classified</u> as either comedies <u>or</u> <u>they are tragedies</u>.
                        A   B   C   D

_____ 5. Tungsten has <u>the highest</u> melting point of all metals, and for this reason it is
                        A

often <u>use</u> in <u>equipment</u> that must <u>withstand</u> high temperatures.
      B   C   D

_____ 6. After <u>leaving</u> the summit <u>meeting</u>, the ambassador felt <u>that his</u> mission had
                 A   B   C

been <u>a</u> most dangerous ever.
     D

_____ 7. People <u>tend to</u> voice <u>theirs</u> opinions first in small <u>groups</u> or among
                 A   B   C

<u>friends and acquaintances</u>.
              D

_____ 8. Inside the Lincoln Memorial <u>is</u> a <u>large statue</u> of Lincoln <u>make</u> from white
                                       A   B   C

marble.
<u>   </u>
D

_____ 9. In the quantitative course, the professor <u>presented</u> <u>a</u> unit with <u>an unique</u>
                                                     A   B   C

approach <u>to solving</u> this sort of problem.
          D

_____ 10. U.S. Census figures <u>indicate</u> that people with only <u>an</u> elementary education
                               A   B

earn <u>just half</u> as much as college <u>graduations</u>.
      C   D

PROBLEMS WITH PREPOSITIONS_____

Prepositions can be used in two ways: in a literal way and in an idiomatic way. In the literal use, the preposition means exactly what you expect.

The boy ran <u>up</u> the hill.

She went <u>in</u> the house.

In the first example, the preposition *up* means that the boy went in the direction *up* rather than *down*. In the second example, the preposition *in* means that she went *into* rather than *out of* the house.

In the idiomatic use, which is what appears most often on the TOEFL, the preposition appears in an idiomatic expression; that is, its meaning in this expression has nothing to do with the literal meaning.

I called <u>up</u> my friend.

He succeeded <u>in</u> passing the course.

In the first example, the word *up* has nothing to do with the direction *up*. *To call up someone* means *to telephone someone*. In the second example, the word *in* has nothing to do with the meaning of *into* or *inside;* it is simply idiomatic that the word *in* is used after the verb *succeed.*

It is impossible to list all potential idiomatic expressions with their prepositions, because there are so many expressions that could appear on the TOEFL. However, in this chapter you can practice recognizing problems with prepositions in TOEFL-type questions. Then, when you are working on the Written Expression section of the TOEFL, you should be aware that idiomatic errors with prepositions are common in that section. There are two common types of problems with prepositions that you should expect: (1) incorrect prepositions, and (2) omitted prepositions.

SKILL 44:   RECOGNIZE INCORRECT PREPOSITIONS

Sometimes an incorrect preposition is given in a sentence in the Written Expression of the TOEFL.

> The game was called <u>on</u>* because of rain.

> I knew I could count <u>in</u>* you to do a good job.

The first example should say that the game was *called off* because of rain. The expression *called off* means *cancelled,* and that is the meaning that makes sense in this example. *To call on someone* is to *visit someone,* and this meaning does not make sense in this example. In the second example, it is not correct in English to *count in someone.* The correct expression is to *count on someone.*

EXERCISE 44:   Each of the following sentences contains at least one preposition. Circle the prepositions. Then indicate if the sentences are correct (C) or incorrect (I).

<u> C </u>   1. (After) school many students participate (in) sports.

<u> I </u>   2. I know I can rely (in) you to be here (on) time.

<u>   </u>   3. If you need more light to read, turn on the lamp next to you.

<u>   </u>   4. Parents always try to bring at their children to be thoughtful.

<u>   </u>   5. I'll have to consult to my attorney before making a decision.

<u>   </u>   6. Walt has lost his keys, so he must look for them.

<u>   </u>   7. I just don't approve at your cheating on the exam.

<u>   </u>   8. Smoking is forbidden, so you should put out your cigarette.

<u>   </u>   9. Failure to pass the test will result to the loss of your license.

<u>   </u> 10. It is unlawful for parolees to associate with known felons.

SKILL 45:   RECOGNIZE WHEN PREPOSITIONS HAVE BEEN OMITTED

Sometimes a necessary preposition has been omitted from a sentence in the Written Expression section of the TOEFL.

> Can you <u>wait</u>* me after the game?

> I <u>plan</u>* attending the meeting.

The first example is incorrect because it is necessary to say *wait **for** me.* The second example is incorrect because it is necessary to say *plan **on** attending.*

EXERCISE 45:   Prepositions have been omitted in some of the following sentences. Mark where prepositions have been omitted. Then indicate if the sentences are correct (C) or incorrect (I).

_I_   1. If you take this job, it will be necessary to deal ∧ other departments.

_C_   2. Each child took one cookie from the plate.

_____   3. In the discussion, Rob sided the rest.

_____   4. The board turned his suggestion for the project because they thought it was too costly.

_____   5. He can always depend his friends.

_____   6. While Mrs. Sampson went shopping, a baby-sitter looked the children.

_____   7. I know Steve believes what you told him.

_____   8. Children should beware strangers.

_____   9. It was difficult to make a decision about buying a house.

_____   10. Tom blamed his brother the dent in the car.

REVIEW EXERCISE (SKILLS 44–45):   Circle the prepositions in the following sentences. Mark where prepositions have been omitted. Then indicate if the sentences are correct (C) or incorrect (I).

_____   1. The students must hand their homework every Monday.

_____   2. It will be difficult to forgive you of breaking your promise.

_____   3. Elizabeth excels math and science.

_____   4. She insisted on going to work in spite of her cold.

_____   5. Bob reminds me to his father because he looks just like him.

_____   6. If you are cold, you should put on your sweater.

_____   7. Mr. Sanders is not here now, but he will call you when he returns.

_____   8. I do not want to interfere your plans.

_____   9. Alan waited Marie after school.

_____   10. Bill laughs me whenever he looks at me.

TOEFL EXERCISE (SKILLS 44–45):   Choose the letter of the underlined word or group of words that is not correct.

_____   1. Amelia Earhart, <u>the first</u> woman to fly solo <u>across</u> the Altantic, disappeared
                                    A   B
             <u>on June 1937</u> while attempting to fly <u>around</u> the world.
                    C   D

_____   2. The <u>occurrence edema</u> <u>indicates</u> the presence <u>of</u> serious <u>illness</u>.
                      A   B   C   D

_____ 3. If approved <u>by</u> the board, the new rules <u>will</u> take effect <u>on</u> the <u>next</u>
               A   B   C   D
       semester.

_____ 4. <u>According legend</u>, Betsy Ross <u>designed and sewed</u> the <u>first</u> American <u>flag</u>.
               A   B   C   D

_____ 5. The <u>middle ear</u> is attached <u>for</u> the back <u>of</u> the throat <u>by</u> the Eustachian
              A   B   C   D
       tube.

_____ 6. Plants that sprout, grow, bloom, <u>produce seeds</u>, and die <u>within</u> <u>one year</u> are
                                       A   B   C
       classified <u>for</u> annuals.
                 D

_____ 7. A marionette is <u>controlled by</u> <u>means strings</u> <u>connected</u> <u>to</u> wooden bars.
                        A   B   C   D

_____ 8. In July <u>of</u> 1861, Pat Garrett <u>killed</u> Billy the Kid <u>in a</u> house
              A   B   C
       <u>close Fort Sumner</u>.
           D

_____ 9. Many comfort heating systems <u>using</u> steam <u>as</u> a working fluid <u>operate</u> <u>at</u>
                                  A   B   C   D
       the convection principle.

_____ 10. Mars' <u>two small</u> moons, Phobos and Deimos, are <u>irregularly</u> <u>shaped</u> and
               A   B   C
       covered <u>for</u> craters.
                D

TOEFL REVIEW EXERCISE (SKILLS 1–45): Choose the letter of the word or group of words that best completes the sentence.

1. _____ Army camps near Washington, D.C., in 1861, Julia Ward Howe wrote the "Battle Hymn of the Republic."
   (A) She visited
   (B) After visiting
   (C) When visited
   (D) When was she visiting

2. Certain authorities claim that the costumes that people wear to parties _____ into their personalities.
   (A) give subtle insights
   (B) they give subtle insights
   (C) which give subtle insights
   (D) subtle insights

3. In any matter, heat tends to flow
   _____ to the cooler parts.
   (A) hotter parts
   (B) there are hotter parts
   (C) from the hotter parts
   (D) toward the hotter parts

Choose the letter of the underlined word or group of words that is not correct.

_____ 4. The body <u>depends</u> <u>in</u> food <u>as</u> <u>its</u> primary source of energy.
                  A   B   C D

_____ 5. Regular <u>programming</u> was <u>interrupted</u> <u>to broadcast</u> a special news <u>bulletins</u>.
                A   B   C   D

_____ 6. Sulfa drugs had been <u>used</u> to treat <u>bacterial infection</u> until penicillin
                              A   B
       <u>becomes</u> <u>widely</u> available.
         C   D

_____ 7. Plans for both the International Monetary Fund <u>or</u> the World Bank were
      A B   C
       <u>drawn up</u> at the Bretton Woods Conference.
         D

_____ 8. Seldom <u>Antarctic icebergs will</u> move <u>far enough</u> north <u>to disturb</u> South
                  A   B   C
       Pacific <u>shipping lanes</u>.
           D

_____ 9. In 1958, <u>a largest</u> <u>recorded</u> wave, <u>with a</u> height of 500 meters, <u>occurred in</u>
                A   B   C   D
       Lituya Bay, Alaska.

_____ 10. Exercise in swimming pools is <u>particularly</u> <u>helpful</u> because <u>of</u> the buoyant
                                    A   B   C
        effect <u>water</u>.
          D

PROBLEMS WITH USAGE

In English certain groups of words have similar uses, and these words are sometimes confused in the Written Expression section of the TOEFL. Although various usage problems are possible on the TOEFL, the following problems are the most common: (1) when to use *make* and *do*, (2) when to use *like, unlike,* and *alike,* and (3) when to use *other, another,* and *others.*

SKILL 46:   DISTINGUISH *MAKE* AND *DO*

Make and *do* can be confused in English because their meanings are so similar. Since the difference between *make* and *do* is tested on the TOEFL, you should learn to distinguish them.

Make often has the idea of *creating* or *constructing*. The following expressions show some of the possible uses of *make*.

1. She likes to make her own clothes.
2. Would you like to make a cake for dessert?
3. If you make a mistake, you should correct it.
4. He was unable to make a response to the threat.

Do often has the idea of *completing* or *performing*. The following expressions show some of the possible uses of *do*.

1. This morning she did all the dishes.
2. The students are doing the assignments.
3. The janitors did the work they were assigned.
4. You can do your laundry at the laundromat.

These are only some of the uses of *make* and *do*. Many uses of *make* and *do* are idiomatic and therefore difficult to classify.

EXERCISE 46:   Each of the following sentences contains *make* or *do*. Circle *make* or *do*. Draw arrows to the nouns that complete the expressions. Then indicate if the sentences are correct (C) or incorrect (I).

I 1. The biology student (did) several mistakes in the lab report.

C 2. I hope that you will be able to (do) me a favor this afternoon.

___ 3. No matter what job she has, she always makes her best.

___ 4. The runner did a strong effort to increase her speed in the mile race.

___ 5. It is comforting to think that your work can make a difference.

___ 6. His grade was not very good because there were several occasions when he had not done his homework.

___ 7. In this job you will make more money than in your previous job.

___ 8. He was unable to do dinner because no one had done the lunch dishes.

___ 9. It is a pleasure to work with someone who always makes the right thing.

___ 10. If you make a good impression at your job interview, you have good chance of getting the job.

SKILL 47:   DISTINGUISH *LIKE*, *ALIKE*, AND *UNLIKE*

Like, alike, and *unlike* are easily confused because they look so similar and they have so many different uses. There are four structures with *like, alike,* and *unlike* that you should be familiar with. (Even if you have difficulty distinguishing the many different uses of *like, alike,* and *unlike,* you should understand that this structure is probably what is being tested when you see one of these words in the Written Expression section of the TOEFL.)

The first structure you should be familiar with involves *alike*. Study the use of *alike* in the following example.

> John and Tom are <u>alike</u>.
>   ADJ

In this example, *alike* is an adjective describing *John and Tom. Alike* has the same meaning as *similar;* this sentence means that *John and Tom are similar.* Notice that *alike* comes after both of the nouns it is comparing.

A second structure that is very common shows the correct use of *like* and *unlike*.

> John is (<u>like</u> Tom.)
>   PREP
>
> John is (<u>unlike</u> Tom.)
>   PREP

In these two examples, *like* means *similar to,* and *unlike* has an opposite meaning. *Like* and *unlike* in these examples are prepositions, which means that each of them must be followed by an object.

A third way that *like* and *unlike* can be used is seen in the following examples.

> (<u>Like</u> Tom,) John is tall.
>   PREP
>
> (<u>Unlike</u> Paul,) John is tall.
>   PREP

Just as in the preceding structure, *like* and *unlike* in these examples are prepositions, so each of them must be followed by an object.

A final structure with *like* is not very common. Study the use of *like* in the following example.

> John and Tom worked in a <u>like</u> manner.
>   ADJ

In this example, *like* means *similar.* It is an adjective (it describes a noun), and when it is used in this way it will come immediately before the noun it describes.

EXERCISE 47: Each of the following sentences contains *like, alike,* or *unlike.* Circle *like, alike,* and *unlike.* Then indicate if the sentences are correct (C) or incorrect (I).

_I_   1. The two routes you have chosen for the trip are (like.)

_C_   2. The science books this semester are (like) the books used last semester.

_____   3. Alike the restaurant where we usually eat, this new restaurant has early bird specials.

_____   4. Unlike the traditional red fire engines, the new fire engines purchased by the department are yellow.

_____   5. The two girls were embarrassed because they were wearing alike dresses.

_____   6. The new piece that the pianist is preparing for the recital is unlike any she has ever played before.

_____   7. Like the Washington Zoo, the San Diego Zoo has several panda bears.

_____   8. The insurance package offered by that company is exactly alike the package our company offers.

_____   9. Any further work done in a like fashion will be rejected.

_____   10. It is unfortunate that the covers for this year's and last year's albums are so alike.

SKILL 48:   DISTINGUISH *OTHER, ANOTHER,* AND *OTHERS*

Other, another, and *others* are very easy to confuse. To decide how to use each of them correctly, you must consider three things: (1) if it is singular or plural, (2) if it is definite (*the*) or indefinite (*a*), and (3) if it is an adjective (it appears with a noun) or if it is a pronoun (it appears by itself).

	SINGULAR	*PLURAL*
INDEFINITE	I have <u>another</u> book. I have <u>another</u>.	I have <u>other</u> books. I have <u>others</u>.
DEFINITE	I have the <u>other</u> book. I have the <u>other</u>.	I have the <u>other</u> books. I have the <u>others</u>.

Notice that you use *another* only to refer to an indefinite, singular idea. *Others* is used only as a plural pronoun (not accompanied by a noun). In all other cases, *other* is correct.

EXERCISE 48: Each of the following sentences contains *other, another,* or *others.* Circle *other, another,* or *others.* Then indicate if the sentences are correct (C) or incorrect (I).

_C_   1. It is essential to complete the first program before working on the (others.)

_I_   2. The waitress will bring you the (another) bowl of soup if you want.

_____ 3. You should pack another pair of shoes in case that pair gets soaked.

_____ 4. It is difficult to find others workers who are willing to work such long hours.

_____ 5. Since the lamp you wanted is out of stock, you must choose another.

_____ 6. The other desk clerk must have put that message in your mailbox.

_____ 7. If your identification card is lost or stolen, you cannot get another.

_____ 8. Because they were not pleased with the hotel accommodations last year, they have decided to try a other hotel this year.

_____ 9. As some students moved into the registration area, others took their place in line.

_____ 10. The printer will not function unless it has another cartridges.

REVIEW EXERCISE (SKILLS 46–48): Circle the words in the following sentences that are commonly confused on the TOEFL. Then indicate if the sentences are correct (C) or incorrect (I).

_____ 1. When the car's odometer reached 100,000 miles, she decided that it was time to buy another car.

_____ 2. Every time someone does an error in the program, several extra hours of work are created.

_____ 3. Like the fashions shown in this magazine, the fashions in the other magazine are quite expensive.

_____ 4. Because the main highway is crowded at this hour, the driver should try to find another routes to the stadium.

_____ 5. Although the two signatures are supposed to be exactly the same, they are not at all like.

_____ 6. The decorators did the shopping for the material and made curtains for the windows.

_____ 7. Before the administrator reads the stack of papers on his desk, he should sign the others that are on the file cabinet.

_____ 8. The committee is doing the arrangements for the Saturday evening banquet.

_____ 9. If you continue to make a like effort, you will be successful at this job.

_____ 10. Perhaps the designer could select others styles if these are inappropriate.

TOEFL EXERCISE (SKILLS 46–48): Choose the letter of the underlined word or group of words that is not correct.

_____ 1. The buffalo and the bison are <u>like</u> <u>except for</u> the <u>size</u> and shape of the
                                              A   B   C

<u>head and shoulders</u>.
      D

_____ 2. <u>Other</u> <u>interesting</u> aspect of tachistopic training in recent years <u>has been</u>
      A   B   C

the <u>newfound use</u> by professional teams.
       D

_____ 3. <u>Only about</u> 3 percent of <u>oil wells</u> <u>actually</u> <u>do</u> a profit.
        A   B   C   D

_____ 4. <u>Dislike</u> sumac <u>with</u> red berries, sumac with white berries <u>is</u> <u>poisonous</u>.
       A   B   C   D

_____ 5. Pittsburgh has reduced <u>its</u> smog by requiring <u>more</u> complete oxidation of
                                 A   B

fuel in cars, and <u>others</u> cities can <u>do</u> the same thing.
                 C   D

_____ 6. <u>Alike</u> <u>all</u> <u>other</u> mammals, dolphins <u>have</u> lungs.
       A   B   C   D

_____ 7. Up to World War II <u>almost all</u> important research in physics had been <u>made</u>
                              A   B

in universities, <u>with only</u> university funds <u>for support</u>.
                 C   D

_____ 8. Because the plan <u>that was</u> made yesterday is <u>no longer</u> feasible, the
                          A   B

manager <u>had to</u> choose another <u>alternatives</u>.
            C   D

_____ 9. Particles with <u>unlike</u> charges attract each other, <u>while</u> particles with <u>alike</u>
                    A   B   C

charges repel each <u>other</u>.
                  D

_____ 10. <u>One another</u> <u>surprising</u> method of forest <u>conservation is</u> <u>controlled cutting</u>
         A   B   C   D

of trees.

TOEFL REVIEW EXERCISE (SKILLS 1–48): Choose the letter of the word or group of words that best completes the sentence.

1. Wild Bill Hickok _____ for the Union Army during the Civil War by posing as a Confederate officer.
   (A) spied
   (B) spying
   (C) a spy
   (D) was spied

2. _____ was unusable as farmland and difficult to traverse, the Badlands is an area in South Dakota.
   (A) So named because it
   (B) Because of
   (C) It
   (D) Naming it

Choose the letter of the underlined word or group of words that is not correct.

_____ 3. Before the chemist could publish his results, it was necessary to finish
            A   B   C
another experiments.
         D

_____ 4. The author Frances Scott Key Fitzgerald is better know as F. Scott
             A   B   C   D
Fitzgerald.

_____ 5. The result of the failure to plan for the future is that a child from an urban
                                                    A   B
area must be took to the country to see nature.
            C   D

_____ 6. This machine can print on a single pieces of paper, but only if the lever is
         A   B   C
facing the front of the machine.
  D

_____ 7. The development of permanent teeth, alike that of deciduous teeth, begins
                                          A   B   C
before birth.
       D

_____ 8. A crowd of several hundred fan watched the ceremony from behind a
                      A   B   C   D
fence.

_____ 9. <u>Unlike</u> <u>other</u> architects of the early modern movement, Alvar Aalto stressed
        A   B

informality, personal expression, <u>romantic</u>, and regionality in <u>his work</u>.
                    C   D

_____ 10. <u>Color blindness</u> may <u>exist at</u> birth or may occur <u>later in</u> life as a result <u>for</u>
         A   B   C   D

disease or injury.

TOEFL POST-TEST
FOLLOWS

TOEFL POST-TEST

SECTION 2
STRUCTURE AND WRITTEN EXPRESSION
Time—25 Minutes

This section is designed to measure your ability to recognize language that is appropriate for standard written English. There are two types of questions in this section, with special directions for each type.

Directions: Questions 1–15 are incomplete sentences. Beneath each sentence you will see four words or phrases, marked (A), (B), (C), and (D). Choose the <u>one</u> word or phrase that best completes the sentence. Then, on your answer sheet, find the number of the question and fill in the space that corresponds to the letter of the answer you have chosen. Fill in the space so that the letter inside the oval cannot be seen.

Example I   Sample Answer

The president _____ the election
by a landslide.
(A) won
(B) he won
(C) yesterday
(D) fortunately

The sentence should read, "The president won the election by a landslide." Therefore, you should choose answer (A).

Example II   Sample Answer

When _____ the conference?
(A) the doctor attended
(B) did the doctor attend
(C) the doctor will attend
(D) the doctor's attendance

The sentence should read, "When did the doctor attend the conference?" Therefore, you should choose answer (B).

After you read the directions, begin work on the questions.

GO ON TO THE NEXT PAGE ▶

1. _____ range in color from pale yellow to bright orange.

   (A) Canaries
   (B) Canaries which
   (C) That canaries
   (D) Canaries that are

2. Carnivorous plants _____ insects to obtain nitrogen.

   (A) are generally trapped
   (B) trap generally
   (C) are trapped generally
   (D) generally trap

3. February normally has twenty-eight days, but every fourth year, _____ has twenty-nine.

   (A) there
   (B) its
   (C) is a leap year
   (D) a leap year, it

4. Evidence suggests that one-quarter of operations _____ bypass surgery may be unnecessary.

   (A) they involve
   (B) involve
   (C) involving
   (D) which they involve

5. _____ a tornado spins in a counterclockwise direction in the northern hemisphere, it spins in the opposite direction in the southern hemisphere.

   (A) However
   (B) Because
   (C) Although
   (D) That

6. The Caldecott Medal, _____ for the best children's picture book, is awarded each January.

   (A) is
   (B) which
   (C) a prize
   (D) is a prize

7. _____ is a medical specialty which deals with the identification and treatment of injuries to persons involved in sports.

   (A) Sports
   (B) Sports medicine
   (C) Because sports medicine
   (D) There is sports medicine

8. _____ and a mechanics instructor, interviewed at the air base, said that they were under orders not to fight.

   (A) A flight instructor
   (B) There were an instructor
   (C) Because of the instructor
   (D) Because the instructor

9. The Wilmington Oil Field, in Long Beach, California, is one of _____ oil fields in the continental United States.

   (A) productive
   (B) the most productive
   (C) most are productive
   (D) productivity

10. The population of Houston was ravaged by yellow fever in 1839 _____ in 1867.

    (A) it happened again
    (B) and again
    (C) was ravaged again
    (D) again once more

11. Thunder occurs when an electrical charge passes through air, causing the heated air to expand and _____ layers of cooler air.

    (A) collides violently with
    (B) violently colliding
    (C) collided with
    (D) collide violently with

GO ON TO THE NEXT PAGE

12. People who reverse the letters of words ____ to read suffer from dyslexia.

    (A) when trying
    (B) if they tried
    (C) when tried
    (D) if he tries

13. According to Bernoulli's Principle, the higher the speed of a fluid gas, ____ the pressure.

    (A) it will be lower
    (B) lower than the
    (C) the lower
    (D) lower it is

14. American public school curriculum is determined at the state or local level ____ the federal level.

    (A) rather than
    (B) nor at the
    (C) is not determined
    (D) whereas

15. In the northern and central parts of the state of Idaho ____ and churning rivers.

    (A) majestic mountains are found
    (B) are majestic moutains found
    (C) are found majestic mountains
    (D) finding majestic mountains

Directions: In questions 16–40 each sentence has four underlined words or phrases. The four underlined parts of the sentence are marked (A), (B), (C), and (D). Identify the one underlined word or phrase that must be changed in order for the sentence to be correct. Then, on your answer sheet, find the number of the question and fill in the space that corresponds to the letter of the answer you have chosen.

Example I   Sample Answer

The four string on a violin are tuned
 A   B   C   D
in fifths.

The sentence should read, "The four strings on a violin are tuned in fifths." Therefore, you should choose answer (B).

Example II   Sample Answer

The research for the book *Roots* taking
     A   B   C
Alex Haley twelve years.
             D

The sentence should read, "The research for the book *Roots* took Alex Haley twelve years." Therefore, you should choose answer (C).

After you read the directions, begin work on the questions.

GO ON TO THE NEXT PAGE ➤

16. Light can travels from the sun to the earth in eight minutes and twenty seconds.
     A   B   C   D

17. Every human typically have twenty-three pairs of chromosomes in most cells.
               A   B   C   D

18. In the sport of fencing, three type of swords are used: the foil, the epee, and the
     A   B   C   D
sabre.

19. The Internal Revenue Service uses computers to check tax return computations, to
                              A   B
determine the reasonableness of deductions, and for verifying the accuracy of
                                         C
reported income.
     D

20. There was four groups of twenty rats each involved in the test.
         A   B   C   D

21. The type of jazz known as "swing" was introduced by Duke Ellington when he
              A   B   C
wrote and records "It Don't Mean a Thing If It Ain't Got That Swing."
          D

22. The bones of mammals, not alike those of other vertebrates, show a high degree of
                   A   B   C   D
differentiation.

23. The United States receives a large amount of revenue from taxation of a tobacco
                      A   B   C   D
products.

24. Much fats are composed of one molecule of glycerin combined with three
     A   B   C
molecules of fatty acids.
          D

25. The capital of the Confederacy was originally in Mobile, but its was later moved to
     A   B   C   D
Richmond.

26. A pearl develops when a tiny grain of sand or some another irritant accidentally
               A   B   C
enters into the shell of a pearl oyster.
     D

GO ON TO THE NEXT PAGE ➤

27. The English horn is <u>an alto</u> oboe with <u>a pitch</u> one fifth lower <u>as</u> <u>that</u> of the soprano
                       A   B   C D

    oboe.

28. In the Milky Way galaxy, <u>the most</u> <u>recent</u> observed supernova <u>appeared</u> <u>in</u> 1604.
                                A   B   C   D

29. <u>Although</u> the name suggests <u>otherwise</u>, the ship <u>known as</u> *Old Ironsides* was built
      A   B   C

    of oak and ceder rather than <u>it was built of</u> iron.
                                 D

30. Never <u>in the history</u> of man <u>there have</u> been <u>more people</u> <u>living</u> on this relatively
            A   B   C   D

    small planet.

31. Because of <u>the mobility</u> of Americans today, <u>it is</u> difficult for <u>him</u> to put down
               A   B   C

    <u>real roots</u>.
      D

32. For five <u>years after</u> the Civil War, Robert E. Lee served <u>to</u> president of Washington
             A   B

    College, <u>which</u> <u>later</u> was called Washington and Lee.
            C   D

33. Doctors <u>successfully</u> used hypnosis <u>during</u> World War II <u>to treat</u> <u>fatigue battle</u>.
              A   B   C   D

34. The main cause of the <u>oceans' tides</u> <u>is</u> the <u>gravitation</u> pull of <u>the moon</u>.
                       A   B   C   D

35. The lobster, <u>like</u> <u>many</u> crustaceans, can cast off a damaged appendage and
               A   B

    regenerate a new appendage to <u>nearly normal</u> <u>sizing</u>.
                                C   D

36. The record albums <u>left</u> <u>sitting</u> on the floor by the window have <u>been</u> damaged
                    A   B   C

    <u>by sun</u>.
      D

37. The fact <u>is</u> that sophisticated technology <u>has become</u> part of the revolution in
            A   B

    <u>travel delivery systems</u> has not made travel schedules <u>less hectic</u>.
              C   D

GO ON TO THE NEXT PAGE

38. Balanchine's <u>plotless</u> ballets <u>such</u> *Jewels* and *The Four Temperaments* <u>present</u>
           A   B   C
    dance <u>purely</u> as a celebration of the movement of the human body.
          D

39. In a solar battery, a photosensitive <u>semiconducting</u> substance <u>such as</u> silicon
                                A   B
    crystal is <u>the source</u> of <u>electrician</u>.
             C   D

40. <u>In early days</u>, hydrochloric acid was <u>done</u> by <u>heating</u> a mixture of sodium chloride
        A   B   C
    <u>with</u> iron sulfate.
     D

THIS IS THE END OF SECTION 2

IF YOU FINISH BEFORE TIME IS CALLED, CHECK YOUR WORK
ON SECTION 2 ONLY.
DO NOT READ OR WORK ON ANY OTHER SECTION OF THE TEST.
THE SUPERVISOR WILL TELL YOU WHEN TO BEGIN
WORK ON SECTION 3.

SECTION THREE:

VOCABULARY AND READING COMPREHENSION

TOEFL PRE-TEST

SECTION 3
VOCABULARY AND READING

Time—45 minutes

This section is designed to measure your comprehension of standard written English. There are two types of questions in this section, with special directions for each type.

<u>Directions:</u> In questions 1–30 each sentence has an underlined word or phrase. Below each sentence are four other words or phrases, marked (A), (B), (C), and (D). You are to choose the <u>one</u> word or phrase that <u>best keeps the meaning</u> of the original sentence if it is substituted for the underlined word or phrase. Then, on your answer sheet, find the number of the question and fill in the space that corresponds to the letter you have chosen. Fill in the space so that the letter inside the oval cannot be seen.

Example   <u>Sample Answer</u>

Both <u>boats</u> and trains are used for
transporting the materials.

(A) planes
(B) ships
(C) canoes
(D) railroads

The best answer is (B) because "Both ships and trains are used for transporting the materials" is closest in meaning to the original sentence. Therefore, you should choose answer (B).

After you read the directions, begin work on the questions.

1. In the 1970s the primary goal of the Federal Reserve policy was to <u>combat</u> inflation.

    (A) regulate
    (B) fight
    (C) avenge
    (D) defend

2. The metallic element beryllium appears at the <u>head</u> of Group IIA in the periodic table.

    (A) top
    (B) peak
    (C) cap
    (D) chief

3. The coastline of Puget Sound is extremely <u>irregular</u>, with an assortment of channels, peninsulas, and cliffed islands.

    (A) rocky
    (B) smooth
    (C) varied
    (D) heavy

4. The diameter of the moon is <u>slightly</u> more than one-fourth that of the earth.

    (A) shortly
    (B) somewhat
    (C) periodically
    (D) radically

GO ON TO THE NEXT PAGE

5. Because of frigid winter temperatures, <u>parts</u> of the St. Lawrence Seaway can be open for operations only about nine months of the year.

(A) paths
(B) locks
(C) sections
(D) series

6. The tilt of the earth <u>rather than</u> the varying distance from the sun is responsible for the changing seasons.

(A) instead of
(B) in preference to
(C) regarding
(D) in addition to

7. The sea otter generally paddles with its <u>hind</u> feet.

(A) back
(B) large
(C) helpful
(D) webbed

8. The National Research Council, initiated during World War I, was continued after the war for the <u>encouragement</u> of research in the natural sciences.

(A) imposition
(B) enchantment
(C) obstruction
(D) promotion

9. From the crest of the Rocky Mountains, water <u>flows</u> eastward to the Atlantic and westward to the Pacific.

(A) drips
(B) floods
(C) runs
(D) drains

10. A microwave oven can cook food in seconds, without heating up the <u>surrounding</u> area.

(A) surface
(B) nearby
(C) circular
(D) enclosed

11. Annie Oakley's life served as <u>a basis</u> for the play *Annie Get Your Gun,* by Herbert and Dorothy Fields.

(A) a foundation
(B) an example
(C) a supporter
(D) a suggestion

12. Navajo rugs are <u>distinguished</u> by their boldly colored geometric patterns.

(A) enlarged
(B) enhanced
(C) hampered
(D) differentiated

13. Desert land formations are the result of both wind action and streams formed after <u>rare</u> showers.

(A) unsettled
(B) unforeseen
(C) unsolicited
(D) uncommon

14. It has been estimated by government officials that Al Capone's operations <u>netted</u> more than $50 million annually.

(A) hit
(B) captured
(C) yielded
(D) paid taxes on

GO ON TO THE NEXT PAGE

VOCABULARY AND READING COMPREHENSION PRE-TEST 195

15. Peddlers traveled through early American <u>settlements</u>, often transporting their wares by cart, by boat, or on horseback.

    (A) outposts
    (B) agreements
    (C) tunnels
    (D) valleys

16. The Phi Beta Kappa Society most probably began as <u>a secret</u> undergraduate society at William and Mary College in Virginia.

    (A) an isolated
    (B) a mysterious
    (C) a profligate
    (D) a lucrative

17. Large deposits of limestone and clay can be found in the northern <u>reaches</u> of the state of Washington.

    (A) rations
    (B) mines
    (C) arrivals
    (D) expanses

18. The island of Hawaii, though irregular in shape, is <u>roughly</u> triangular.

    (A) approximately
    (B) ruggedly
    (C) gratingly
    (D) perceptibly

19. The United States government has been studying the possibility of using underground salt mines to <u>house</u> radioactive wastes.

    (A) hide
    (B) store
    (C) protect
    (D) bury

20. The innateness theory of language suggests that language is a characteristic of all humans and that any human <u>race</u> is therefore able to learn a language.

    (A) competitive group
    (B) language group
    (C) ethnic group
    (D) normal group

21. Bighorn rams have <u>massive</u>, tightly curled horns.

    (A) imposing
    (B) molded
    (C) tenuous
    (D) rounded

22. Most butterfly larvae spin cocoons to <u>camouflage</u> the helpless pupa.

    (A) enhance
    (B) reinforce
    (C) support
    (D) disguise

23. The Pawnee Rock was a famous <u>landmark</u> for pioneers traveling on the old Santa Fe Trail.

    (A) distinction
    (B) milestone
    (C) footnote
    (D) landscape

24. Thresher sharks herd their <u>prey</u> with their tails, sometimes stunning them with one stroke.

    (A) fins
    (B) attackers
    (C) victims
    (D) cattle

GO ON TO THE NEXT PAGE

25. <u>Conventional</u> theories have always assumed that phobic behaviors have psychological explanations.

    (A) convenient
    (B) scientific
    (C) arbitrary
    (D) orthodox

26. A dermatologist may use a <u>filtered</u> ultraviolet light to aid in the diagnosis of certain types of fungus infections.

    (A) screened
    (B) luminous
    (C) radiant
    (D) resplendent

27. One survey showed that employees working in a plutonium plant had <u>markedly</u> higher rates of bone marrow cancer than the population at large.

    (A) ludicrously
    (B) conspicuously
    (C) haphazardly
    (D) shockingly

28. The United States issued silver certificates in three different <u>denominations</u> until 1963.

    (A) bills
    (B) checks
    (C) values
    (D) names

29. One efficient and inexpensive method to keep winter roads free of ice is to <u>sprinkle</u> salt on them.

    (A) scatter
    (B) blot
    (C) swab
    (D) splinter

30. <u>Mercilessly</u> hunted for their oil and hides, northern elephant seals were almost completely wiped out by 1890.

    (A) relentlessly
    (B) thanklessly
    (C) redolently
    (D) meticulously

GO ON TO THE NEXT PAGE

Directions: In the rest of this section you will read several passages. Each one is followed by several questions about it. For questions 31–60, you are to choose the one best answer, (A), (B), (C), or (D), to each question. Then, on your answer sheet, find the number of the question and fill in the space that corresponds to the letter of the answer you have chosen.

Answer all questions following a passage on the basis of what is stated or implied in that passage.

Read the following passage:

John Quincy Adams, who served as the sixth president of the United States from 1825 to 1829, is today recognized for his masterful statesmanship and diplomacy. He dedicated his life to public service, both in the presidency and in the various other political offices he held. Throughout his political career he demonstrated his unswerving belief in freedom of speech, the anti-slavery cause, and the right of Americans to be free from European and Asian domination.

Example I   Sample Answer

To what did John Quincy Adams   Ⓐ ● Ⓒ Ⓓ
devote his life?

(A) Improving his personal life
(B) Serving the public
(C) Increasing his fortune
(D) Working on his private business

According to the passage, John Quincy Adams "dedicated his life to public service." Therefore, you should choose answer (B).

Example II   Sample Answer

The passage implies that John   Ⓐ Ⓑ Ⓒ ●
Quincy Adams held

(A) no political offices
(B) only one political office
(C) exactly two political offices
(D) at least three political offices

The passage states that John Quincy Adams served in "the presidency and various other political offices." Therefore, you should choose answer (D).

After you read the directions, begin work on the questions.

GO ON TO THE NEXT PAGE ➤

Questions 31–35

Carbon tetrachloride, a colorless and inflammable liquid, is widely used in industry today as a solvent in spite of the fact that it has been banned for home use. In the past, carbon tetrachloride was a common ingredient in cleaning compounds, but it was found to be dangerous: when heated, it changes into a poisonous gas. Because of this dangerous characteristic, the United States government revoked permission for the home use of carbon tetrachloride in 1970. The U.S. has taken similar action with various other chemical compounds.

31. The author's main point in this passage is that

    (A) carbon tetrachloride can be very dangerous when it is heated
    (B) the government banned carbon tetrachloride in 1970
    (C) although carbon tetrachloride can legally be used in industry, it is not allowed in home products
    (D) carbon tetrachloride used to be a regular part of cleaning compounds

32. According to the passage, before 1970 carbon tetrachloride was

    (A) used by itself as a cleanser
    (B) banned in industrial use
    (C) often used as a component of cleaning products
    (D) not allowed in home cleaning products

33. It is stated in the passage that when carbon tetrachloride is heated, it becomes

    (A) harmful
    (B) colorless
    (C) a cleaning compound
    (D) inflammable

34. It can be inferred from the passage that one role of the U.S. government is to

    (A) regulate product safety
    (B) prohibit any use of carbon tetrachloride
    (C) instruct industry on cleaning methodologies
    (D) ban the use of any chemicals

35. Which of the following is NOT true, according to the passage?

    (A) Carbon tetrachloride is extensively used in industry.
    (B) The properties of carbon tetrachloride change when its temperature is raised.
    (C) The government banned carbon tetrachloride because of the potential danger.
    (D) Carbon tetrachloride is still widely used in the home.

GO ON TO THE NEXT PAGE

Questions 36–41

The next artist in this survey of American artists is James Whistler; he is included in this survey of American artists because he was born in the United States, although the majority of his art work was completed in Europe. Whistler was born in Massachusetts in 1834, but nine years later his father moved the family to St. Petersburg, Russia, to work on the construction of a railroad. The family returned to the United States in 1849. Two years later Whistler entered the U.S. military academy at West Point, but he was unable to graduate. At the age of twenty-one, Whistler went to Europe to study art despite familial objections, and he remained in Europe until his death.

Whistler worked in various art forms, including etchings and lithographs. But he is most famous for his paintings, particularly *Arrangement in Gray and Black No. 1: Portrait of the Artist's Mother* or *Whistler's Mother*, as it is more commonly known. This painting shows a side view of Whistler's mother dressed in black and posing against a gray wall. The asymmetrical nature of the portrait, with his mother seated off-center, is highly characteristic of Whistler's work.

36. The paragraph preceding this passage most likely discusses

(A) a survey of eighteenth-century art
(B) a different American artist
(C) Whistler's other famous paintings
(D) European artists

37. Which of the following best states the topic of the passage?

(A) James Whistler's life story
(B) American artists
(C) An overview of the life and works of an artist
(D) The paintings of James Whistler

38. It is implied in the passage that Whistler's family was

(A) unable to find any work at all in Russia
(B) highly supportive of his desire to pursue art
(C) working class
(D) military

39. According to the passage, Whistler lived in America for approximately how many years of his life?

(A) 6
(B) 9
(C) 15
(D) 21

40. It is stated in the passage that Whistler did all the following EXCEPT

(A) live in Russia
(B) graduate from a military academy
(C) study art
(D) make lithographs and etchings

41. Which of the following is NOT true according to the passage?

(A) Whistler worked with a variety of art forms.
(B) *Whistler's Mother* is not the official name of his painting.
(C) Whistler is best known for his etchings.
(D) *Whistler's Mother* is painted in somber tones.

GO ON TO THE NEXT PAGE

Questions 42–49

The locations of stars in the sky relative to one another do not appear to the naked eye to change, and as a result stars are often considered to be fixed in position. In reality, though, stars are always moving, but because of the tremendous distances between stars themselves and from stars to earth, the changes are barely perceptible here. It takes approximately 200 years for a fast-moving star like Bernard's star to move a distance in the skies equal to the diameter of the Earth's moon. When the apparently negligible movement of the stars is contrasted with the movement of the planets, the stars are seemingly unmoving.

42. Which of the following is the best title for this passage?

(A) What the Eye Can See in the Sky
(B) Bernard's Star
(C) Planetary Movement
(D) The Evermoving Stars

43. According to the passage, the distances between the stars and earth are

(A) barely perceptible
(B) huge
(C) fixed
(D) moderate

44. The word "perceptible" (line 4) is closest in meaning to which of the following words?

(A) Noticeable
(B) Persuasive
(C) Conceivable
(D) Astonishing

45. The passage states that in 200 years Bernard's star can move

(A) around the earth's moon
(B) next to the earth's moon
(C) a distance equal to the distance from the earth to the moon
(D) a distance equivalent in measurement to the diameter of the moon

46. The passage implies that from the earth it appears that the planets

(A) are fixed in the sky
(B) move more slowly than the stars
(C) show approximately the same amount of movement as the stars
(D) travel through the sky considerably more rapidly than the stars

47. Which of the following is NOT true according to the passage?

(A) Stars do not appear to the eye to move.
(B) The large distances between stars and the earth tend to magnify movement to the eye.
(C) Bernard's star moves quickly in comparison with other stars.
(D) Although stars move, they seem to be fixed.

48. The paragraph following the passage most probably discusses

(A) the movement of the planets
(B) Bernard's star
(C) the distance from the earth to the moon
(D) why stars are always moving

49. This passage would most probably be assigned reading in which course?

(A) Astrology
(B) Geophysics
(C) Astronomy
(D) Geography

GO ON TO THE NEXT PAGE

VOCABULARY AND READING COMPREHENSION PRE-TEST 201

Questions 50–56

It has been noted that traditionally courts have granted divorces on fault grounds: one spouse is deemed to be at fault in causing the divorce. More and more today, however, divorces are being granted on a no-fault basis.

Proponents of no-fault divorce argue that when a marriage fails, it is rarely the case that one marriage partner is completely to blame and the other blameless. A failed marriage is much more often the result of mistakes by both partners.

Another argument in favor of no-fault divorce is that proving fault in court, in a public arena, is a destructive process that only serves to lengthen the divorce process and that dramatically increases the negative feelings present in a divorce. If a couple can reach a decision to divorce without first deciding which partner is to blame, the divorce settlement can be negotiated more easily and equitably and the post-divorce healing process can begin more rapidly.

50. According to the passage, no-fault divorces

(A) are on the increase
(B) are the traditional form of divorce
(C) are less popular than they used to be
(D) were granted more in the past

51. It is implied in the passage that

(A) there recently has been a decrease in no-fault divorces
(B) not all divorces today are no-fault divorces
(C) a no-fault divorce is not as equitable as a fault divorce
(D) people recover more slowly from a no-fault divorce

52. The word "proponents" (line 4) is closest in meaning to which of these?

(A) Advocates
(B) Adversaries
(C) Authorities
(D) Enemies

53. The passage states that a public trial to prove the fault of one spouse can

(A) be satisfying to the wronged spouse
(B) lead to a shorter divorce process
C) reduce negative feelings
(D) be a harmful process

54. Which of the following is NOT listed in this passage as an argument in favor of no-fault divorce?

(A) Rarely is only one marriage partner to blame for a divorce.
(B) A no-fault divorce generally costs less in legal fees.
(C) Finding fault in a divorce increases negative feelings.
(D) A no-fault divorce settlement is generally easier to negotiate.

55. What does this passage mainly discuss?

(A) Traditional grounds for divorce
(B) Who is at fault in a divorce
(C) The increase in no-fault divorces
(D) The various reasons for divorces

56. The tone of this passage is

(A) emotional
(B) enthusiastic
(C) expository
(D) reactionary

GO ON TO THE NEXT PAGE

Questions 57–60

The idea of determinism, that no event occurs in nature without natural causes, has been postulated as a natural law yet is under attack on both scientific and philosophical grounds. Scientific laws assume that a specific set of conditions will unerringly lead to a predetermined outcome. However, studies in the field of physics have demonstrated that the location and speed of miniscule particles such as electrons are the result of random behaviors rather than predictable results determined by pre-existing conditions. As a result of these studies, the principle of indeterminacy was formulated in 1925 by Werner Heisenberg. According to this principle, only the probable behavior of an electron can be predicted. The inability to absolutely predict the behavior of electrons casts doubt on the universal applicability of a natural law of determinism. Philosophically, the principal opposition to determinism emanates from those who see man as a creature in possession of a free will. Human decisions may be influenced by previous events, but man's ultimate freedom may possibly lead him to an unforeseen choice, one not preordained by preceding events.

57. It is implied in the passage that a natural law

   (A) is something that applies to science only
   (B) can be incontrovertibly found in the idea of determinism
   (C) is philosophically unacceptable
   (D) is a principle to which there is no exception

58. The idea of determinism is refuted in this passage based on

   (A) scientific proof
   (B) data from the science and philosophy of determinism
   (C) principles or assumptions from different fields of study
   (D) philosophical doubt about man's free will

59. According to the passage, which of the following is NOT true about the principle of indeterminacy?

   (A) It was formulated based on studies in physics.
   (B) It is philosophically unacceptable.
   (C) It has been in existence for more than a decade.
   (D) It is concerned with the random behavior of electrons.

60. It is implied in the passage that free will is

   (A) accepted by all philosophers
   (B) a direct outcome of Werner's principle of indeterminacy
   (C) the antithesis of determinism
   (D) a natural law

THIS IS THE END OF SECTION 3

IF YOU FINISH BEFORE TIME IS CALLED, CHECK YOUR WORK
ON SECTION 3 ONLY.
DO NOT READ OR WORK ON ANY OTHER SECTION OF THE TEST.

STOP STOP STOP STOP STOP STOP STOP

VOCABULARY AND READING

The third section of the TOEFL is the Vocabulary and Reading Comprehension Section. This section consists of 60 questions (some tests may be longer). You have 45 minutes to complete the 60 questions in this section.

There are two types of questions in this section of the TOEFL:

1. **Vocabulary** (questions 1–30) consists of 30 sentences in which a word or group of words has been underlined. Each sentence is followed by four answer choices. You must choose the answer that is closest in meaning to the underlined word or words.
2. **Reading Comprehension** (questions 31–60) consists of five or six reading passages, each followed by a number of questions. The questions must be answered according to what is stated or implied in the passages.

It is up to you to decide how much of your time you will spend on vocabulary and how much on reading. The biggest mistake that students make in this section is to spend too much time on vocabulary (because it comes first) and not enough time on reading. Repeated experiments with students have demonstrated again and again that when students are given extra time to go over the Vocabulary section, they do not improve their scores; either they know the meaning of the word the first time they read the question or they do not.

However, when students are given extra time on the Reading Comprehension Section, their scores do improve. Therefore, the most important message to students for this section of the TOEFL is to **complete the Vocabulary section quickly and efficiently and move directly on to Reading Comprehension. Use any extra time to go over the reading questions.**

GENERAL STRATEGIES

1. **Begin with vocabulary questions 1–30.** Complete this section quickly and efficiently. You can do this by looking at the underlined word and the answers. You do not need to read the complete sentences carefully.

2. **Continue with reading questions 31–60.** Work slowly and carefully through the Reading Section.

3. **If you have time remaining, then return to the vocabulary questions.** You should return to the vocabulary questions only if you have spent all the time that you need on the reading questions.

4. **Never leave any questions blank on your answer sheet.** Even if you are unsure of the correct response, you should answer the question.

VOCABULARY SKILLS

Each vocabulary question consists of a sentence with an underlined word or group of words. This sentence is followed by four answer choices. You must choose the answer that is closest in meaning to the underlined word or group of words. You must also be sure not to change the meaning of the sentence.

Example

The earth is <u>divided</u> into two hemispheres.
(A) chopped
(B) joined
(C) separated
(D) mixed

Of the four answer choices, answer (C) *separated* is closest in meaning to the underlined word *divided*. Also, the sentence *The earth is **separated** into two hemispheres* has approximately the same meaning as *The earth is **divided** into two hemispheres*. Therefore, answer (C) is the best answer.

There are four ideas that you should remember while you are working on the vocabulary questions. These ideas will help you plan the best strategies for the vocabulary questions:

1. The questions progress from easy to difficult.
2. The vocabulary questions do not test grammar.
3. The context does not help very much and in fact is sometimes confusing.
4. You must be careful of second meanings of words.

Each of these ideas will be explained in detail in the following section.

1. **The questions progress from easy to difficult.**
Of the 30 questions in the Vocabulary Section, the first few questions are rather easy. The questions become progressively harder throughout the section, and the last few questions are extremely difficult. Unless your vocabulary is very strong, you should not expect to know the meanings of the last vocabulary words. You should answer each question (even if you do not know the meaning of a word) because there is no penalty for guessing on the TOEFL. However, do not make the mistake of spending too much time on the vocabulary, particularly on words that you do not know. If you spend a lot of time on the really difficult vocabulary questions, you will probably not get too many correct. Worse than that, you will use up valuable time that could be put to better use on the reading questions.

2. **The vocabulary questions do not test grammar.**
In the vocabulary questions the answer choices will always be the same part of speech as the underlined word or group of words. If the underlined word is a noun, then the four answer choices will all be nouns; if the underlined word is a verb, then the four answer choices will all be verbs. You will not have any questions in which you must choose between different parts of speech. The following example is a typical TOEFL vocabulary question.

Example

Disneyland <u>first</u> (an adverb) opened for business in 1955.
(A) later   (an adverb)
(B) originally   (an adverb)
(C) next   (an adverb)
(D) finally   (an adverb)

In this example, notice that the underlined word *first* is an adverb, and each of the answer choices are adverbs. The word that is closest in meaning to *first* is *originally*. Therefore, you should choose answer (B).

The next example shows what you will **not** see in the Vocabulary section of the TOEFL. You will not have any questions in which you must choose between different parts of speech.

An Example Of What You Will Not Find On The TOEFL

The shop was having financial <u>difficulties</u> (a noun) because of its huge inventory.
(A) worsen   (a verb)
(B) problems   (a noun)
(C) serious   (an adjective)
(D) terribly   (an adverb)

You will not find any examples in the Vocabulary section of the TOEFL in which you must choose a correct answer because it is the same part of speech as the underlined word. Therefore, do not waste your time looking at the grammatical construction of the sentences in the Vocabulary section.

3. **The context does not help much.**
The context of the TOEFL vocabulary questions does not help you very much to understand the underlined vocabulary word. In fact, the context is often designed to lead you to an incorrect answer.

Example

In the middle of the desert, they found a <u>refreshing</u> spring.
(A) hot
(B) dry
(C) sandy
(D) cooling

In this example, if you do not know the meaning of *refreshing*, you might look at the context and see the word *desert*. Since a desert is hot, dry, and sandy, you might choose answers (A), (B), or (C). However, the answer that is closest in meaning to *refreshing* is answer (D) *cooling*. Therefore, you should choose answer (D). You should not let yourself be confused by the mention of *desert* in the context around the underlined vocabulary word.

4. **Beware of second meanings.**
Words in English often have more than one meaning. The word *embrace,* for example, has a primary meaning of *hug,* but it can also mean *include.* In the Vocabulary section of the TOEFL, the primary meaning of a word can be an incorrect answer and a secondary meaning of that word can be the correct answer. (In this case, the immediate context can be of some help in determining which of several possible meanings is correct.)

Example

His essay <u>embraced</u> all the main points of his philosophy.
(A) hugged
(B) entertained
(C) interlaced
(D) included

Although *embraced* in some sentences can mean *hugged,* in this sentence it means *included.* Therefore, the best answer is (D).

STRATEGIES FOR THE VOCABULARY QUESTIONS

1. **Work quickly through the Vocabulary Section.** The questions progress from easy to difficult. Do not spend too much time on the difficult questions.

2. **Do not look for grammatical clues to help you decide which vocabulary word goes in the blank.** The Vocabulary Section does not test grammar.

3. **Do not spend a lot of time looking for contextual clues to the meanings of words.** The context usually doesn't help you understand the meaning of the word.

4. **Be careful of secondary meanings of words.** Words in English often have more than one meaning. The word "embrace," for example, has a primary meaning of "hug," but it can also mean "include." You must be aware that in the Vocabulary Section of the TOEFL, the primary meaning of a word can be an incorrect answer and a secondary meaning of that word can be the correct answer.

5. **Never leave any answers blank.** Be sure to answer every question in the Vocabulary Section even if you do not know the meanings of the words.

EXERCISE 1:   You should do this exercise two times.

First, do the exercise as quickly as possible. Look only at the underlined word and a few words around it to determine the context. Do not waste time by studying the rest of the sentence. Do not look at the grammatical construction of the sentence. You should complete the ten questions in this exercise in two minutes or less.

Then, look at the exercise a second time, but this time spend all the time that you want on each question. Study the context. Read and reread each sentence. Do you change your mind about the answers when you complete the exercise slowly, or do you choose the same answers regardless of how quickly or slowly you do the exercise?

1. When <u>viewed</u> from the earth, planets move in a westward direction through the sky.
   (A) reflected
   (B) seen
   (C) reconstructed
   (D) envisioned

2. The Appalachian Mountains run parallel to the Atlantic <u>shore</u>, from the Gulf of St. Lawrence to Alabama.
   (A) ocean
   (B) cliffs
   (C) islands
   (D) coast

3. Your eyes need <u>approximately</u> 20 to 30 minutes to adjust to darkness.
   (A) potentially
   (B) appropriately
   (C) roughly
   (D) exactly

4. <u>Prior to</u> the battle between the ironclad warships *Monitor* and *Merrimack* in 1862, warships had been constructed entirely of oak.
   (A) Upon
   (B) Because of
   (C) Before
   (D) With the advent of

5. Sir Francis Drake circumnavigated the <u>globe</u> from 1577 to 1580.
   (A) earth
   (B) continent
   (C) equator
   (D) latitude

6. During the nineteenth century, early chemists discovered more than half of the 100 <u>known</u> elements.
   (A) basic
   (B) recognized
   (C) saluted
   (D) met

7. A potato <u>consists of</u> 80 percent water, 17 percent starch, and 3 percent protein.
   (A) retains
   (B) thrives on
   (C) is composed of
   (D) is enhanced with

8. Magnolia is a family of trees and <u>shrubs</u> that are native to North America and Asia.
   (A) flowers
   (B) leaves
   (C) trunks
   (D) bushes

9. The peachtree is <u>native</u> to Georgia.
   (A) indigenous
   (B) transported
   (C) allocated
   (D) imported

10. Pearls come in various colors, but black pearls are generally <u>considered</u> the most valuable.
    (A) designated
    (B) deemed
    (C) classified as
    (D) appointed

When you have completed this exercise, you should begin to decide on a strategy to use on the Vocabulary section of the TOEFL. If you have the same number of correct answers when you work slowly or quickly, you should of course work very quickly in the Vocabulary section of the TOEFL. If you have more correct answers when you work more slowly, then it is of course to your advantage to work more slowly in this section of the TOEFL. However, remember that you need to work fairly quickly on the vocabulary questions so that you will have enough time for the reading comprehension questions.

EXERCISE 2:   Follow the same directions for this exercise that you used in Exercise 1.

1. The steamship *Clermont* made a trip from New York to Albany on the Hudson River on August 17, 1807.
   (A) voyage
   (B) distance
   (C) maneuver
   (D) vacation

2. The first U.S. census took 18 months to complete in spite of the fact that there were fewer than 4 million people living in the country.
   (A) as a result of
   (B) despite
   (C) because of
   (D) including

3. Shirley Chisholm is famous as the first black woman to be elected to the U.S. Congress.
   (A) disowned
   (B) renowned
   (C) proposed
   (D) recorded

4. The stars vary tremendously in size, brightness, and temperature.
   (A) advantageously
   (B) diversely
   (C) enormously
   (D) creatively

5. Emergency food and clothing are needed at the earthquake site.
   (A) location
   (B) center
   (C) shelter
   (D) damage

6. About one-third of Canada's people inhabit the province of Ontario.
   (A) inherit
   (B) reside in
   (C) depart from
   (D) are born in

7. A fluorescent lamp uses a much smaller amount of electricity than an incandescent lamp to produce a similar amount of light.
   (A) comparable
   (B) regular
   (C) simultaneous
   (D) gigantic

8. The false theory of spontaneous generation was disproved by Louis Pasteur.
   (A) sagacious
   (B) circumstantial
   (C) automatic
   (D) surreptitious

9. If severe hemorrhaging is not stopped, death can result in minutes.
   (A) coughing
   (B) trembling
   (C) paralysis
   (D) bleeding

10. After gold was discovered in California in 1848, the population there swelled.
    (A) retracted
    (B) acquiesced
    (C) curtailed
    (D) burgeoned

EXERCISE 3:   Follow the same directions in this exercise as you used in Exercise 1.

1. The Arctic tern breeds in the Arctic <u>regions</u> of North America and then migrates 17,000 kilometers to the waters of Antarctica.
   - (A) aspects
   - (B) areas
   - (C) islands
   - (D) marshes

2. Weather satellites can <u>monitor</u> the extent of the earth's snow and ice cover.
   - (A) check
   - (B) cut
   - (C) increase
   - (D) photograph

3. The Panama Canal, <u>linking</u> the Atlantic and Pacific oceans, was opened in 1914.
   - (A) joining
   - (B) closing
   - (C) crossing
   - (D) retaining

4. It is believed that the earth's core consists of iron and nickel oxides, <u>whereas</u> the crust is mainly granite.
   - (A) while
   - (B) or
   - (C) whenever
   - (D) whereby

5. Penicillin is widely used to <u>treat</u> bacterial infections.
   - (A) transmit
   - (B) repair
   - (C) deflect
   - (D) cure

6. Although fumes still escape from Mount Ranier's volcanic core, the volcano was <u>largely</u> formed a long time ago.
   - (A) hugely
   - (B) mainly
   - (C) repeatedly
   - (D) lengthily

7. The Peloponnesian War was a <u>series</u> of battles between the Greek city-states of Sparta and Athens.
   - (A) combination
   - (B) succession
   - (C) postponement
   - (D) forfeiture

8. Like the income statement, the statement of changes in retained earnings <u>refers to</u> a period of time rather than a single date.
   - (A) includes
   - (B) digests
   - (C) applies to
   - (D) selects

9. The highest <u>rank</u> in the United States army is that of general.
   - (A) grade
   - (B) commander
   - (C) appointment
   - (D) executive

10. Because of the moon's <u>weak</u> gravity, it has little or no atmosphere.
    - (A) potent
    - (B) feeble
    - (C) negative
    - (D) harmless

READING SKILLS

The Reading Comprehension Section of the TOEFL consists of five or six reading passages, each followed by four to eight questions. Topics of the reading passages are varied, but they are often informational subjects that might be studied in an American university: American history, literature, art, architecture, geology, geography, and astronomy, for example.

Time is definitely a factor in the Reading section. Many students who take the TOEFL note that they are unable to finish all the questions in this section. Therefore, you need to make the most efficient use of your time in this section to get the highest possible score.

The following method is the best way of attacking a reading passage and its accompanying questions to get the most questions correct in a limited amount of time:

STRATEGIES FOR THE READING PASSAGES

1. **Skim the reading passage to determine the main idea and the overall organization of ideas in the passage.** You do not need to understand every detail in each passage to answer the questions correctly. It is therefore a waste of time to read the passage with the intent of understanding every single detail before you try to answer the questions.

2. **Look ahead at the questions to determine what types of questions you must answer.** If you know the types of questions you must answer, you will know where to look in the passage to find the answers to the questions.

3. **Find the section of the passage that deals with each question.** If you understand the overall organization of ideas in the passage and you know what types of questions you must answer, you will know exactly where to look in the passage to find the correct answers. You can study the section of the passage that deals with each question thoroughly and carefully.

4. **Choose the best answer to each question from the four answer choices listed in your test booklet.** You can choose the best answer or answers according to what is given in the appropriate section of the passage, eliminate definitely wrong answers, and mark your best guess on the answer sheet.

The following skills will help you to implement these strategies in the Reading section.

212

LOOKING AHEAD AT THE READINGS _____

SKILL 1: RECOGNIZE THE OVERALL ORGANIZATION OF A PASSAGE

The first step when you come to a reading passage is to skim the passage. When you look ahead at a passage, you are looking for the main idea and the overall organization of details. TOEFL reading passages are generally very well organized, and the organization therefore is often easy to spot.

Because time is a factor in the Reading section, you do not have time to read and reread each passage. You do not have time to read a passage carefully, read the questions carefully, and then read the passage carefully again to find the answers to the questions. This is the method many students use, and it is the students who use this method of rereading the passages who do not have enough time to finish the Reading section.

Therefore, the first time you look at a reading passage, **do not read each detail carefully. Just look for the main idea and the overall organization of details.** You can probably find the main idea by looking for a topic sentence at the beginning of each paragraph. You can probably find the overall organization of details by skimming the passage for clues as to how the details are organized. Most (but not all) TOEFL passages have a very clear flow of ideas that can be spotted quickly.

Example

> There are two very common types of calendars, one determined by the sun and the other by the moon. The solar calendar is based on the solar year. Since the solar year is 365.2422 days long, solar calendars consist of regular years of 365 days and have an extra day every fourth year, or leap year, to make up for the additional fractional amount. In a solar calendar, the waxing and waning of the moon can take place at various stages of each month. The lunar calendar is synchronized to the lunar month rather than the solar year. Since the lunar month is twenty-nine and a half days long, most lunar calendars have alternating months of twenty-nine and thirty days. A twelve-month lunar year thus has 354 days, eleven days shorter than a solar year.

In this example you should start by reading the first sentence carefully because it is probably the topic sentence. Careful reading of this sentence indicates that this passage is about two very common types of calendars.

After you find the topic sentence and you understand that the passage is about two different types of calendars, you should pass your eyes quickly over the rest of the passage to determine how the details are organized. You are looking for *two very common types of calendars,* so it is easy to find the *solar calendar* (line 2) and the *lunar calendar* (line 6). You can therefore quickly recognize that this passage is organized in the following way:

- a topic sentence discussing two types of calendars
- three sentences about the solar calendar
- three sentences about the lunar calendar

EXERCISE 1:   Skim each passage looking for the main idea and the organization of details. (1) Circle the topic sentence(s). (2) Then underline any words that show you how the details are organized. The first one has been done for you.

PASSAGE ONE

The United States does not have a national university, but the idea has been around for quite some time. George Washington first recommended the idea to Congress; he even selected an actual site in Washington, D.C., and then left an endowment for the proposed national university in his will. During the century following the Revolution the idea of a national university continued to receive the support of various U.S. presidents, and philanthropist Andrew Carnegie pursued the cause at the beginning of the present century. Although the original idea has not yet been acted upon, it continues to be proposed in bills before Congress.

PASSAGE TWO

Within organizations, management may see conflict from one of two contrasting points of view. According to the traditional view of conflict, all conflict is harmful to an organization. Managers with this traditional view of conflict see it as their role in an organization to rid the organization of any possible sources of conflict. The interactionist view of conflict, on the other hand, holds that conflict can serve an important function in an organization by reducing complacency among workers and causing positive changes to occur. Managers who hold an interactionist view of conflict may actually take steps to stimulate conflict within the organization.

PASSAGE THREE

Chamber music received its name because it was originally intended to be performed in small rooms in private homes rather than huge concert halls or theaters. Today it has evolved into small ensemble music in which each performer in the ensemble plays an individual part. The compositions written for this type of performance can easily be classified into three distinct periods, each with its style of music and instrumentation. In the earliest period (1450–1650), the viol and other instrumental families developed considerably, and instrumental music took its first steps toward equal footing with vocal music. In the second period (1650–1750), trio sonatas dominated. These ensemble compositions were often written for two violins and a cello; the harpsichord was also featured in various compositions of this period. In the modern period (after 1750), the preponderance of chamber music was written for the string quartet, an ensemble composed of two violins, a viola, and a cello.

PASSAGE FOUR

Vaccines are prepared from harmful viruses or bacteria and administered to patients to provide immunity to specific diseases. The various types of vaccines are classified according to the method by which they are derived.

The most basic class of vaccines actually contains disease-causing micro-organisms that have been killed with a solution containing formaldehyde. In this type of vaccine, the microorganisms are dead and therefore cannot cause disease; however, the antigens found in and on the microorganisms can still stimulate the formation of antibodies. Examples of this type of vaccine are those that fight influenza, typhoid fever, and cholera.

A second type of vaccine contains the toxins produced by the microorganisms rather than the microorganisms themselves. This type of vaccine is prepared when the microorganism itself does little damage but the toxin with the microorganism is extremely harmful. For example, the bacteria that cause diphtheria can thrive in the throat without much harm, but when toxins are released from the bacteria, muscles can become paralyzed and death can ensue.

A final type of vaccine contains living microorganisms that have been rendered harmless. With this type of vaccine, a large number of antigen molecules are produced and the immunity that results is generally longer lasting than the immunity from other types of vaccines. The Sabin oral antipolio vaccine and the BCG vaccine against tuberculosis are examples of this type of vaccine.

SKILL 2:   RECOGNIZE THE DIFFERENT TYPES OF QUESTIONS

There are four types of questions about the reading passages. It is important to recognize the various types because you will use a different strategy to find the correct answer to each of them. In this skill you will practice recognizing the various types of questions and learn strategies for answering them. TOEFL reading questions can be classified in the following way:

	DIRECTLY ANSWERED QUESTIONS	INDIRECTLY ANSWERED QUESTIONS
ABOUT THE WHOLE PASSAGE	What is the *main idea?* What is the *topic?* What is the *subject?* What is the best *title?*	What is the *tone?* What is the *author's purpose?* In which *course* . . . ? The passage *suggests* that . . .
ABOUT PART OF THE PASSAGE	*According to the passage* . . . It is *indicated* that . . . It is *stated* that . . . Which is *not* true?	It can be *inferred* that . . . It is *implied* that . . . What *most likely* happened? What does this *word* mean? What *probably* came before/later?

Questions about the main idea, topic, subject, or title are classified as **directly answered** in the passage in this classification system. This is because the great majority of TOEFL passages begin with a topic sentence, so that questions about the main idea, topic, subject, or title are considered to be directly answered in the topic sentence.

When you first look at a question in the reading section, you should think about what type of question it is. You should ask yourself if it is about the whole passage or only part of the passage. You should ask yourself if it is directly or indirectly answered in the passage.

Example

You will read the question:
  What is the topic of this passage?

You will ask yourself:
  1. Is this question about the whole passage or just one part of the passage? (It is asking about the whole passage, not just one detail.)
  2. Is this question answered directly or indirectly in the passage? (It is probably answered directly in the main idea or topic sentence of the passage.)

EXERCISE 2:   Study each of the following questions from reading passages. First, mark if the question is about the whole passage or one part of the passage. Then, mark if the question will probably be answered directly or indirectly in the passage. Underline any words that help you to answer these questions. The first one has been done for you.

  1. <u>According to the passage</u>, what is the average number of students per class at the university?

      This question is about   (a) _____ the whole passage
                                     (b) _✓_ part of the passage
      This question is answered   (c) _✓_ directly in the passage
                                     (d) _____ indirectly in the passage

  2. It can be inferred from the passage that the author approves of which of the following?

      This question is about   (a) _____ the whole passage
                                     (b) _____ part of the passage
      This question is answered   (c) _____ directly in the passage
                                     (d) _____ indirectly in the passage

  3. Which of the following best states the main idea of the passage?

      This question is about   (a) _____ the whole passage
                                     (b) _____ part of the passage
      This question is answered   (c) _____ directly in the passage
                                     (d) _____ indirectly in the passage

  4. It is stated in the passage that the sleep cycle of a carnivorous animal is . . .

      This question is about   (a) _____ the whole passage
                                     (b) _____ part of the passage
      This question is answered   (c) _____ directly in the passage
                                     (d) _____ indirectly in the passage

5. The word "adhocracy" (line 2) is closest in meaning to which of the following words?

This question is about   (a) _____ the whole passage
                          (b) _____ part of the passage
This question is answered (c) _____ directly in the passage
                          (d) _____ indirectly in the passage

6. What is the author's purpose in this passage?

This question is about   (a) _____ the whole passage
                          (b) _____ part of the passage
This question is answered (c) _____ directly in the passage
                          (d) _____ indirectly in the passage

7. Which of the following is implied in the passage about the role of women in factories during the war?

This question is about   (a) _____ the whole passage
                          (b) _____ part of the passage
This question is answered (c) _____ directly in the passage
                          (d) _____ indirectly in the passage

8. This passage would probably be assigned reading in which course?

This question is about   (a) _____ the whole passage
                          (b) _____ part of the passage
This question is answered (c) _____ directly in the passage
                          (d) _____ indirectly in the passage

9. Which of the following best describes the tone of this passage?

This question is about   (a) _____ the whole passage
                          (b) _____ part of the passage
This question is answered (c) _____ directly in the passage
                          (d) _____ indirectly in the passage

10. The passage indicates that which species is almost extinct?

This question is about   (a) _____ the whole passage
                          (b) _____ part of the passage
This question is answered (c) _____ directly in the passage
                          (d) _____ indirectly in the passage

ANSWERING DIFFERENT TYPES OF QUESTIONS

SKILL 3: FIND DIRECT ANSWERS ABOUT THE WHOLE PASSAGE

Some questions in the Reading section ask about the passage as a whole rather than just one small detail of the passage, and these questions can often be answered by carefully studying the topic sentence of the paragraph. The following are examples of this kind of question.

QUESTIONS ABOUT THE TOPIC OF THE PASSAGE

- WHAT IS THE TOPIC OF THIS PASSAGE?
- WHAT IS THE SUBJECT OF THIS PASSAGE?
- WHAT DOES THIS PASSAGE MAINLY DISCUSS?

If a question asks about the topic or subject of a passage, it is asking about what is discussed throughout the passage.

QUESTIONS ABOUT THE MAIN IDEA OF THE PASSAGE

- WHAT IS THE MAIN IDEA OF THE PASSAGE?
- WHAT IS THE AUTHOR'S MAIN POINT IN THIS PASSAGE?

A question about the main idea of a passage is a little more involved than a question about the topic. The main idea of a passage is the topic of a passage and the author's idea about that topic. For example, if the topic of a passage is George Washington's childhood, then the main idea might be that George Washington's childhood was happy or that George Washington's childhood had a profound effect on George's later career.

QUESTIONS ABOUT THE TITLE OF THE PASSAGE

- WHICH OF THE FOLLOWING WOULD BE THE BEST TITLE?

A question about the best title for a passage is asking almost the same information as a topic question, but it is written as a title with capital letters. For example, if the topic of a passage is George Washington's childhood, then the best title for the passage might be *George Washington's Childhood* or *The Childhood of the First American President*.

STRATEGIES FOR ANSWERING DIRECT QUESTIONS ABOUT THE WHOLE PASSAGE

All of these kinds of questions are asking for the same type of information: they are asking for information about the passage as a whole. When you answer these kinds of questions, you should remember that (1) information about the whole passage is generally given in the first sentence (the topic sentence) of each paragraph, and (2) the incorrect answers are often true details from the passage. The following strategies work best for questions about the topic, main idea, or title.

STRATEGIES: DIRECT QUESTIONS ABOUT THE WHOLE PASSAGE

1. Read the first sentence of each paragraph carefully to determine the topic and main idea of the passage.

2. Pass your eyes quickly over the rest of the passage to check that the first sentence is the topic sentence of the passage.

3. Eliminate any definitely wrong answers and choose the best of the remaining ones.

Example One

In the philosophy of John Dewey a sharp distinction is made between "intelligence" and "reasoning." According to Dewey, intelligence is the only absolute way to achieve a balance between realism and idealism, between practicality and wisdom of life. Intelligence involves "interacting with other things and knowing them," while reasoning is merely the act of an observer, ". . . a mind that beholds or grasps objects outside the world of things. . . ." With reasoning, a level of mental certainty can be achieved, but it is through intelligence that control is taken of events that shape one's life.

What is the topic of this passage?

(A) The intelligence of John Dewey
(B) Distinctions made by John Dewey
(C) Dewey's ideas on the ability to reason
(D) How intelligence differs from reasoning in Dewey's works

When you are looking for the topic of a passage with only one paragraph, you should read the first sentence of the passage carefully because it is probably a topic sentence. The first sentence of this passage discusses a distinction between the ideas of "intelligence" and "reasoning" in the philosophy of John Dewey, so this is probably the topic. A quick check of the rest of the sentences in the passage confirms that the topic is in fact the difference between "intelligence" and "reasoning."

Now you should check each of the answers to determine which one comes closest to the topic you have determined. Answer (A) mentions only intelligence, so it is not the topic. Answer (B) is too general: it mentions distinctions that John Dewey makes, but it does not say specifically what type of distinctions. Answer (C) mentions only reasoning, when the passage discusses a distinction between reasoning and intelligence, so answer (C) is incomplete. The best answer is therefore (D); the idea of **how intelligence differs from reasoning** comes from the first sentence of the passage, which mentions *a sharp distinction . . . between "intelligence" and "reasoning."*

Example Two

Nitrogen fixation is a process by which additional nitrogen is continuously fed into biological circulation. In this process, certain algae and bacteria convert nitrogen into ammonia (NH_3). This newly created ammonia is then for the most part absorbed by plants.
The opposite process of denitrification returns nitrogen to the air. During the process of denitrification, bacteria cause some of the nitrates from the soil to convert into gaseous nitrogen or nitrous oxide (N_2O). In this gaseous form the nitrogen returns to the atmosphere.

Which of the following would be the best title for this passage?

(A) The Process of Nitrogen Fixation
(B) Two Nitrogen Processes
(C) The Return of Nitrogen to the Air
(D) The Effects of Nitrogen on Plant Life

In a passage with more than one paragraph, you should be sure to read the first sentence of each paragraph to determine the subject, title, or main idea. In Example Two, the first sentence of the first paragraph indicates that the first paragraph is about the process of nitrogen fixation. If you look only at the first paragraph, you might choose the incorrect answer (A), which would be a good title for the first paragraph only. The first sentence of the second paragraph indicates that the process of denitrification is discussed in the second paragraph. Answer (C) is incorrect because **the return of nitrogen to the air** is the process of denitrification, and this is discussed in the second paragraph only. Answer (D) is incorrect because **the effects of nitrogen on plant life** is not discussed in this passage. The best answer to this question is answer (B); the two nitrogen processes are nitrogen fixation, which is discussed in the first paragraph, and denitrification, which is discussed in the second paragraph.

EXERCISE 3:   Study each of the passages and choose the best answers to the questions that follow. In this exercise, each paragraph is followed by *two* main idea, topic, or title questions so that the students can practice this type of question. On the TOEFL one paragraph would probably not have two such questions because they are so similar.

PASSAGE ONE (Questions 1–2)

Fort Knox, Kentucky, is the site of a U.S. army post, but it is even more renowned for the Fort Knox Bullion Depository, the massive vault that contains the bulk of the U.S. government's gold deposits. Completed in 1936, the vault is housed in a two-story building constructed of granite, steel, and concrete; the vault itself is made of steel and concrete and has a door that weighs more than twenty tons. Naturally, the most up-to-date security devices available are in place at Fort Knox, and the army post nearby provides further protection.

1. Which of the following best describes the topic of the passage?
    (A) The city of Fort Knox, Kentucky
    (B) The federal gold depository
    (C) The U.S. army post at Fort Knox
    (D) Gold bullion

2. Which of the following would be the best title for this passage?
    (A) The Massive Concrete Vault
    (B) Fort Knox Security
    (C) Where the U.S. Keeps Its Gold
    (D) A Visit to Kentucky

PASSAGE TWO (Questions 3–4)

One identifying characteristic of minerals is their relative hardness, which can be determined by scratching one mineral with another. In this type of test, a harder mineral can scratch a softer one, but a softer mineral is unable to scratch the harder one. The Mohs' hardness scale is used to rank minerals according to hardness. Ten minerals are listed in this scale, ranging from talc with a hardness of 1 to diamond with a hardness of 10. On this scale, quartz (number 7) is harder than feldspar (number 6) and is therefore able to scratch it; however, feldspar is unable to make a mark on quartz.

3. Which of the following best describes the subject of this passage?
   (A) The hardness of diamonds
   (B) Identifying minerals by means of a scratch test
   (C) Feldspar on the Mohs' scale
   (D) Recognizing minerals in their natural state

4. The main idea of this passage is that
   (A) the hardness of a mineral can be determined by its ability to make a mark on other minerals
   (B) diamonds, with a hardness of 10 on the Mohs' scale, can scratch all other minerals
   (C) a softer mineral cannot be scratched by a harder mineral
   (D) talc is the first mineral listed on the Mohs' scale

PASSAGE THREE (Questions 5–6)

Hurricanes generally occur in the North Atlantic from May through November, with the peak of the hurricane season in September; only rarely will they occur December through April in that part of the ocean. The main reason for the occurrence of hurricanes during this period is that the temperature on the water's surface is at its warmest and the humidity of the air is at its highest.

Of the tropical storms that occur each year in the North Atlantic, only about five, on the average, are powerful enough to be called hurricanes. To be classified as a hurricane, a tropical storm must have winds reaching speeds of at least 117 kilometers per hour, but the winds are often much stronger than that; the winds of intense hurricanes can easily surpass 240 kilometers per hour.

5. This passage mainly discusses
   (A) how many hurricanes occur each year
   (B) the strength of hurricanes
   (C) the weather in the North Atlantic
   (D) hurricanes in one part of the world

6. The best title for this passage would be
   (A) The North Atlantic Ocean
   (B) Storms of the Northern Atlantic
   (C) Hurricanes: the Damage and Destruction
   (D) What Happens May through November

PASSAGE FOUR (Questions 7–8)

A hoax, unlike an honest error, is a deliberately concocted plan to present an untruth as the truth. It can take the form of a fraud, a fake, a swindle, or a forgery, and can be accomplished in almost any field: successful hoaxes have been foisted on the public in fields as varied as politics, religion, science, art, and literature.

A famous scientific hoax occurred in 1912 when Charles Dawson claimed to have uncovered a human skull and jawbone on the Piltdown Common in southern England. These human remains were said to be more than 500,000 years old and were unlike any other remains from that period; as such they represented an important discovery in the study of human evolution. These remains, popularly known as the Piltdown Man and scientifically named *Eoanthropus dawsoni* after their discoverer, confounded scientists for more than forty years. Finally in 1953 a chemical analysis was used to date the bones, and it was found that the bones were modern bones that had been skillfully aged. A further twist to the hoax was that the skull belonged to a human and the jaws to an orangutan.

7. The topic of this passage could best be described as
   (A) the Piltdown Man
   (B) Charles Dawson's discovery
   (C) *Eoanthropus dawsoni*
   (D) a definition and example of a hoax

8. The author's main point is that
   (A) various types of hoaxes have been perpetrated
   (B) Charles Dawson discovered a human skull and jawbone
   (C) Charles Dawson was not an honest man
   (D) the human skull and jawbone were extremely old

SKILL 4:   FIND DIRECT ANSWERS ABOUT PART OF THE PASSAGE

Many questions in the Reading section of the TOEFL ask about one small part of the passage rather than the passage as a whole. This means that you can find the answers directly in the passage. The following are examples of this type of question:

QUESTIONS ABOUT WHAT IS IN THE PASSAGE

- ACCORDING TO THE PASSAGE . . .
- IT IS STATED IN THE PASSAGE THAT . . .

This type of question asks for information that is explicitly given in the passage. The answers to these questions are generally given in order in the passage, and the correct answer is often a restatement of what is given in the passage. This means that the correct answer often expresses the same idea as what is written in the passage, but the words are not exactly the same. For example, if the passage states that *George Washington's family was rich,* then the correct answer to a question about the financial status of Washington's family might state that *his relatives were wealthy.*

QUESTIONS ABOUT WHAT IS NOT IN THE PASSAGE

- WHICH OF THE FOLLOWING IS **NOT** TRUE?
- WHICH OF THE FOLLOWING IS **NOT** STATED IN THE PASSAGE?
- ALL OF THE FOLLOWING ARE TRUE EXCEPT . . .

This type of question asks about what is not in the passage or what is not true according to the passage. In this type of question, three of the answers are true and one of the answers is not mentioned in the passage or is not true according to the passage. The correct answer is the answer that is **not** true or that is **not** mentioned in the passage. Many students, however, will make a mistake and choose one of the true answers.

STRATEGIES FOR ANSWERING DIRECT QUESTIONS ABOUT PART OF THE PASSAGE

When answering this type of question, you should remember that (1) these detail questions are generally answered in order in the passage, and (2) the correct answers can use exactly the same words as the passage but generally are **restatements** of what is said. The following method works best for questions about what is or is not in the passage.

STRATEGIES: DIRECT QUESTIONS ABOUT PART OF THE PASSAGE

1. Decide where to look in the passage for the correct answer, based on your understanding of the organization of details in the passage and the knowledge that questions are generally answered in order in the passage.

2. Eliminate any definitely wrong answers and choose the best of the remaining ones.

3. If the question says **NOT** or **EXCEPT**, choose the answer that is not true or not stated in the passage. Answers that are true according to the passage are not correct in this type of question.

Example

> Williamsburg is a historic city in Virginia situated on a peninsula between two rivers, the York and the James. It was settled by English colonists in 1633, twenty-six years after the first permanent English colony in America was settled at Jamestown. In the beginning the colony at Williamsburg was named Middle Plantation because of its location in the middle of the peninsula. The site for Williamsburg had been selected by the colonists because the soil drainage was better there than at the Jamestown location, and there were fewer mosquitoes.

1. According to the passage, Williamsburg is located

   (A) on an island
   (B) in the middle of a river
   (C) where the York and the James meet
   (D) on a piece of land with rivers on two sides

The answers to questions are generally found in order in the passage, so you should look for the answer to the first question near the beginning of the passage. Since the question asks about where *Williamsburg is located,* you should see that the first sentence in the passage answers the question because *situated* means *located.* Answer (A) is an incorrect answer because Williamsburg is not located on an island; the passage states that it is *situated on a peninsula.* Answer (B) is incorrect because Williamsburg is *between two rivers,* not *in the middle of a river.* Answer (C) is incorrect because the passage says nothing about whether or not the two rivers meet at Williamsburg. The best answer to this question is answer (D); *rivers on two sides* is closest in meaning to *between two rivers.*

2. The passage states that the name Middle Plantation

   (A) is a more recent name than Williamsburg
   (B) derived from the location of the colony on the peninsula
   (C) refers to the middle part of England that was home to the colonists
   (D) was given to the new colony because it was located in the middle of several
        plantations

The answer to the second question will probably be located in the passage after the answer to the first question. Because the question is about *the name Middle Plantation,* you should skim through the passage to find the part that discusses this topic. The answer to this passage is found in the statement *Williamsburg was named Middle Plantation because of its location in the middle of the peninsula.* Answer (B) is correct because it is closest in meaning to this statement. Answer (A) is incorrect because it is false; the area was named Middle Plantation *in the beginning,* and the name Williamsburg is *more recent.* Answer (C) is incorrect because the passage says nothing about naming the area after the colonists' home in England. Answer (D) is incorrect because the passage says nothing about any other plantations in the area of Williamsburg.

3. Which of the following is NOT true, according to the passage?

   (A) Jamestown was settled before Williamsburg.
   (B) Williamsburg was settled by English colonists.
   (C) Soil drainage was not as good at Jamestown as at Williamsburg.
   (D) There were more mosquitoes at Williamsburg than at Jamestown.

In a question about what is **not** true, three of the answers are true and only one is **not** true; the correct answer is the one that is **not** true. Answer (A) is true because the passage states that Williamsburg *was settled . . . twenty-six years after the . . . colony . . . at Jamestown.* Since answer (A) is true, it is not correct. Answer (B) is also true because the passage clearly states that Williamsburg *was settled by English colonists.* Since answer (B) is true, it is not correct. Answer (C) is true because the passage states that *soil drainage was better* at Williamsburg *than at the Jamestown location.* Since answer (C) is true, it is not correct. The best answer to this question is answer (D) because it is **not** true: according to the passage *there were fewer mosquitoes* at Williamsburg than at Jamestown.

EXERCISE 4: Study each passage and choose the best answers to the questions that follow.

PASSAGE ONE (Questions 1–3)

Ice ages, those periods when ice covered extensive areas of the earth, are known to have occurred at least six times. Past ice ages can be recognized from rock strata that show evidence of foreign materials deposited by moving walls of ice or melting glaciers. Ice ages can also be recognized from land formations that have been produced from moving walls of ice, such as U-shaped valleys, sculptured landscapes, and polished rock faces.

1. According to the passage, what happens during an ice age?
    (A) Rock strata are recognized by geologists.
    (B) Evidence of foreign materials is found.
    (C) Ice covers a large portion of the earth's surface.
    (D) Ice melts six times.

2. The passage covers how many different methods of recognizing past ice ages?
    (A) One
    (B) Two
    (C) Three
    (D) Four

3. According to the passage, what in the rock strata is a clue to geologists of a past ice age?
    (A) Ice
    (B) Melting glaciers
    (C) U-shaped valleys
    (D) Substances from other areas

PASSAGE TWO (Questions 4–6)

The human heart is divided into four chambers, each of which serves its own function in the cycle of pumping blood. The atria are the thin-walled upper chambers that gather blood as it flows from the veins between heartbeats. The ventricles are the thick-walled lower chambers that receive blood from the atria and push it into the arteries with each contraction of the heart. The left atrium and ventricle work separately from those on the right. The role of the chambers on the right side of the heart is to receive oxygen-depleted blood from the body tissues and send it on to the lungs; the chambers on the left side of the heart then receive the oxygen-enriched blood from the lungs and send it back out to the body tissues.

4. All of the following are true about ventricles EXCEPT that
    (A) they have relatively thick walls.
    (B) they send blood to the atria.
    (C) they are lower than the atria.
    (D) there are two ventricles, a right one and a left one.

5. When is blood pushed into the arteries from the ventricles?
    (A) As the heart beats
    (B) Between heartbeats
    (C) Before each contraction of the heart
    (D) Before it is received by the atria

6. According to the passage, which part of the heart gets blood from the body tissues and passes it on to the lungs?
    (A) The atria
    (B) The ventricles
    (C) The right atrium and ventricle
    (D) The left atrium and ventricle

PASSAGE THREE (Questions 7–9)

The Golden Age of railroads refers to the period from the end of the Civil War to the beginning of World War I when railroads flourished and in fact maintained a near monopoly in mass transportation in the United States. One of the significant developments during the period was the notable increase in uniformity, particularly through the standardization of track gauge and time.

At the end of the Civil War, only about half of the nation's railroad track was laid at what is now the standard gauge of 1.4 meters; much of the rest, particularly in southern states, had a 1.5-meter gauge. During the post-war years tracks were converted to the 1.4-meter gauge, and by June 1, 1886, the standardization of tracks was completed, resulting in increased efficiency and economy in the rail system.

A further boon to railroad efficiency was the implementation of Standard Time in 1883. With the adoption of Standard Time, four time zones were established across the country, thus simplifying railroad scheduling and improving the efficiency of railroad service.

7. Which of the following is NOT true about the Golden Age of railroads, according to the passage?
    (A) It occurred prior to the first World War.
    (B) Most of U.S. mass transportation was controlled by the railroads.
    (C) Track gauge was standardized before the Golden Age of railroads.
    (D) Standard Time was implemented during the Golden Age of railroads.

8. According to the passage, the establishment of uniformity of track gauge resulted in which of the following?
    (A) The Civil War
    (B) Improved economy in the transportation system
    (C) Standardization of time zones
    (D) Railroad schedules

9. According to the passage, when was Standard Time implemented in the United States?
    (A) Before the Civil War
    (B) On June 1, 1886
    (C) After World War I
    (D) Before standardized track gauge was established throughout the U.S.

REVIEW EXERCISE (SKILLS 1–4): Study each of the passages and choose the best answers to the questions that follow.

PASSAGE ONE (Questions 1–4)

Lincoln's now famous Gettysburg Address was not, on the occasion of its delivery, recognized as the masterpiece it is today. Lincoln was not even the primary speaker at the ceremonies, held at the height of the Civil War in 1863, to dedicate the battlefield at Gettysburg. The main speaker was orator Edward Everett, whose two-hour speech was followed by Lincoln's shorter remarks. Lincoln began his small portion of the program with words that today are immediately recognized by most Americans: "Four score and seven years ago our fathers brought forth on this continent a new nation, conceived in liberty and dedicated to the proposition that all men are created equal." At the time of the speech, little notice was given to what Lincoln had said, and Lincoln considered his appearance at the ceremonies rather unsuccessful. It was after his speech appeared in print that it began receiving the growing recognition that today places it among the greatest speeches of all time.

1. The main idea of this passage is that
   (A) the Gettysburg Address has always been regarded as a masterpiece
   (B) at the time of its delivery the Gettysburg Address was truly appreciated as a masterpiece
   (C) it was not until sometime after 1863 that Lincoln's speech at Gettysburg took its place in history
   (D) Lincoln is better recognized today than he was at the time of his presidency

2. Which of the following is true about the ceremonies at Gettysburg during the Civil War?
   (A) Lincoln was the main speaker.
   (B) Lincoln gave a two-hour speech.
   (C) Lincoln was the opening speaker of the ceremonies.
   (D) Lincoln's first public words were: "Four score and seven years ago. . . ."

3. According to the passage, when Lincoln spoke at the Gettysburg ceremonies,
   (A) his words were immediately recognized by most Americans
   (B) he spoke for only a short period of time
   (C) he was enthusiastically cheered
   (D) he was extremely proud of his performance

4. When did Lincoln's Gettysburg Address begin to receive public acclaim?
   (A) After it had been published
   (B) Immediately after the speech
   (C) Not until the present day
   (D) After Lincoln received growing recognition

PASSAGE TWO (Questions 5–8)

Hay fever is a seasonal allergy to pollens; the term hay fever, however, is a less than adequate description since an attack of this allergy does not incur fever and since such an attack can be brought on by sources other than hay-producing grasses. Hay fever is generally caused by air-borne pollens, particularly ragweed pollen. The amount of pollen in the air is largely dependent on geographical location, weather, and season. In the eastern section of the United States, for example, there are generally three periods when pollen from various sources can cause intense hay fever suffering: in the springtime months of March and April when pollen from trees is prevalent, in the summer months of June and July when grass pollen fills the air, and at the end of August when ragweed pollen is at its most concentrated levels.

5. Which of the following would be the best title for the passage?
   (A) The Relationship Between Season and Allergies
   (B) Misconceptions and Facts about Hay Fever
   (C) Hay Fever in the Eastern U.S.
   (D) How Ragweed Causes Hay Fever

6. According to the passage, which of the following helps to explain why the term hay fever is somewhat of a misnomer?
   (A) A strong fever occurs after an attack.
   (B) The amount of pollen in the air depends on geographical location.
   (C) Hay fever is often caused by ragweed.
   (D) Grass pollen is prevalent in June and July.

7. Which of the following is NOT discussed in the passage as a determining factor of the amount of pollen in the air?
   (A) Place
   (B) Climate
   (C) Time of year
   (D) Altitude

8. Which of the following is NOT true about hay fever in the eastern U.S.?
   (A) Suffering from hay fever is equally severe year-round.
   (B) Pollen from trees causes hay fever suffering in the spring.
   (C) Grass pollen fills the air earlier in the year than ragweed pollen.
   (D) Ragweed pollen is most prevalent at the end of the summer.

PASSAGE THREE (Questions 9–12)

According to the theory of continental drift, the continents are not fixed in position but instead move slowly across the surface of the earth, constantly changing in position relative to one another. This theory was first proposed in the eighteenth century when mapmakers noticed how closely the continents of the earth fit together when matched up. It was suggested then that the present-day continents had once been one large continent that had broken up into pieces which drifted apart.

Today the modern theory of plate tectonics has developed from the theory of continental drift. The theory of plate tectonics suggests that the crust of the earth is divided into six large, and many small, tectonic plates that drift on the lava that composes the inner core of the earth. These plates consist of ocean floor and continents that quite probably began breaking up and moving relative to one another more than 200 million years ago.

9. The topic of this passage is
    (A) continental drift
    (B) the theory of plate tectonics
    (C) the development of ideas about the movement of the earth's surface
    (D) eighteenth-century mapmakers

10. The passage states that the theory of continental drift developed as a result of
    (A) the fixed positions of the continents
    (B) the work of mapmakers
    (C) the rapid movement of continents
    (D) the fit of the earth's plates

11. Which of the following is NOT true about the theory of plate tectonics?
    (A) It is not as old as the theory of continental drift.
    (B) It evolved from the theory of continental drift.
    (C) It postulates that the earth's surface is separated into plates.
    (D) It was proposed by mapmakers.

12. According to the passage, what constitutes a tectonic plate?
    (A) The inner core of the earth
    (B) Only the continents
    (C) Lava
    (D) The surface of the land and the floor of the oceans

SKILL 5: FIND INDIRECT ANSWERS ABOUT PART OF THE PASSAGE

Some questions will ask for answers that are not given directly in the passage. To answer these questions correctly, you will have to draw conclusions from information that is given in the passage. These questions can be about the whole passage (as in Skill 6), or they can be about only one small part of the passage. The following are examples of indirectly answered questions about only part of the passage:

QUESTIONS ABOUT WHAT IS IMPLIED IN THE PASSAGE

- IT IS IMPLIED IN THE PASSAGE THAT . . .
- THE AUTHOR INFERS THAT . . .
- IT IS MOST LIKELY THAT . . .
- WHAT PROBABLY HAPPENED . . .

The words *implied, inferred, most likely,* or *probably* are clues to you that the question is not answered directly in the passage. To answer such a question, you will have to draw a conclusion from something in the passage. For example, if the passage states that George Washington attended private schools, owned five horses, and enjoyed wearing the latest fashions, you could draw the conclusion that he was rich even though the passage does not say so directly.

Keep in mind when you are looking for some information to help you answer this type of question that the questions in the Reading section of the TOEFL are generally answered in order in the passage. For example, if the answer to question 35 is implied in the passage, the information that will help you answer this question will come in the passage after the answer to question 34 and before the answer to question 36.

QUESTIONS ABOUT THE MEANINGS OF VOCABULARY WORDS

- THE WORD "INEVITABLE" IN LINE 6 MEANS . . .

A question about the meaning of a particular vocabulary word is generally not answered directly in the Reading section of the TOEFL. For this type of question you must draw a conclusion about the meaning of the word from information in the passage. For example, the passage might state that *George Washington was very disheartened during the long winter at Valley Forge because of the tremendous losses his troops had suffered,* and the question might ask the meaning of the word *disheartened.* To answer this question, you should study the context around the word that is being tested. The sentence indicates that Washington's troops had suffered tremendous losses, so Washington probably felt discouraged. The word *disheartened* means *discouraged.*

QUESTIONS ABOUT WHAT COMES BEFORE OR AFTER THE PASSAGE

- WHAT INFORMATION IS PROBABLY IN THE PARAGRAPH PRECEDING THE PASSAGE?
- THE PARAGRAPH FOLLOWING THE PASSAGE MOST LIKELY CONTAINS WHAT INFORMATION?

A question about what probably came before the passage or what most likely comes next in the passage is not answered directly in the passage. You can draw a conclusion from the information in the passage to answer this type of question.

To answer a question about what probably came before this passage, you should look at the beginning of the passage: the first sentence of the passage is probably a transition from the previous paragraph and will tell you what probably came before. For example, perhaps a passage begins with *after serving as the Commander-in-Chief of the Revolutionary forces, George Washington was elected as the first President of the United States.* This probably means that the previous paragraph was about how George Washington served as Commander-in-Chief of the Revolutionary forces and the passage that follows is about his election as the first U.S. president.

To answer a question about what probably comes after the passage, you should look at the end of the passage: the last sentence is probably a transition from this passage to the next paragraph. For example, a passage might end with *after his election to the presidency, George Washington began looking for new ways to strengthen the young nation.* The next paragraph is probably about George Washington's new ways to strengthen the young nation.

STRATEGIES FOR ANSWERING INDIRECT QUESTIONS ABOUT PART OF THE PASSAGE

For this type of question you should remember that (1) *implied, inferred, most likely,* and *probably* are clues that the question is not answered directly in the passage, and (2) the questions are generally answered in order in the passage.

STRATEGIES:
INDIRECT QUESTIONS ABOUT PART OF THE PASSAGE

1. Decide where to look in the passage for the correct answer based on your understanding of the organization of details in the passage and the knowledge that questions are generally answered in order in the passage.

2. Draw a conclusion from the information that is given to answer the question. Do not expect to find a direct answer to the question.

Example

Another program instrumental in the popularization of science was *Cosmos.* This series, broadcast on public television, dealt with topics and issues from varied fields of science. The principal writer and narrator of the program was Carl Sagan, a noted astronomer and Pulitzer Prize winning author.

1. The paragraph preceding this passage most probably discusses

   (A) a different scientific television series
   (B) Carl Sagan's scientific achievements
   (C) the Pulitzer Prize won by Carl Sagan
   (D) public television

A question about what probably came **before** the passage is generally answered in the **beginning** of the passage; you should therefore carefully study the first line of this passage to answer the question. Since this passage about the scientific television program *Cosmos* begins with *another program,* it should be clear that the paragraph preceding this passage probably discusses another scientific television program. Therefore the best answer to this question is answer (A).

2. The word "issues" (line 2) is closest in meaning to which of the following words?

   (A) Editions
   (B) Volumes
   (C) Solutions
   (D) Matters of public concern

A question about the meaning of a vocabulary word is generally not answered directly in the passage; you must instead determine as much as you can about the meaning of the word from the context. Since the passage states that the television program discusses *top-*

ics and issues, hopefully you can understand that the best answer to this question is answer (D) *matters of public concern.* Be very careful to read the context in this type of question. *Issues* can mean *editions* (answer A) or *volumes* (answer B) when it refers to *publications.* However, in this context, *issues* does not mean *editions* or *volumes.* Answer (C) is incorrect because *issues* are more related to *problems* than to *solutions.*

3. Which of the following would probably NOT be the title of a *Cosmos* show?

   (A) Is There Life on Mars?
   (B) Exploring the Human Brain
   (C) How to Deal with World Poverty
   (D) When Will the Next Big Earthquake Occur?

Since the question says *probably,* the answer is not given directly in the passage; however, you can draw a conclusion from something in the passage to answer the question. The passage states that *Cosmos* was about *topics and issues from varied fields of science.* Answer (A) about Mars, answer (B) about the human brain, and answer (D) about earthquakes are science topics and could therefore possibly serve as topics of *Cosmos* shows. Since *World Poverty* (answer C) is more a question of sociology or economics than science, the best answer to this question is answer (C).

EXERCISE 5: Study each of the passages and choose the best answers to the questions that follow.

PASSAGE ONE (Questions 1–4)

> The most conservative sect of the Mennonite Church is the Old Order Amish, with 33,000 members living mainly today in the states of Pennsylvania, Ohio, and Indiana. Their lifestyle reflects their belief in the doctrines of separation from the world and simplicity of life. The Amish have steadfastly rejected the societal changes that have occurred in the previous three hundred years, preferring instead to remain securely rooted in a seventeenth-century lifestyle. They live without radios, televisions, telephones, electric lights, and cars; they dress in plainly styled and colored old-fashioned clothes; and they farm their lands with horses and tools rather than modern farm equipment. They have a highly communal form of living, with barn raisings and quilting bees as commonplace activities.

1. The paragraph preceding this passage most probably discusses
   (A) other more liberal sects of Mennonites
   (B) where Mennonites live
   (C) the communal Amish lifestyle
   (D) the most conservative Mennonites

2. The word "steadfastly" (line 4) is closest in meaning to
   (A) quickly
   (B) staunchly
   (C) negatively
   (D) simply

3. Which of the following would probably NOT be found on an Amish farm?
    (A) A hammer
    (B) A cart
    (C) A long dress
    (D) A refrigerator

4. It can be inferred from the passage that a quilting bee
    (A) involves a group of people
    (B) is necessary when raising bees
    (C) always follows a barn raising
    (D) provides needed solitude

PASSAGE TWO (Questions 5–8)

Various other Indian tribes also lived on the Great Plains. The Sioux, a group of seven American Indian tribes, are best known for their fiercely combative posture against the encroaching white civilization in the 1800's. Although they are popularly referred to today as Sioux, these Indian tribes did not call themselves Sioux; the name of Sioux was given to them by an enemy tribe. The seven Sioux tribes called themselves by some variation of the word Dakota, which means "allies" in their language. Four tribes of the eastern Sioux community living in Minnesota were known by the name Dakota. The Nakota included two tribes that left the eastern woodlands and moved out onto the plains. The Teton Sioux, or Lakota, moved even further west to the plains of the present-day states of North Dakota, South Dakota, and Wyoming.

5. The paragraph preceding this passage most probably discusses
    (A) how the Sioux battled the white man
    (B) one of the Plains Indian tribes
    (C) where the Sioux lived
    (D) American Indian tribes on the east coast

6. The word "encroaching" (line 3) is closest in meaning to which of the following?
    (A) Attacking
    (B) Dominant
    (C) Intruding
    (D) Withdrawing

7. It is implied in the passage that the seven Sioux tribes called each other by some form of the word "Dakota" because they were
    (A) united in a cause
    (B) all living in North Dakota
    (C) fiercely combative
    (D) enemies

8. It can be inferred from the passage that the present-day states of North and South Dakota
    (A) are east of Minnesota
    (B) are home to the four tribes known by the name "Dakota"
    (C) received their names from the Indian tribes living there
    (D) are part of the eastern woodlands

PASSAGE THREE (Questions 9–12)

The extinction of many species of birds has undoubtedly been hastened by modern man; since 1600 it has been estimated that approximately 100 bird species have become extinct over the world. In North America, the first species known to be annihilated was the great auk, a flightless bird that served as an easy source of food and bait for Atlantic fishermen through the beginning of the nineteenth century.

Shortly after the great auk's extinction, two other North American species, the Carolina parakeet and the passenger pigeon, began dwindling noticeably in numbers. The last Carolina parakeet and the last passenger pigeon in captivity both died in September 1914. In addition to these extinct species, several others such as the bald eagle, the peregrine falcon, and the California condor are today recognized as endangered; steps are being taken to prevent their extinction.

9. The passage implies that the great auk disappeared
   (A) before 1600
   (B) in the 1600s
   (C) in the 1800s
   (D) in the last fifty years

10. It can be inferred from the passage that the great auk was killed because
   (A) it was eating the fishermen's catch
   (B) fishermen wanted to eat it
   (C) it flew over fishing areas
   (D) it baited fishermen

11. The word "annihilated" (line 4) is closest in meaning to which of the following?
   (A) Wiped out
   (B) Decreased
   (C) Hurt
   (D) Damaged

12. The paragraph following this passage most probably discusses
   (A) what is being done to save endangered birds
   (B) what the bald eagle symbolizes to Americans
   (C) how several bird species became endangered
   (D) other extinct species

REVIEW EXERCISE (SKILLS 1–5): Study each of the passages and choose the best answers to the questions that follow.

PASSAGE ONE (Questions 1–5)

The Mason-Dixon Line, often considered by Americans to be the demarcation between the North and the South, is in reality the boundary that separates the state of Pennsylvania from Maryland and parts of West Virginia. Prior to the Civil War, this southern boundary of Pennsylvania separated the non-slave states to the north from the slave states to the south.

The Mason-Dixon Line was established well before the Civil War, as a result of a boundary dispute between Pennsylvania and Maryland. Two English astronomers, Charles Mason and Jeremiah Dixon, were called in to survey the area and officially mark the boundary between the two states. The survey was completed in 1767, and the boundary was marked with stones.

1. The best title for this passage would be
   (A) Dividing the North and the South
   (B) The Meaning of the Mason-Dixon Line
   (C) Two English Astronomers
   (D) The History of the Mason-Dixon Line

2. It can be inferred from the passage that before the Civil War
   (A) Pennsylvania was south of the Mason-Dixon Line
   (B) Pennsylvania was a non-slave state
   (C) the states south of the Mason-Dixon Line had the same opinion about slavery as Pennsylvania
   (D) the slave states were not divided from the non-slave states

3. According to the passage, the Mason-Dixon Line was established because of a disagreement
   (A) about borders
   (B) about slaves
   (C) between two astronomers
   (D) over surveying techniques

4. The word "survey" (line 8) is closest in meaning to which of the following?
   (A) View
   (B) Understand
   (C) Map out
   (D) Separate

5. The passage indicates that the Mason-Dixon Line was identified with
   (A) pieces of rock
   (B) a fence
   (C) a stone wall
   (D) a border crossing

PASSAGE TWO (Questions 6–10)

Manic depression is another psychiatric illness that mainly affects the mood. A patient suffering from this disease will alternate between periods of manic excitement and extreme depression, with or without relatively normal periods in between. The changes in mood suffered by a manic-depressive patient go far beyond the day-to-day mood changes experienced by the general population. In the period of manic excitement, the mood elevation can become so intense that it can result in extended insomnia, extreme irritability, and heightened aggressiveness. In the period of depression, which may last for several weeks or months, a patient experiences feelings of general fatigue, uselessness, and hopelessness, and in serious cases may contemplate suicide.

6. The paragraph preceding this passage most probably discusses
   (A) when manic depression develops
   (B) a different type of mental disease
   (C) how moods are determined
   (D) how manic depression can result in suicide

7. According to the passage, a manic-depressive patient in a manic phase would be feeling
   (A) highly emotional
   (B) unhappy
   (C) listless
   (D) relatively normal

8. The passage indicates that most people
   (A) never undergo mood changes
   (B) experience occasional shifts in mood
   (C) switch wildly from highs to lows
   (D) become highly depressed

9. The word "intense" (line 6) is closest in meaning to
   (A) lengthy
   (B) haughty
   (C) strong
   (D) extensive

10. The passage implies that
    (A) changes from excitement to depression occur frequently and often
    (B) only manic-depressive patients experience aggression
    (C) the depressive phase of this disease can be more harmful than the manic phase
    (D) suicide is inevitable in cases of manic depression

PASSAGE THREE (Questions 11–15)

The 1960 presidential campaign featured the politically innovative and highly influential series of televised debates in the contest between the Republicans and the Democrats. Senator John Kennedy established an early lead among the Democratic hopefuls and was nominated on the first ballot at the Los Angeles convention to be the representative of the Democratic party in the presidential election. Richard Nixon, then serving as Vice-President of the United States under Eisenhower, received the nomination of the Republican party. Both Nixon and Kennedy campaigned vigorously throughout the country and then took the unprecedented step of appearing in face-to-face debates on television. Political experts contend that the debates were a pivotal force in the elections. In front of a viewership of more than 100 million citizens, Kennedy masterfully overcame Nixon's advantage as the better-known and more experienced candidate and reversed the public perception of him as too inexperienced and immature for the presidency.

11. Which of the following best expresses the main idea of the passage?
    (A) Kennedy defeated Nixon in the 1960 presidential election.
    (B) Television debates were instrumental in determining the outcome of the 1960 presidential election.
    (C) Television debates have long been a part of campaigning.
    (D) Kennedy was the leading Democratic candidate in the 1960 presidential election.

12. The passage implies that Kennedy
    (A) was a long shot to receive the Democratic presidential nomination
    (B) won the Democratic presidential nomination fairly easily
    (C) was not a front runner in the race for the Democratic presidential nomination
    (D) came from behind to win the Democratic presidential nomination

13. The passage states that the television debates between presidential candidates in 1960
    (A) did not establish a precedent
    (B) were the final televised presidential debates
    (C) were fairly usual in the history of presidential campaigns
    (D) were the first presidential campaign debates to be televised

14. The word "pivotal" (line 10) is closest in meaning to
    (A) circular
    (B) influential
    (C) nebulous
    (D) uneven

15. The passage states that in the debates with Nixon, Kennedy demonstrated to the American people that he was
    (A) old enough to be president
    (B) more experienced than Nixon
    (C) better known than Nixon
    (D) too inexperienced to serve as president

SKILL 6:   FIND INDIRECT ANSWERS ABOUT THE WHOLE PASSAGE

Some questions about the whole passage will ask for answers that are not given directly in the passage. To answer these questions correctly, you must draw conclusions from information in the passage. The following are examples of questions about the whole passage that are not answered directly for you in the passage:

QUESTIONS ABOUT TONE

- WHAT IS THE TONE OF THE PASSAGE?

A question about the tone is asking if the author is showing any emotion in his or her writing. The majority of the passages on the TOEFL are factual passages presented without any emotion; the tone of this type of passage could be simply **informational, explanatory,** or **factual.** Sometimes on the TOEFL, however, the author shows some emotion in his or her writing, and you must be able to recognize that emotion to answer a question about tone correctly. If the author is being funny, then the tone might be **humorous;** if the author is making fun of something, the tone might be **sarcastic;** if the author feels strongly that something is wrong or right, the tone might be **impassioned.**

QUESTIONS ABOUT PURPOSE

- WHAT IS THE AUTHOR'S PURPOSE IN THIS PASSAGE?

A question about purpose is asking what the author is trying to do in the passage. You can draw a conclusion about the author's purpose by referring to the main idea and the organization of details in the passage. For example, if the main idea is that George Washington's early life greatly influenced his later career and if the details give a history of his early life, the author's purpose could be **to show how George Washington's early life influenced his later career.** However, the answer to a purpose question is often considerably more general than the main idea. A more general author's purpose for the main idea about George Washington would be **to demonstrate the influence of early experiences on later life** (without any mention of George Washington).

QUESTIONS ABOUT THE COURSE

- IN WHICH COURSE WOULD THIS READING PROBABLY BE ASSIGNED?

A question about the course is asking you to decide which university course might have this passage as assigned reading. You should draw a conclusion about the course by referring to the topic of the passage and the organization of details. For example, if the passage is about George Washington and the details give historical background on his early life, then this would probably be assigned reading in an American history class. However, if the passage is about George Washington and the details show the various influences that George had on the formation of the American government, then the passage might be assigned reading in a government or political science class.

STRATEGIES FOR ANSWERING INDIRECT QUESTIONS ABOUT THE WHOLE PASSAGE

Questions about tone, purpose, or course are all asking you to draw a conclusion about the whole passage. When you are answering this type of question, you should remember that

(1) the answer is not given directly, and (2) the answer must refer to the passage as a whole rather than one detail in the passage. The following strategies work best for questions about tone, purpose, or course.

STRATEGIES:
INDIRECT QUESTIONS ABOUT THE WHOLE PASSAGE

1. **Tone:** As you read the passage, look for clues that the author is showing some emotion rather than just presenting facts.

2. **Purpose:** Draw a conclusion about the purpose from the main idea of the passage and the overall organization of details.

3. **Course:** Draw a conclusion about the course from the topic of the passage and the organization of details.

Example

Military awards have long been considered symbolic of royalty, and thus when the United States was a young nation just finished with revolution and eager to distance itself from anything tasting of monarchy, there was strong sentiment against military decoration. For a century, from the end of the Revolutionary War until the Civil War, the United States awarded no military honors. The institution of the Medal of Honor in 1861 was a source of great discussion and concern. From the Civil War until World War I, the Medal of Honor was the only military award given by the United States government, and today it is awarded only in the most extreme cases of heroism. Although the United States is still somewhat wary of granting military awards, several awards have been instituted since World War I.

1. The tone of the passage is
    (A) angered
    (B) humorous
    (C) outraged
    (D) informational

To determine the tone of a passage, you should look for any indications of emotion on the part of the author. In this passage the author uses historical facts to make a point about America's sentiment against military awards; the author does not make any kind of emotional plea. Therefore, the best answer to this question is answer (D). There is nothing in this passage to indicate any anger (A), or humor (B), or outrage (C) on the part of the author.

2. The author's purpose in this passage is to
   (A) describe the history of military awards from the Revolutionary War to the Civil War
   (B) demonstrate an effect of America's attitude toward royalty
   (C) give an opinion of military awards
   (D) outline various historical symbols of royalty

To answer this question correctly, refer to the main idea of this passage as outlined in the first sentence. The main idea is that there has been strong sentiment against military awards in the United States because military awards are symbols of royalty. The author gives historical facts about military awards as details to support the main idea. Since the purpose is determined from the main idea and the overall organization of details, the author's purpose is to describe, explain, or demonstrate that America's sentiment against military awards is because of its negative sentiment against royalty.

The best answer to this question is therefore answer (B) because this answer is closest in meaning to the purpose that you have determined from the main idea and organization of details. Notice that the correct answer is considerably more general than the main idea: according to answer (B), the purpose is to *demonstrate an effect* (America's dislike of military awards) *of America's attitude toward royalty*. Answer (A) is incorrect because it refers to only one part of the passage, military awards from the Revolutionary War to the Civil War, while the passage discusses military awards from the Revolutionary War to the present. Answer (C) is incorrect because the author is not giving his or her own opinion of military awards in this passage, but is instead attempting to describe the sentiment of the American people. Answer (D) is incorrect because the author does not attempt to describe the various symbols of royalty in this passage. Only one symbol of royalty (military awards) is discussed, but there are many other royal symbols.

3. This passage would probably be assigned reading in a course on
   (A) military science
   (B) sociology
   (C) American history
   (D) interior decoration

To draw a conclusion about the course, you should refer to the topic of the passage and the overall organization of details. Since this passage is about the American military awards, and the details discuss the history of American military awards from the Revolutionary War until today, the best answer is (C).

EXERCISE 6: Study each of the passages and choose the best answers to the questions that follow.

PASSAGE ONE (Questions 1–3)

In Cold Blood (1966) is a well-known example of the "nonfiction novel," a recently popular type of writing based upon factual events in which the author attempts to describe the underlying forces, thoughts, and emotions that lead to actual events. In Truman Capote's book, the author describes the sadistic murder of a family on a Kansas farm, often showing the point of view of the killers. To research the book, Capote interviewed the murderers, and he maintains that his book presents a faithful reconstruction of the incident.

1. The purpose of this passage is to
   (A) discuss an example of a new literary genre
   (B) tell the story of *In Cold Blood*
   (C) explain Truman Capote's reasons for writing *In Cold Blood*
   (D) describe how Truman Capote researched his nonfiction novel

2. Which of the following best describes the tone of the passage?
   (A) Cold
   (B) Sadistic
   (C) Emotional
   (D) Descriptive

3. This passage would probably be assigned reading in which of the following courses?
   (A) Criminal Law
   (B) American History
   (C) Modern American Novels
   (D) Literary Research

PASSAGE TWO (Questions 4–6)

Up to now confessions that have been obtained from defendants in a hypnotic state have not been admitted into evidence by courts in the United States. Experts in the field of hypnosis have found that such confessions are not completely reliable. Subjects in a hypnotic state may confess to crimes they did not commit for one of two reasons. Either they fantasize that they had committed the crimes or they believe that others want them to confess.

A landmark case concerning a confession obtained under hypnosis went all the way to the U.S. Supreme Court. In the case of *Leyra* vs. *Denno,* a suspect was hypnotized by a psychiatrist for the district attorney; in a post-hypnotic state the suspect signed three separate confessions to a murder. The Supreme Court ruled that the confessions were invalid because of the mental coercion used to obtain them. The suspect was then released because the confessions had been the only evidence against him.

4. Which of the following best describes the author's purpose in this passage?
   (A) To describe the history of hypnosis
   (B) To demonstrate why confessions made under hypnosis are not reliable
   (C) To clarify the role of the Supreme Court in invalidating confessions from hypnotized subjects
   (D) To explain the legal status of hypnotically induced confessions

5. The tone of this passage could best be described as
   (A) outraged
   (B) judicious
   (C) hypnotic
   (D) informative

6. This passage would probably be assigned reading in a course on
   (A) American Law
   (B) Psychiatric Healing
   (C) Parapsychology
   (D) Philosophy

PASSAGE THREE (Questions 7–9)

The rate at which the deforestation of the world is proceeding is alarming. In 1950 approximately 25 percent of the earth's land surface had been covered with forests, and less than 25 years later the amount of forest land was reduced to 20 percent. This decrease from 25 percent to 20 percent from 1950 to 1973 represents an astounding loss of 20 million square kilometers of forests. Predictions are that an additional 20 million square kilometers of forest land will be lost by 2020.

The majority of deforestation is occurring in tropical forests in developing countries, fueled by the developing countries' need for increased agricultural land and the desire on the part of developed countries to import wood and wood products. More than 90 percent of the plywood used in the United States, for example, is imported from developing countries with tropical forests. By the mid-1980's, solutions to this expanding problem were being sought, in the form of attempts to establish an international regulatory organization to oversee the use of tropical forests.

7. The author's main purpose in this passage is to
   (A) cite statistics about an improvement on the earth's land surface
   (B) explain where deforestation is occurring
   (C) make the reader aware of a worsening world problem
   (D) blame developing countries for deforestation

8. Which of the following best describes the tone of the passage?
   (A) Concerned
   (B) Disinterested
   (C) Placid
   (D) Exaggerated

9. This passage would probably be assigned reading in which of the following courses?
   (A) Geology
   (B) Geography
   (C) Geometry
   (D) Marine Biology

REVIEW EXERCISE (SKILLS 1–6): Study each of the passages and choose the best answers to the questions that follow.

PASSAGE ONE (Questions 1–5)

Another noteworthy trend in twentieth-century music in the U.S. has been the use of folk and popular music as a base for more serious compositions. The motivation for these borrowings from traditional sources might be a desire on the part of a composer to return to simpler forms, to enhance patriotic feelings, or to establish an immediate rapport with an audience. For whatever reason, composers such as Charles Ives and Aaron Copland offered compositions featuring novel musical forms flavored with refrains from traditional Americana. Ives employed the whole gamut of patriotic songs, hymns, jazz, and popular songs in his compositions, while Copland drew upon folk music, particularly as sources for his ballets *Billy the Kid, Rodeo,* and *Appalachian Spring.*

1. The paragraph preceding this passage most probably discusses
   (A) nineteenth-century music
   (B) one development in music of this century
   (C) the works of Aaron Copland
   (D) the history of folk and popular music

2. Which of the following best describes the main idea of the passage?
   (A) Traditional music has flavored some American musical compositions in this century.
   (B) Ives and Copland have used folk and popular music in their compositions.
   (C) A variety of explanations exist as to why a composer might use traditional sources of music.
   (D) Traditional music is composed of various types of folk and popular music.

3. It can be inferred from this passage that the author is not sure
   (A) when Ives wrote his compositions
   (B) that Ives and Copland actually borrowed from traditional music
   (C) why certain composers borrowed from folk and popular music
   (D) if Copland really featured new musical forms

4. Which of the following is not listed in the passage as a source for Ives' compositions?
   (A) National music
   (B) Religious music
   (C) Jazz
   (D) American novels

5. The passage would most probably be assigned reading in which of the following courses?
   (A) American History
   (B) The History of Jazz
   (C) Modern American Music
   (D) Composition

PASSAGE TWO (Questions 6–10)

The rattlesnake has a reputation as a dangerous and deadly snake with a fierce hatred for mankind. Although the rattlesnake is indeed a venomous snake capable of killing a human, its nature has perhaps been somewhat exaggerated in myth and folklore.

The rattlesnake is not inherently aggressive and generally strikes only when it has been put on the defensive. In its defensive posture the rattlesnake raises the front part of its body off the ground and assumes an S-shaped form in preparation for a lunge forward. At the end of a forward thrust, the rattlesnake pushes its fangs into the victim, thereby injecting its venom.

There are more than thirty species of rattlesnakes, varying in length from 20 inches to six feet and also varying in toxicity of venom. In the United States there are only a few deaths annually from rattlesnakes, with a mortality rate of less than 2 percent of those attacked.

6. Which of the following would be the best title for this passage?
   (A) The Exaggerated Reputation of the Rattlesnake
   (B) The Dangerous and Deadly Rattlesnake
   (C) The Venomous Killer of Humans
   (D) Myth and Folklore about Killers

7. According to the passage, which of the following is true about rattlesnakes?
   (A) They are always ready to attack.
   (B) They are always dangerous and deadly.
   (C) Their fierce nature has been underplayed in myth and folklore.
   (D) Their poison can kill people.

8. When a rattlesnake is ready to defend itself, it
   (A) lies in an S-shape on the ground
   (B) lunges with the back part of its body
   (C) is partially off the ground
   (D) assumes it is prepared by thrusting its fangs into the ground

9. It can be inferred from the passage that
   (A) all rattlesnake bites are fatal
   (B) all rattlesnake bites are not equally harmful
   (C) the few deaths from rattlesnake bites are from the six-foot snakes
   (D) deaths from rattlesnake bites have been steadily increasing

10. The author's purpose in this passage is to
   (A) warn readers about the extreme danger from rattlesnakes
   (B) explain a misconception about rattlesnakes
   (C) describe a rattlesnake attack
   (D) clarify how a rattlesnake kills humans

PASSAGE THREE (Questions 11–15)

A massive banking crisis occurred in the United States in 1933. In the two preceding years, a large number of banks had failed, and fear of lost savings prompted many depositors to remove their funds from banks. Problems became so serious in the state of Michigan that Governor William A. Comstock was forced to declare a moratorium on all banking activities in the state on February 14, 1933. The panic in Michigan quickly spread to other states, and by March 6, President Franklin D. Roosevelt had declared a banking moratorium throughout the United States that left the entire country without banking services.

Congress immediately met in a special session to solve the banking crisis and on March 9 passed the Emergency Banking Act of 1933 to assist financially healthy banks to reopen. By March 15, banks controlling 90 percent of the country's financial reserves were again open for business.

11. The author's purpose in this passage is to
   (A) discuss a problem and its resolution
   (B) warn depositors about potential banking problems
   (C) assess blame for a problem that had occurred
   (D) praise Congress for its actions

12. The passage states that all the following occurred prior to 1933 EXCEPT that
   (A) many banks went under
   (B) many bank patrons were afraid of losing their deposits
   (C) a lot of money was withdrawn from accounts
   (D) Governor Comstock cancelled all banking activities in Michigan

13. The word "moratorium" (line 5) is closest in meaning to which of the following?
   (A) Death
   (B) Temporary cessation
   (C) Murder
   (D) Slow decline

14. Which of the following is implied in the passage?
   (A) Congress did not give any special priority to the banking situation.
   (B) The Emergency Banking Act helped all banks to reopen.
   (C) Ninety percent of the banks reopened by the middle of March.
   (D) Ten percent of the country's money was in financially unhealthy banks.

15. Which of the following best describes the tone of the passage?
   (A) Panicked
   (B) Critical
   (C) Historical
   (D) Angry

TOEFL POST-TEST
FOLLOWS

TOEFL POST-TEST

SECTION 3
VOCABULARY AND READING

Time—45 minutes

This section is designed to measure your comprehension of standard written English. There are two types of questions in this section, with special directions for each type.

<u>Directions:</u> In questions 1–30 each sentence has an underlined word or phrase. Below each sentence are four other words or phrases, marked (A), (B), (C), and (D). You are to choose the <u>one</u> word or phrase that <u>best keeps the meaning</u> of the original sentence if it is substituted for the underlined word or phrase. Then, on your answer sheet, find the number of the question and fill in the space that corresponds to the letter you have chosen. Fill in the space so that the letter inside the oval cannot be seen.

Example   <u>Sample Answer</u>

Both <u>boats</u> and trains are used for   Ⓐ
transporting the materials.   ●
(A) planes   ©
(B) ships   Ⓓ
(C) canoes
(D) railroads

The best answer is (B) because "Both ships and trains are used for transporting the materials" is closest in meaning to the original sentence. Therefore, you should choose answer (B).

After you read the directions, begin work on the questions.

1. Alpha rays tend to lose energy <u>quickly</u> when they pass through matter.

    (A) after a while
    (B) at last
    (C) rapidly
    (D) heartily

2. Although the average rainfall annually for the entire earth is 34 inches, some areas near the equator have <u>received</u> 400 inches in one year.

    (A) gotten
    (B) surpassed
    (C) emitted
    (D) deserved

3. A large <u>part</u> of the city of Chicago was destroyed in the fire.

    (A) selection
    (B) portion
    (C) block
    (D) district

4. <u>Altogether</u> there are more than 25,000 radio stations in the world.

    (A) Approximately
    (B) Estimatedly
    (C) Assuredly
    (D) In total

GO ON TO THE NEXT PAGE

5. Key West is the <u>farthest</u> of the Florida Keys from the mainland.

   (A) largest
   (B) most distant
   (C) greatest
   (D) widest

6. The Bunker Hill Monument was erected on Breed's Hill in <u>remembrance</u> of one of the first battles of the American Revolution.

   (A) memory
   (B) reverence
   (C) construction
   (D) suppression

7. Some locomotives can <u>push</u> trains, thus eliminating the need to turn trains around at the end of the track.

   (A) pull
   (B) lead
   (C) propel
   (D) obstruct

8. A <u>constant</u> supply of water is necessary for the cultivation of rice.

   (A) tremendous
   (B) deep
   (C) heavy
   (D) steady

9. The first chickens were brought to the North American <u>continent</u> by Spanish explorers.

   (A) country
   (B) land mass
   (C) hemisphere
   (D) boundary

10. The use of mechanical refrigerators became <u>widespread</u> in the United States in the 1920's.

    (A) well known
    (B) commonplace
    (C) misinterpreted
    (D) chilled

11. Nuclear-<u>generated</u> electricity is in use in most parts of the United States.

    (A) related
    (B) inherited
    (C) produced
    (D) motivated

12. Whether a reptile is active at night or during the day can be determined from the <u>shape</u> of its pupil.

    (A) size
    (B) weight
    (C) diameter
    (D) form

13. The eastern third of the state of Rhode Island is <u>far</u> more heavily populated than the western portion.

    (A) distantly
    (B) considerably
    (C) minimally
    (D) doubtlessly

14. A railroad company cannot make a decision to discontinue passenger service along a <u>particular</u> line without permission from the Interstate Commerce Commission.

    (A) specific
    (B) low income
    (C) part of a
    (D) peculiar

GO ON TO THE NEXT PAGE

15. The Freemasons are one of the oldest <u>fraternities</u> in the world.

    (A) universities
    (B) sociologists
    (C) exhibitions
    (D) brotherhoods

16. At the mouth of a river, the flow of water lessens <u>dramatically</u>.

    (A) theatrically
    (B) slightly
    (C) tremendously
    (D) opportunely

17. Local medical officials <u>expect</u> an increased number of reported cases of the flu in the weeks to come.

    (A) reject
    (B) anticipate
    (C) evoke
    (D) spark

18. In the 1930's eight companies <u>banded</u> together to build the Hoover Dam.

    (A) joined
    (B) sang
    (C) worked
    (D) incorporated

19. Sedimentary rock consists of <u>layers</u> of what millions of years ago was loose material.

    (A) mixtures
    (B) carcasses
    (C) strata
    (D) crystals

20. Louisiana forbids shrimping in its marshes and lakes in the summer to <u>protect</u> breeding grounds.

    (A) preserve
    (B) detain
    (C) premier
    (D) condescend

21. The <u>restoration</u> of the Willard House in Washington, D.C., took five years to complete.

    (A) depreciation
    (B) craftsmanship
    (C) termination
    (D) renovation

22. The candidate responded with a <u>cunning</u> smile to the question about his campaign strategy.

    (A) wily
    (B) polite
    (C) sincere
    (D) transient

23. Radar guns are used by police in many parts of the United States to <u>enforce</u> speed laws.

    (A) expose
    (B) uphold
    (C) shove
    (D) deregulate

24. After a molecule has lost an electron, it has a positive <u>charge</u>.

    (A) attack
    (B) altercation
    (C) credit
    (D) current

25. Rapid City, South Dakota, was named after Rapid Creek, which <u>streams</u> through the city.

    (A) fixates
    (B) inclines
    (C) glides
    (D) breezes

26. Norman Rockwell's paintings and illustrations show <u>meticulous</u> attention to detail.

    (A) inordinate
    (B) mesmerizing
    (C) careful
    (D) exultant

GO ON TO THE NEXT PAGE ➤

27. If a person receives a subpoena, he or she is <u>compelled</u> to appear in court to testify.

    (A) required
    (B) challenged
    (C) doomed
    (D) disposed

28. The program was <u>suspended</u> because of a shortage of patrol officers.

    (A) supplanted
    (B) discontinued
    (C) relinquished
    (D) quelled

29. On March 5, 1770, there was <u>a skirmish</u> between some angry residents of Boston and a squad of British soldiers.

    (A) a battalion
    (B) a blemish
    (C) a clash
    (D) an encroachment

30. The United States government has a <u>bilateral</u> trade agreement with various other governments.

    (A) homogeneous
    (B) precipitous
    (C) tangible
    (D) reciprocal

<u>Directions:</u> In the rest of this section you will read several passages. Each one is followed by several questions about it. For questions 31–60, you are to choose the one best answer, (A), (B), (C), or (D), to each question. Then, on your answer sheet, find the number of the question and fill in the space that corresponds to the letter of the answer you have chosen.

Answer all questions following a passage on the basis of what is <u>stated</u> or <u>implied</u> in that passage.

Read the following passage:

John Quincy Adams, who served as the sixth president of the United States from 1825 to 1829, is today recognized for his masterful statesmanship and diplomacy. He dedicated his life to public service, both in the presidency and in the various other political offices he held. Throughout his political career he demonstrated his unswerving belief in freedom of speech, the anti-slavery cause, and the right of Americans to be free from European and Asian domination.

Example I   Sample Answer

To what did John Quincy Adams   Ⓐ
devote his life?   ●
                                                                    Ⓒ
(A) Improving his personal life   Ⓓ
(B) Serving the public
(C) Increasing his fortune
(D) Working on his private business

According to the passage, John Quincy Adams "dedicated his life to public service." Therefore, you should choose answer (B).

GO ON TO THE NEXT PAGE

Example II   Sample Answer

The passage implies that John   Ⓐ
Quincy Adams held   Ⓑ
                                                                   Ⓒ
(A) no political offices   ●
(B) only one political office
(C) exactly two political offices
(D) at least three political offices

The passage states that John Quincy Adams served in "the presidency and various other political offices." Therefore, you should choose answer (D).

After you read the directions, begin work on the questions.

Questions 31–35

A solar eclipse occurs when a new moon moves in front of the sun and hides the sun from the earth. During a new moon, the moon is at its fullest, thus allowing the moon to obscure the sun. Although the moon is considerably smaller in size than the sun, the moon is able to cover the sun because of their relative distances from the earth. A total eclipse can last up to seven minutes, during which time the moon's shadow moves across the earth at a speed of about .6 kilometers per second.

31. This passage mainly

   (A) describes how long an eclipse
        will last
   (B) gives facts about the moon
   (C) explains how the moon is able
        to obscure the sun
   (D) informs the reader about solar
        eclipses

32. According to the passage, a new
    moon

   (A) has just been created
   (B) is as full as it can be
   (C) is not big enough to hide the
        sun
   (D) eclipses the sun by moving
        behind it

33. According to the passage, how can
    the moon hide the sun during an
    eclipse?

   (A) The fact that the moon is closer
        to the earth than the sun
        makes up for the moon's
        smaller size.
   (B) The moon can only obscure the
        sun because of the moon's
        great distance from the
        earth.
   (C) Because the sun is relatively
        close to the earth, the sun can
        be eclipsed by the moon.
   (D) The moon hides the sun
        because of the moon's
        considerable size.

GO ON TO THE NEXT PAGE →

34. The passage indicates that the duration of a solar eclipse

    (A) is more than seven minutes
    (B) is always seven minutes
    (C) is no more than seven minutes
    (D) was exactly seven minutes the last time it occurred

35. The passage states that which of the following happens during an eclipse?

    (A) The moon hides from the sun.
    (B) The moon is obscured by the sun.
    (C) The moon begins moving at a speed of .6 kilometers per second.
    (D) The moon's shadow crosses the earth.

Questions 36–41

Most people think of deserts as dry, flat areas with little vegetation and little or no rainfall, but this is hardly true. Many deserts have varied geographical formations ranging from soft, rolling hills to stark, jagged cliffs, and most deserts have a permanent source of water. Although deserts do not receive a high amount of rainfall—to be classified as a desert, an area must get less than 25 centimeters of rainfall per year—there are many plants that thrive on only small amounts of water, and deserts are often full of such plant life.

36. What is the main idea of the passage?

    (A) Deserts are dry, flat areas with few plants.
    (B) There is little rainfall in the desert.
    (C) Many kinds of vegetation can survive with little water.
    (D) Deserts are not really flat areas with little plant life.

37. The passage implies that

    (A) the typical conception of a desert is incorrect
    (B) all deserts are dry, flat areas
    (C) most people are well informed about deserts
    (D) the lack of rainfall in deserts causes the lack of vegetation

38. The passage describes the geography of deserts as

    (A) flat
    (B) sandy
    (C) varied
    (D) void of vegetation

39. According to the passage, what causes an area to be classified as a desert?

    (A) The type of plants
    (B) The geographical formations
    (C) The amount of precipitation
    (D) The source of water

40. Which of the following statements is NOT supported by the passage?

    (A) Deserts can have flourishing plant life.
    (B) Deserts can have a permanent supply of water.
    (C) An area with 30 centimeters of rainfall per year would not be called a desert.
    (D) The rainfall in deserts is intense.

41. What is most likely the topic of the paragraph following this passage?

    (A) The geography of deserts
    (B) Plants that do not require much water
    (C) The water sources of deserts
    (D) The amount of rainfall in a desert

GO ON TO THE NEXT PAGE

Questions 42–46

American jazz is a conglomeration of sounds borrowed from such varied sources as American and African folk music, European classical music, and Christian gospel songs. One of the recognizable characteristics of jazz is its use of improvisation: certain parts of the music are written out and played the same way by various performers, and other improvised parts are created spontaneously during a performance and vary widely from performer to performer.

The earliest form of jazz was ragtime, lively songs or *rags* performed on the piano, and the best-known of the ragtime performers and composers was Scott Joplin. Born in 1868 to former slaves, Scott Joplin earned his living from a very early age playing the piano in bars around the Mississippi. One of his regular jobs was in the Maple Leaf Club in Sedalia, Missouri. It was there that he began writing the more than 500 compositions that he was to produce, the most famous of which was "The Maple Leaf Rag."

42. The word "conglomeration" (line 1) could best be replaced by

(A) disharmony
(B) mixture
(C) purity
(D) treasure

43. When a musician improvises, he

(A) plays the written parts of the music
(B) performs similarly to other musicians
(C) makes up music as he plays
(D) plays a varied selection of musical compositions

44. According to the passage, ragtime was

(A) generally performed on a variety of instruments
(B) the first type of jazz
(C) extremely soothing and sedate
(D) performed only at the Maple Leaf Club in Sedalia

45. Which of the following statements is true according to the passage?

(A) Scott Joplin was a slave when he was born.
(B) Scott Joplin's parents were slaves when Scott was born.
(C) Scott Joplin had formerly been a slave, but he no longer was after 1868.
(D) Scott Joplin's parents had been slaves before Scott was born.

46. The name of Scott Joplin's most famous composition probably came from

(A) the name of a saloon where he performed
(B) the maple tree near his Sedalia home
(C) the name of the town where he was born
(D) the school where he learned to play the piano

GO ON TO THE NEXT PAGE

Questions 47–52

The three phases of the human memory are the sensory memory, the short-term memory, and the long-term memory. This division of the memory into phases is based on the time span of the memory.

Sensory memory is instantaneous memory. It is an image or memory that enters your mind fleetingly; it comes and goes in under a second. The memory will not last longer than that unless the information enters the short-term memory.

Information can be held in the short-term memory for about twenty seconds or as long as you are actively using it. If you repeat a fact to yourself, that fact will stay in your short-term memory as long as you keep repeating it. Once you stop repeating it, either it is forgotten or it moves into long-term memory.

Long-term memory is the almost limitless memory tank that can hold ideas and images for years and years. Information can be added to your long-term memory when you actively try to put it there through memorization or when an idea or image enters your mind on its own.

47. The best title for this passage would be

   (A) The Difference Between Sensory and Short-Term Memory
   (B) How Long It Takes to Memorize
   (C) How to Classify the Stages of Human Memory
   (D) The Time Span of Human Phases

48. The three phases of memory discussed in this passage are differentiated according to

   (A) location in the brain
   (B) the period of time it takes to remember something
   (C) how the senses are involved in the memory
   (D) how long the memory lasts

49. According to the passage, which type of memory is the shortest?

   (A) Sensory memory
   (B) Active memory
   (C) Short-term memory
   (D) Long-term memory

50. The word "fleetingly" (line 5) is closest in meaning to which of the following?

   (A) Easily
   (B) Haphazardly
   (C) Temporarily
   (D) Fundamentally

51. According to the passage, when will information stay in your short-term memory?

   (A) For as long as twenty minutes
   (B) As long as it is being used
   (C) After you have repeated it many times
   (D) When it has moved into long-term memory

52. According to the passage, what is the capacity of long-term memory?

   (A) Limited
   (B) Infinite
   (C) Equal to the capacity of short-term memory
   (D) Very large

GO ON TO THE NEXT PAGE

VOCABULARY AND READING COMPREHENSION POST-TEST   253

Questions 53–60

Whereas literature in the first half of the eighteenth century in America had been largely religious and moral in tone, by the latter half of the century the revolutionary fervor that was coming to life in the colonies began to be reflected in the literature of the time, which in turn served to further influence the population. Although not all writers of this period supported the revolution, the two best-known and most influential writers, Ben Franklin and Thomas Paine, were both strongly supportive of that cause.

Ben Franklin first attained popular success through his writings in his brother's newspaper, the *New England Current*. In these articles he used a simple style of language and common sense argumentation to defend the point of view of the farmer and the Leather Apron man. He continued with the same common sense practicality and appeal to the common man with his work on *Poor Richard's Almanac* from 1733 until 1758. Firmly established in his popular acceptance by the people, Franklin wrote a variety of extremely effective articles and pamphlets about the colonists' revolutionary cause against England.

Thomas Paine was an Englishman working as a magazine editor in Philadelphia at the time of the Revolution. His pamphlet *Common Sense*, which appeared in 1776, was a force in encouraging the colonists to declare their independence from England. Then throughout the long and desperate war years he published a series of *Crisis* papers (from 1776 until 1783) to encourage the colonists to continue on with the struggle. The effectiveness of his writing was probably due to his emotional yet oversimplified depiction of the cause of the colonists against England as a classic struggle of good and evil.

53. The paragraph preceding this passage most likely discusses

    (A) how literature influences the population
    (B) religious and moral literature
    (C) literature supporting the cause of the American Revolution
    (D) what made Thomas Paine's literature successful

54. The word "fervor" (line 3) is closest in meaning to

    (A) war
    (B) anxiety
    (C) spirit
    (D) action

55. Which of the following statements is NOT supported by the passage?

    (A) The literature at the time of the Revolution was a reflection of the sentiments felt by the general population.
    (B) Revolutionary literature influenced the public.
    (C) The Revolution would not have taken place without the impetus of literature.
    (D) The increasing revolutionary zeal of the second half of the eighteenth century was reflected in the literature.

GO ON TO THE NEXT PAGE →

56. It is implied in the passage that

(A) some writers in the American colonies supported England during the Revolution
(B) Franklin and Paine were the only writers to influence the Revolution
(C) because Thomas Paine was an Englishman, he supported England against the colonists
(D) authors who supported England did not remain in the colonies during the Revolution

57. Benjamin Franklin's Leather Apron man probably represents

(A) a cook
(B) a cleaning man
(C) a farm worker
(D) a skilled laborer

58. According to the passage, the tone of *Poor Richard's Almanac* is

(A) pragmatic
(B) erudite
(C) theoretical
(D) scholarly

59. Thomas Paine's style of writing could best be described as

(A) practical
(B) ineffective
(C) impassioned
(D) desperate

60. The purpose of this passage is to

(A) discuss American literature in the first half of the eighteenth century
(B) give biographical data on two American writers
(C) explain which authors supported the Revolution
(D) describe the literary influence during Revolutionary America

THIS IS THE END OF SECTION 3

IF YOU FINISH BEFORE TIME IS CALLED, CHECK YOUR WORK
ON SECTION 3 ONLY.
DO NOT READ OR WORK ON ANY OTHER SECTION OF THE TEST.

STOP STOP STOP STOP STOP STOP STOP

SECTION FOUR

TEST OF WRITTEN ENGLISH

THE TEST OF WRITTEN ENGLISH

The Test of Written English (TWE) is a writing section that appears on the TOEFL several times a year. You should check the *Bulletin of Information for TOEFL and TSE* for the dates that the TWE will be administered. If you are required to take the TWE, be sure to sign up for the TOEFL in one of the months that it is given.

On the TWE you will be given a specific question and you will be asked to answer that question in essay format in 30 minutes. The TWE will be given at the beginning of the TOEFL, before the Listening Comprehension, Structure and Written Expression, and Vocabulary and Reading Sections.

The TWE is currently emphasizing two different types of questions: (1) contrast questions and (2) interpretation of graphical data. In a contrast question you will be asked to discuss both sides of an issue and then indicate which position you agree with. In a graphical question you will be asked to interpret some type of graphical data and perhaps draw some conclusions about the data.

Because you must write a complete essay in such a short period of time, it is best for you to aim to write a basic, clear, concise, and well-organized essay. The following strategies should help you to write this type of essay:

STRATEGIES FOR THE TEST OF WRITTEN ENGLISH

1. **Read the question carefully and answer the question exactly as it is asked.** Take several minutes at the beginning of the test to be sure that you understand the question and to outline a response that answers it.

2. **Organize your response very clearly.** You should think of having an introduction, body paragraphs that develop the introduction, and a conclusion to end your essay. Use transitions to help the reader understand the organization of ideas.

3. **Whenever you make any kind of general statement, be sure to support that idea with examples, reasons, facts, or similar details.**

4. **Stick to vocabulary and sentence structures that you know.** This is not the time to try out new words or structures.

5. **Finish writing your essay five minutes early so that you have time to proof what you wrote.**

THE SCORE

The score of the TWE is included on the same form as your regular TOEFL score, but it is not part of your overall TOEFL score. It is a separate score on a scale of 1 to 6, where 1 is the worst score and 6 is the best score. The following table outlines what each of the scores essentially means:

	TEST OF WRITTEN ENGLISH SCORES
6	The writer has very strong organizational, structural, and grammatical skills.
5	The writer has good organizational, structural, and grammatical skills. However, the essay contains some errors.
4	The writer has adequate organizational, structural, and grammatical skills. The essay contains a number of errors.
3	The writer shows evidence of organizational, structural, and grammatical skills that still need to be improved.
2	The writer shows a minimal ability to convey ideas in written English.
1	The writer is not capable of conveying ideas in written English.

SAMPLE ESSAYS

This section contains six essays, one demonstrating each of the six possible scores. These essays can give you some idea of the type of essay you need to write to achieve a good score. They can also demonstrate some of the major errors you should avoid when you take the TWE.

The strengths and weaknesses of each essay have been outlined at the end of each. It would be helpful to study each answer in order to understand what is good and what is not so good in each of these essays.

This is the question that was used in the sample essays:

Some people place a high value on loyalty to the employer. To others, it is perfectly acceptable to change jobs every few years to build a career. Discuss these two positions. Then indicate which position you agree with and why.

The following essay received a score of 6.

Different cultures place varying values on loyalty to the employer. In some countries, most notably in Asia, there is a high degree of loyalty to one company. However, in most European countries and the United States, loyalty to one's employer is not highly valued; instead it is considered more rationel and reasonable for an employee to change jobs whenever it is waranted to achieve the optimal overall career. Both of these positions have advantages and disadvantages.

In cultures that value loyalty to the employer, a kind of family relationship seems to develop between employer and employee. It is a reciprocal arrangement which the employer is concerned with asisting the employee to develop to his full potential and the employee is concerned about optimizing the welfare of the company. The negative aspect to absolute loyalty to one company is that an employee may stay in one job that he has outgrow and may miss out on opportunities to develop in new directions. From the the employer's point of view, the employee may be burdened with employees whose skills no longer match the needs of the company.

In cultures in which it is quite acceptable to change jobs every few years, employees can build the career they choose for themself. They can stay with one company as long as it is mutually beneficial to company and employee. As long as good relationship exists and the employee's career is advancing at an acceptable pace, the employee can remain with a company. But at any time the employee is free to move to another company, perhaps to achieve a higher position, to move into a new area, or to find a work situation that is more suitable to his personality. The disadvantage of this situation is employees tend to move around a lot.

Although both these systems have advantages and disadvantages, it is much better for employees have the opportunity to move from job to job if it is necessary to have a better career.

THE "6" ESSAY

Strengths of This Essay

1. It answers the question well.

2. It is clearly organized.

3. The ideas are well developed.

4. It has good, correct sentence structure.

5. It has only a few spelling and grammar errors.

Weaknesses of This Essay

1. The concluding paragraph is rather weak.

The following essay received a score of 5.

Some people place high value on loyalty to employer. They believe the company is responsible for the employee's career. The company will make decisions for the employee about his job. The company will decide to raise employee to new position or keep him in the old position. In this way the company will have overall plan for the good of the company and everyone in the company.

Other people believe it is perfectly acceptable to change jobs every few years to build a career. They believe employee is responsible for his own career. The employee will make decisions about his career. Employee will decide when to move to other company. Employee will choose what is good for employee rather than the company.

The best system is one when employer takes responsibility for the careers of employees. Employer should take responsibility. It is his duty. Employee knows that employer is watching out for his career. Then employee will work hard and do good job. He will be loyal to the company. This system works out best for everyone. It is best for both the company and employees.

THE "5" ESSAY

Strengths of This Essay

1. It answers the question well.

2. It is clearly organized.

3. It has correct sentence structure.

Weaknesses of This Essay

1. The sentence structure is very simple.

2. There are some grammatical errors, particularly with articles.

The following essay received a score of 4.

Every one is not in agreement about how loyal people should be to their employers. Some people place a high value on loyalty to the employer. These people believe that they should work hard for their employer and so their employer will take care of them. To others it is perfectly acceptable to change jobs every few years to build a career. They believe that having only one employer and one job in a career will not be the best for them.

In my culture people stay with one employer for their whole life. They have a job they will work their hardest at that job because it is the only job they will have. They do not look for another job they already have one because that would be unloyal. This way is better because when you old the company will take care you and your family.

THE "4" ESSAY

Strengths of This Essay

1. It answers the question fairly well.

2. It is clearly organized.

Weaknesses of This Essay

1. It copies too much directly from the question.

2. The ideas are not very well developed.

3. There are several examples of incorrect sentence structure.

The following essay received a score of 3.

Some people stay with one employeer for their entire career, but anothers build a career by changing jobs every few years. There are three reasens people should staying with on employer for their entire career.

First, the people should staying with one employer because it is best for the workers. If workers stay with one employer they will not having to move and they can learning all abou the company and advence in the company.

Second, people should staying with one employer because it is best for the compeny. The people will knowing how to do their jobs and they will having a big producton and the compeny will be very success.

Finally, people should staying with one employer because it is best for soceity. If people stay with one compeny then all the compenies will being very success. If all the compenie are very success then soceity will be success.

THE "3" ESSAY

Strengths of This Essay

1. It is clearly organized.

2. It has good, correct sentence structure.

Weaknesses of This Essay

1. It does not answer the question completely.

2. There are errors in spelling and grammar.

The following essay received a score of 2.

First, there is a disadvantage to place a high value on loyalty to the employer if your employer is no a good employer and your job is no a good job then you should no be loyal to a bad employer. Many employer are no good employers and if you are loyal to a bad employer it is a waste because a bad employer he will no be good to you.

Next, there is a advantage to change jobs every few years to build a carere if you get boring with your job and you want to move from one job to other so yo can get a better job instead of stay in your old boring job.

Finally, people should decide for themself where they want to work, if they decide one plce when they very young, how can they be sure whe they are older that they will still want to work there?

THE "2" ESSAY

Strengths of This Essay

1. The overall organization is clear.

2. The writer's main point is clear.

Weaknesses of This Essay

1. The sentence structure is poor.

2. There are numerous errors in spelling and grammar.

3. The ideas are not very well developed.

The following essay received a score of 1.

I think people should staying only one job for his hole careere. Because it is importent loyal to your jop. If you not loyal. Th company didn't be able has good business. If the employees keep change. New employees alway needs be train, and so on.

THE "1" ESSAY

Weaknesses of This Essay

1. It does not answer all the question.

2. The ideas are disorganized and difficult to follow.

3. There are many errors in spelling and grammar.

4. There are many errors in sentence structure.

5. It is too short.

PRACTICE TESTS _____

ESSAY QUESTION #1

Time—30 minutes

Some parents have the opinion that children should be strongly pushed to achieve, while other parents have the opinion that it is best to allow children to progress at their own pace. Discuss each position. Then indicate which you agree with and why.

Write your answer on the forms found on pages 273 and 274.

ESSAY QUESTION #2

Time—30 minutes

Study the chart describing the characteristics of three different jobs. Then respond to the question below.

Three Available Jobs

	JOB A	JOB B	JOB C
PAY	****	***	**
JOB VARIETY	**	*	****
JOB SECURITY	**	***	**
AUTONOMY	***	****	***

**** = High   ** = Moderately Low
*** = Moderately High   * = Low

Of the three jobs that are described in the chart, which one would you choose? Explain your choice.

Write your answer on the forms found on pages 277 and 278.

ESSAY QUESTION #3

Time—30 minutes

People are watching more and more television, and as a result television is having an increasing effect on society. Discuss the beneficial and harmful effects of television on society. Then indicate what you believe the role of television should be and why.

Write your answer on the forms found on pages 279 and 280.

ESSAY QUESTION #4

Time—30 minutes

Study the following graphs describing three different plans that a university has for spending its funds. Then respond to the question.

Plans for Spending University Funds

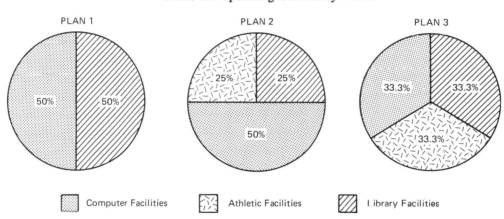

Which of the three plans should the university choose for its spending. Explain your choice.

Write your answer on the forms found on pages 281 and 282.

SCORING YOUR PRE-TESTS AND POST-TESTS_____

When your TOEFL is scored, you will receive a score between 20 and 70 in each of the three sections (Listening, Structure and Written Expression, Vocabulary and Reading). You will also receive an overall score between 200 and 700. You can use the following chart to estimate the scores on your TOEFL Pre-Tests and Post-Tests.

NUMBER CORRECT	CONVERTED SCORE SECTION 1	CONVERTED SCORE SECTION 2	CONVERTED SCORE SECTION 3
60	—	—	67
59	—	—	66
58	—	—	65
57	—	—	64
56	—	—	63
55	—	—	62
54	—	—	61
53	—	—	61
52	—	—	60
51	—	—	59
50	68	—	58
49	66	—	58
48	64	—	57
47	63	—	56
46	62	—	56
45	61	—	55
44	60	—	54
43	59	—	54
42	58	—	53
41	57	—	52
40	57	68	52
39	56	65	51
38	55	64	50
37	54	63	50
36	53	61	49
35	53	59	48
34	52	58	48
33	51	57	47
32	51	56	47
31	50	54	46
30	49	53	45
29	49	52	45
28	48	51	44
27	48	50	43

NUMBER CORRECT	CONVERTED SCORE SECTION 1	CONVERTED SCORE SECTION 2	CONVERTED SCORE SECTION 3
26	47	49	43
25	47	48	42
24	46	47	41
23	45	46	40
22	45	45	40
21	44	44	39
20	43	43	38
19	43	42	37
18	42	41	36
17	42	40	35
16	41	39	34
15	40	38	33
14	39	37	32
13	38	36	31
12	37	35	30
11	36	34	29
10	35	34	28
9	33	33	27
8	32	31	26
7	31	30	26
6	30	28	25
5	29	26	24
4	28	25	24
3	27	24	23
2	25	23	22
1	22	21	21
0	20	20	20

You should first use the chart to determine your converted score for each section. Suppose that you got 30 correct in the first section, 28 correct in the second section, and 43 correct in the third section. The 30 correct in the first section means a converted score of 49. The 28 correct in the second section means a converted score of 51. The 43 correct in the third section means a converted score of 54. (See the chart on the next page.)

	SECTION 1	*SECTION 2*	*SECTION 3*
NUMBER CORRECT	30	28	43
CONVERTED SCORE	49	51	54

Next you should determine your overall score in the following way:

1. Add the three converted scores together.

$$49 + 51 + 54 = 154$$

2. Divide the sum by 3.

$$154/3 = 51.3$$

3. Then multiply by 10.

$$51.3 \times 10 = 513$$

The overall TOEFL score in this example is 513.

CHARTING YOUR PROGRESS

Each time you take a Pre-Test or Post-Test, you should record the results in the chart that follows. In this way you will be able to keep track of the progress you make. You will also be aware of the areas of the TOEFL that you still need to improve.

	LISTENING COMPRE-HENSION	*STRUCTURE AND WRITTEN EXPRESSION*	*VOCABULARY AND READING*	*OVERALL SCORE*
PRE-TEST				
POST-TEST				

TEST OF ENGLISH AS A FOREIGN LANGUAGE

SIDE 1

THIS IS A SAMPLE ANSWER SHEET

DO NOT WRITE IN THIS AREA.

0 2 1 5 2 3 5

1. NAME: Print your name as it appears on your admission ticket: first print your family name (surname), then your given name, and then your middle name. Leave one box blank between names. Then, below each box, fill in the oval that contains the same letter.

Use a No. 2 (H.B.) pencil only. Do not use ink. Be sure each mark is dark and completely fills the intended oval. Erase errors or stray marks completely.

2. REGISTRATION NUMBER

Start here

YOUR REGISTRATION NUMBER IS PRINTED TO THE RIGHT AND IS IN MACHINE READABLE FORM.

DO NOT RE-ENTER THE NUMBER HERE.

3. INSTITUTION AND DEPARTMENT CODES: Give the code numbers of the institutions and departments to which you want your official score report sent. Be sure to fill in the corresponding oval below each box.

| INSTITUTION CODE | DEPT. CODE | INSTITUTION CODE | DEPT. CODE | INSTITUTION CODE | DEPT. CODE |

4. DO YOU PLAN TO STUDY FOR A DEGREE IN THE U.S.A. OR CANADA?
○ YES   ○ NO

5. REASON FOR TAKING TOEFL (FILL IN ONLY ONE OVAL)

○ 1. To enter a college or university as an undergraduate student.
○ 2. To enter a college or university as a graduate student.
○ 3. To enter a school other than a college or university.
○ 4. To become licensed to practice my profession in the U.S.A. or Canada.
○ 5. To demonstrate my proficiency in English to the company for which I work or expect to work.
○ 6. Other than the above (please specify)

6. NUMBER OF TIMES YOU HAVE TAKEN TOEFL BEFORE
○ NONE ○ THREE
○ ONE   ○ FOUR OR MORE
○ TWO

7. CENTER (Print.)

COUNTRY   CITY   CENTER NUMBER

8. PLEASE PRINT IN BLOCK LETTERS YOUR NAME AND MAILING ADDRESS.

FAMILY NAME (SURNAME)   GIVEN (FIRST) NAME   MIDDLE NAME

STREET ADDRESS OR P.O. BOX NO

CITY   STATE OR PROVINCE

POSTAL OR ZIP CODE   COUNTRY

9. SIGNATURE AND DATE: Please copy the following statement in the space provided below; use handwriting.

"I hereby agree to the conditions set forth in the Bulletin of Information and affirm that I am the person whose name and address are given on this answer sheet." Also sign your name on the line provided and enter today's date (in numbers).

SIGNED:

(WRITE YOUR NAME AS IF SIGNING A BUSINESS LETTER)

DATE: MO   DAY   YEAR

DO NOT MARK IN THIS AREA.

TEST FORM:

Reprinted by permission

271

SIDE 2
FORM
TEST BOOK SERIAL NUMBER
SEAT NUMBER

Choose only one answer for each question. Carefully and completely fill in the oval corresponding to the answer you choose so that the letter inside the oval cannot be seen. Completely erase any other marks you may have made. Choose only one answer for each question.

CORRECT	WRONG	WRONG	WRONG	WRONG
Ⓐ Ⓑ ● Ⓓ	Ⓐ Ⓑ Ⓒ Ⓓ	Ⓐ Ⓑ Ⓒ Ⓓ	Ⓐ Ⓑ Ⓒ Ⓓ	Ⓐ Ⓑ Ⓒ Ⓓ

NAME (Print) _____
FAMILY NAME (SURNAME)   GIVEN (FIRST NAME)   MIDDLE NAME

SEX	DATE OF BIRTH
☐ MALE ☐ FEMALE	MO / DAY / YEAR

REGISTRATION NUMBER

SIGNATURE

THIS IS A SAMPLE ONLY

SECTION 1

1 Ⓐ Ⓑ Ⓒ Ⓓ
2 Ⓐ Ⓑ Ⓒ Ⓓ
3 Ⓐ Ⓑ Ⓒ Ⓓ
4 Ⓐ Ⓑ Ⓒ Ⓓ
5 Ⓐ Ⓑ Ⓒ Ⓓ
6 Ⓐ Ⓑ Ⓒ Ⓓ
7 Ⓐ Ⓑ Ⓒ Ⓓ
8 Ⓐ Ⓑ Ⓒ Ⓓ
9 Ⓐ Ⓑ Ⓒ Ⓓ
10 Ⓐ Ⓑ Ⓒ Ⓓ
11 Ⓐ Ⓑ Ⓒ Ⓓ
12 Ⓐ Ⓑ Ⓒ Ⓓ
13 Ⓐ Ⓑ Ⓒ Ⓓ
14 Ⓐ Ⓑ Ⓒ Ⓓ
15 Ⓐ Ⓑ Ⓒ Ⓓ
16 Ⓐ Ⓑ Ⓒ Ⓓ
17 Ⓐ Ⓑ Ⓒ Ⓓ
18 Ⓐ Ⓑ Ⓒ Ⓓ
19 Ⓐ Ⓑ Ⓒ Ⓓ
20 Ⓐ Ⓑ Ⓒ Ⓓ
21 Ⓐ Ⓑ Ⓒ Ⓓ
22 Ⓐ Ⓑ Ⓒ Ⓓ
23 Ⓐ Ⓑ Ⓒ Ⓓ
24 Ⓐ Ⓑ Ⓒ Ⓓ
25 Ⓐ Ⓑ Ⓒ Ⓓ
26 Ⓐ Ⓑ Ⓒ Ⓓ
27 Ⓐ Ⓑ Ⓒ Ⓓ
28 Ⓐ Ⓑ Ⓒ Ⓓ
29 Ⓐ Ⓑ Ⓒ Ⓓ
30 Ⓐ Ⓑ Ⓒ Ⓓ
31 Ⓐ Ⓑ Ⓒ Ⓓ
32 Ⓐ Ⓑ Ⓒ Ⓓ
33 Ⓐ Ⓑ Ⓒ Ⓓ
34 Ⓐ Ⓑ Ⓒ Ⓓ
35 Ⓐ Ⓑ Ⓒ Ⓓ
36 Ⓐ Ⓑ Ⓒ Ⓓ
37 Ⓐ Ⓑ Ⓒ Ⓓ
38 Ⓐ Ⓑ Ⓒ Ⓓ
39 Ⓐ Ⓑ Ⓒ Ⓓ
40 Ⓐ Ⓑ Ⓒ Ⓓ
41 Ⓐ Ⓑ Ⓒ Ⓓ
42 Ⓐ Ⓑ Ⓒ Ⓓ
43 Ⓐ Ⓑ Ⓒ Ⓓ
44 Ⓐ Ⓑ Ⓒ Ⓓ
45 Ⓐ Ⓑ Ⓒ Ⓓ
46 Ⓐ Ⓑ Ⓒ Ⓓ
47 Ⓐ Ⓑ Ⓒ Ⓓ
48 Ⓐ Ⓑ Ⓒ Ⓓ
49 Ⓐ Ⓑ Ⓒ Ⓓ
50 Ⓐ Ⓑ Ⓒ Ⓓ

SECTION 2

1 Ⓐ Ⓑ Ⓒ Ⓓ
2 Ⓐ Ⓑ Ⓒ Ⓓ
3 Ⓐ Ⓑ Ⓒ Ⓓ
4 Ⓐ Ⓑ Ⓒ Ⓓ
5 Ⓐ Ⓑ Ⓒ Ⓓ
6 Ⓐ Ⓑ Ⓒ Ⓓ
7 Ⓐ Ⓑ Ⓒ Ⓓ
8 Ⓐ Ⓑ Ⓒ Ⓓ
9 Ⓐ Ⓑ Ⓒ Ⓓ
10 Ⓐ Ⓑ Ⓒ Ⓓ
11 Ⓐ Ⓑ Ⓒ Ⓓ
12 Ⓐ Ⓑ Ⓒ Ⓓ
13 Ⓐ Ⓑ Ⓒ Ⓓ
14 Ⓐ Ⓑ Ⓒ Ⓓ
15 Ⓐ Ⓑ Ⓒ Ⓓ
16 Ⓐ Ⓑ Ⓒ Ⓓ
17 Ⓐ Ⓑ Ⓒ Ⓓ
18 Ⓐ Ⓑ Ⓒ Ⓓ
19 Ⓐ Ⓑ Ⓒ Ⓓ
20 Ⓐ Ⓑ Ⓒ Ⓓ
21 Ⓐ Ⓑ Ⓒ Ⓓ
22 Ⓐ Ⓑ Ⓒ Ⓓ
23 Ⓐ Ⓑ Ⓒ Ⓓ
24 Ⓐ Ⓑ Ⓒ Ⓓ
25 Ⓐ Ⓑ Ⓒ Ⓓ
26 Ⓐ Ⓑ Ⓒ Ⓓ
27 Ⓐ Ⓑ Ⓒ Ⓓ
28 Ⓐ Ⓑ Ⓒ Ⓓ
29 Ⓐ Ⓑ Ⓒ Ⓓ
30 Ⓐ Ⓑ Ⓒ Ⓓ
31 Ⓐ Ⓑ Ⓒ Ⓓ
32 Ⓐ Ⓑ Ⓒ Ⓓ
33 Ⓐ Ⓑ Ⓒ Ⓓ
34 Ⓐ Ⓑ Ⓒ Ⓓ
35 Ⓐ Ⓑ Ⓒ Ⓓ
36 Ⓐ Ⓑ Ⓒ Ⓓ
37 Ⓐ Ⓑ Ⓒ Ⓓ
38 Ⓐ Ⓑ Ⓒ Ⓓ
39 Ⓐ Ⓑ Ⓒ Ⓓ
40 Ⓐ Ⓑ Ⓒ Ⓓ

SECTION 3

1 Ⓐ Ⓑ Ⓒ Ⓓ
2 Ⓐ Ⓑ Ⓒ Ⓓ
3 Ⓐ Ⓑ Ⓒ Ⓓ
4 Ⓐ Ⓑ Ⓒ Ⓓ
5 Ⓐ Ⓑ Ⓒ Ⓓ
6 Ⓐ Ⓑ Ⓒ Ⓓ
7 Ⓐ Ⓑ Ⓒ Ⓓ
8 Ⓐ Ⓑ Ⓒ Ⓓ
9 Ⓐ Ⓑ Ⓒ Ⓓ
10 Ⓐ Ⓑ Ⓒ Ⓓ
11 Ⓐ Ⓑ Ⓒ Ⓓ
12 Ⓐ Ⓑ Ⓒ Ⓓ
13 Ⓐ Ⓑ Ⓒ Ⓓ
14 Ⓐ Ⓑ Ⓒ Ⓓ
15 Ⓐ Ⓑ Ⓒ Ⓓ
16 Ⓐ Ⓑ Ⓒ Ⓓ
17 Ⓐ Ⓑ Ⓒ Ⓓ
18 Ⓐ Ⓑ Ⓒ Ⓓ
19 Ⓐ Ⓑ Ⓒ Ⓓ
20 Ⓐ Ⓑ Ⓒ Ⓓ
21 Ⓐ Ⓑ Ⓒ Ⓓ
22 Ⓐ Ⓑ Ⓒ Ⓓ
23 Ⓐ Ⓑ Ⓒ Ⓓ
24 Ⓐ Ⓑ Ⓒ Ⓓ
25 Ⓐ Ⓑ Ⓒ Ⓓ
26 Ⓐ Ⓑ Ⓒ Ⓓ
27 Ⓐ Ⓑ Ⓒ Ⓓ
28 Ⓐ Ⓑ Ⓒ Ⓓ
29 Ⓐ Ⓑ Ⓒ Ⓓ
30 Ⓐ Ⓑ Ⓒ Ⓓ
31 Ⓐ Ⓑ Ⓒ Ⓓ
32 Ⓐ Ⓑ Ⓒ Ⓓ
33 Ⓐ Ⓑ Ⓒ Ⓓ
34 Ⓐ Ⓑ Ⓒ Ⓓ
35 Ⓐ Ⓑ Ⓒ Ⓓ
36 Ⓐ Ⓑ Ⓒ Ⓓ
37 Ⓐ Ⓑ Ⓒ Ⓓ
38 Ⓐ Ⓑ Ⓒ Ⓓ
39 Ⓐ Ⓑ Ⓒ Ⓓ
40 Ⓐ Ⓑ Ⓒ Ⓓ
41 Ⓐ Ⓑ Ⓒ Ⓓ
42 Ⓐ Ⓑ Ⓒ Ⓓ
43 Ⓐ Ⓑ Ⓒ Ⓓ
44 Ⓐ Ⓑ Ⓒ Ⓓ
45 Ⓐ Ⓑ Ⓒ Ⓓ
46 Ⓐ Ⓑ Ⓒ Ⓓ
47 Ⓐ Ⓑ Ⓒ Ⓓ
48 Ⓐ Ⓑ Ⓒ Ⓓ
49 Ⓐ Ⓑ Ⓒ Ⓓ
50 Ⓐ Ⓑ Ⓒ Ⓓ
51 Ⓐ Ⓑ Ⓒ Ⓓ
52 Ⓐ Ⓑ Ⓒ Ⓓ
53 Ⓐ Ⓑ Ⓒ Ⓓ
54 Ⓐ Ⓑ Ⓒ Ⓓ
55 Ⓐ Ⓑ Ⓒ Ⓓ
56 Ⓐ Ⓑ Ⓒ Ⓓ
57 Ⓐ Ⓑ Ⓒ Ⓓ
58 Ⓐ Ⓑ Ⓒ Ⓓ
59 Ⓐ Ⓑ Ⓒ Ⓓ
60 Ⓐ Ⓑ Ⓒ Ⓓ

SAMPLE

SCORE CANCELLATION

If you want to cancel your scores from this administration, complete A and B below. The scores will not be sent to you or your designated recipients, and they will be deleted from your permanent record. To cancel your scores from this test administration, you must:

A. fill in both ovals here   and B. sign your name in full below

◯ — ◯

ONCE A SCORE IS CANCELED, IT CANNOT BE REINSTATED ON YOUR PERMANENT RECORD.

1R	2R	3R	TCS	FOR ETS USE ONLY	F
1CS	2CS	3CS			

REGISTRATION NUMBER		TEST CENTER		TEST BOOK SERIAL NUMBER		TEST DATE

Begin your essay here. If you need more space, use the other side.

TOPIC

Q1381-07

273

DO NOT WRITE IN THIS AREA.

0 0 7 3 2 0 7

THIS IS A SAMPLE ANSWER SHEET

Reprinted by permission.

DO NOT WRITE BELOW THIS LINE. FOR ETS USE ONLY.

ORS

NO

OFF

TEST OF ENGLISH AS A FOREIGN LANGUAGE

THIS IS A SAMPLE ANSWER SHEET

DO NOT WRITE IN THIS AREA.

0 2 1 5 2 3 5

1. NAME: Print your name as it appears on your admission ticket. First print your family name (surname), then your given name, and then your middle name. Leave one box blank between names. Then, below each box, fill in the oval that contains the same letter.

Use a No. 2 (H.B.) pencil only. Do not use ink. Be sure each mark is dark and completely fills the intended oval. Erase errors or stray marks completely.

2. REGISTRATION NUMBER
→ Start here

YOUR REGISTRATION NUMBER IS PRINTED TO THE RIGHT AND IS IN MACHINE READABLE FORM.

DO NOT RE-ENTER THE NUMBER HERE.

3. INSTITUTION AND DEPARTMENT CODES: Give the code numbers of the institutions and departments to which you want your official score report sent. Be sure to fill in the corresponding oval below each box.

INSTITUTION CODE — DEPT. CODE

4. DO YOU PLAN TO STUDY FOR A DEGREE IN THE U.S.A. OR CANADA?
○ YES   ○ NO

5. REASON FOR TAKING TOEFL
(FILL IN ONLY ONE OVAL)

○ 1. To enter a college or university as an undergraduate student.
○ 2. To enter a college or university as a graduate student.
○ 3. To enter a school other than a college or university.
○ 4. To become licensed to practice my profession in the U.S.A. or Canada.
○ 5. To demonstrate my proficiency in English to the company for which I work or expect to work.
○ 6. Other than the above (please specify)

6. NUMBER OF TIMES YOU HAVE TAKEN TOEFL BEFORE
○ NONE   ○ THREE
○ ONE   ○ FOUR OR MORE
○ TWO

7. CENTER (Print.)
CITY
COUNTRY
CENTER NUMBER

8. PLEASE PRINT IN BLOCK LETTERS YOUR NAME AND MAILING ADDRESS.
FAMILY NAME (SURNAME)   GIVEN (FIRST) NAME   MIDDLE NAME
STREET ADDRESS OR P.O. BOX NO.
CITY   STATE OR PROVINCE
POSTAL OR ZIP CODE   COUNTRY

9. SIGNATURE AND DATE: Please copy the following statement in the space provided below; use handwriting.

"I hereby agree to the conditions set forth in the Bulletin of Information and affirm that I am the person whose name and address are given on this answer sheet."

Also sign your name on the line provided and enter today's date (in numbers).

SIGNED:
(WRITE YOUR NAME AS IF SIGNING A BUSINESS LETTER)
DATE: MO   DAY   YEAR

DO NOT MARK IN THIS AREA.
TEST FORM:

Choose only one answer for each question. Carefully and completely fill in the oval corresponding to the answer you choose so that the letter inside the oval cannot be seen. Completely erase any other marks you may have made.

	CORRECT	WRONG	WRONG	WRONG	WRONG
	Ⓐ	Ⓐ	Ⓐ	Ⓐ	Ⓐ
	Ⓑ	Ⓑ	Ⓑ	Ⓑ	Ⓑ
	●	Ⓒ	Ⓒ	Ⓒ	Ⓒ
	Ⓓ	Ⓓ	Ⓓ	Ⓓ	Ⓓ

FORM

SEX
☐ MALE
☐ FEMALE

TEST BOOK SERIAL NUMBER

DATE OF BIRTH
MO DAY YEAR

SEAT NUMBER

NAME (Print)
FAMILY NAME (SURNAME)   GIVEN (FIRST) NAME   MIDDLE NAME

REGISTRATION NUMBER

SIGNATURE

SECTION 1

SECTION 2

SECTION 3

THIS IS A SAMPLE ANSWER SHEET

SCORE CANCELLATION

If you want to cancel your scores from this administration, complete A and B below. The scores will not be sent to you or your designated recipients, and they will be deleted from your permanent record.
To cancel your scores from this test administration, you must:

A. fill in both ovals here   and   B. sign your name in full below

○–○

ONCE A SCORE IS CANCELED, IT CANNOT BE REINSTATED ON YOUR PERMANENT RECORD.

Reprinted by permission.

FOR ETS USE ONLY

1R	2R	3R
1CS	2CS	3CS
		TCS
		E

REGISTRATION NUMBER		TEST CENTER		TEST BOOK SERIAL NUMBER		TEST DATE

Begin your essay here. If you need more space, use the other side.

TOPIC

0   0   7   3   2   0   7

THIS IS A SAMPLE ANSWER SHEET

Reprinted by permission.

DO NOT WRITE BELOW THIS LINE. FOR ETS USE ONLY.

ORS

NO ○

OFF ○

® **TOEFL ESSAY PAGE** SIDE 3

REGISTRATION NUMBER		TEST CENTER		TEST BOOK SERIAL NUMBER		TEST DATE

Begin your essay here. If you need more space, use the other side.

TOPIC

Q1381-07

279

SIDE 4
Continuation of essay

DO NOT WRITE IN THIS AREA.

0   0   7   3   2   0   7

THIS IS A SAMPLE ANSWER SHEET

Reprinted by permission.

DO NOT WRITE BELOW THIS LINE. FOR ETS USE ONLY.

ORS

NO ◯

OFF ◯

TOEFL **ESSAY PAGE** SIDE 3

REGISTRATION NUMBER		TEST CENTER		TEST BOOK SERIAL NUMBER		TEST DATE

Begin your essay here. If you need more space, use the other side.

TOPIC

Q1381-07

281

DO NOT WRITE IN THIS AREA.

0   0   7   3   2   0   7

THIS IS A SAMPLE ANSWER SHEET

Reprinted by permission.

DO NOT WRITE BELOW THIS LINE. FOR ETS USE ONLY.

ORS

NO

OFF